SOCIAL WORK, PSYCHOLOGY & WELFARE MANAGEMENT

SOCIAL WORK, PSYCHOLOGY
&
WELFARE MANAGEMENT

Edited by
Ranjna K. Devi

OMEGA PUBLICATIONS
NEW DELHI-110 002 (INDIA)

OMEGA PUBLICATIONS
4378/4B, G-4 JMD House
Murari Lal Street, Ansari Road
Daryaganj, New Delhi - 110 002
Phone : 011-23278062,9811787417
e-mail : omega_publications@yahoo.com

Edition : 2023

ISBN : 978-81-8455-184-6

Price : 1295/-

PRINTED IN INDIA

Published by Mahender Garg for Omega Publications, New Delhi- 110002
Printed at Tarun Offest Press Delhi-110053

Preface

Social work theory has to provide a framework for these issues. Psychology has an important contribution to make towards an understanding of: (i) the theoretical and practical issues surrounding interviewing, assessment and therapeutic skills; (ii) human development and human interactions; and (iii) the scope of applied psychology in the provision of social work and other welfare services.

There were however, two compelling reasons why this approach to psychology was adopted by the social work profession in preference to any other psychodynamic theory clearly *does* address itself to understanding the psychological and emotional processes which occur in the life of an individual, and when people interact with each other and mainstream psychology, on the whole, has not demonstrated an overwhelming interest in making a contribution to the formulation of social work theory, or to social work training. The separate development of mainstream psychology and psychodynamic theory has meant there has been very little in the way of cross-fertilisation despite both apparently being concerned with 'people'. Traditionally psychologists have concentrated on establishing their discipline as a credible 'science', and on developing methods by which they could conduct empirical studies. Now psychology is flourishing in higher education institutions and psychologists are being called upon to fulfil a number of functions in industry, the health and educational services, as well as taking a traditional research role.

In this study, we discussed about social work, psychology & welfare management. The following themes are taken here with an elaborate discussion—Social Work and Psychology: An Introduction; Historical Development of Psychiatric Social Work; Mental Health and Social Work: Co-operation and Contention; Role of Social Work in Health Care; Social Treatment of Mental and Emotional Problems; Management of Social Welfare; Humanistic Psychology; Developmental Theory; and Effects of the Physical Structure of the School Environment; and Bibliography etc.

We are grateful to our publisher for materialising this effort meticulously. We would feel amply rewarded, if comments, constructive criticisms for erudite readers could be communicated to us for enhancement of utility of this project. Comments and suggestions from the users are welcome to enhance it utility, which we may corroborate in subsequent editions. Definitely, the users will find it useful and informative.

—Editor

Contents

self-actualisation is weak, it rarely disappears altogether—even in adulthood. It persists underground, in the unconscious, and speaks to us as an inner voice waiting to be heard. Inner signals can lead even the neurotic adult back to buried capacities and unfulfilled potentials. Our inner core is a pressure we call the "will to health," and it is this urge on which all successful psychotherapy is based (pp. 192-93).

7. There are a few people—"self-actualisers"—who have remained deeply responsive to their inner natures and urges toward growth. These people are less molded and flattened by cultural pressures, and have preserved the capacity to look at the world in a spontaneous, fresh, childlike manner (pp. 207-8).

Humanistic thought has taken various forms through the decades. During the Enlightenment, humanism became linked to an environmental outlook and the scientific enterprise. The hope was that the creation of improved environments, aided by scientific knowledge, would lead to better living conditions for us all. In contemporary psychology, the behaviourists continue to pursue the goals of the Enlightenment.

In recent years, however, the behaviouristic approach has struck many humanistic psychologists as too one-sided. Maslow and others have objected that behaviourism leaves out too much that gives human life its richness and dignity. By focusing on how external behaviour comes under environmental control, it has ignored our inner world and our spontaneous urges toward health and independence. If we are to create better environments, they must not simply be those that control behaviour but those that foster and support the intrinsic creative forces.

1

Social Work and Psychology: An Introduction

Generic social work is a very young profession, dating from 1971 and the effects of the Seebohm Report. The need to establish a theoretical framework and define the limits and scope for social work practice has been the subject of fierce debate. This has been reflected in the content of the Certificate of Qualification in Social Work (CQSW) courses, set up to train these new professionals and attempting to equip students to cope with a range of social problems affecting a variety of client groups (Richards and Righton, 1972). The aims of social work training are as diverse as the tasks that social workers are expected to perform; but broadly speaking they concentrate on three main areas:

- Enabling social workers to understand the social and political context of their work.
- Acquiring assessment and therapeutic skills.
- Considering theoretical knowledge of human development, social interactions and the scope of their own and other professional disciplines.

Social work theory has to provide a framework for these issues. Psychology has an important contribution to make towards an understanding of:

- the theoretical and practical issues surrounding interviewing, assessment and therapeutic skills.
- human development and human interactions.
- the scope of applied psychology in the provision of social work and other welfare services.

Although this might at first glance appear to be a statement of the obvious, for several historical reasons the contribution of psychology towards social work knowledge has been contentious. In order to make more sense of the confusion over psychology teaching provided for social work students, it is worth looking at the background to the development of social work as a profession, prior to the Seebohm reorga-nisation. During the 1950s there was an expansion of social work practice, and a move towards professional training, particularly for the Psychiatric Social Workers (PSWs).

The PSWs were the most professionally autonomous group of social workers and due to a quirk in the history of social work development they derived their theoretical knowledge from American psychodynamically oriented therapists and social workers. Thus they developed and promoted the method of intervention known as 'social casework' based on this approach. It proved fairly flexible, incorporating a framework for understanding the social as well as the psychological context of a client's distress. And so, because it appeared easily adaptable to changing fashions in social work theory, and because it was the first theoretical offering to the growing profession, it survived. The result was that to social workers, psychology meant psychodynamic theory (see CCETSW Discussion Paper No. 2, 1967).

There were however, two compelling reasons why this approach to psychology was adopted by the social work profession in preference to any other:

- Psychodynamic theory clearly *does* address itself to understanding the psychological and emotional processes which occur in the life of an individual, and when people interact with each other.
- Mainstream psychology, on the whole, has not demonstrated an overwhelming interest in making a contribution to the formulation of social work theory, or to social work training.

The separate development of mainstream psychology and psychodynamic theory has meant there has been very little in the way of cross-fertilisation despite both apparently being concerned with 'people'.

Traditionally psychologists have concentrated on establishing their discipline as a credible 'science', and on developing methods by which they could conduct empirical studies. Now psychology is flourishing in higher education institutions and psychologists are being called upon to fulfil a number of functions in industry, the health and educational services, as well as taking a traditional research role.

Early applied psychology derived from experiments in industry involving the nature of work groups: studies concerned with productivity, group identity and relationships provided information to management on the way people might be manipulated to increase production.

This association with the 'needs of management' ensured that psychology acquired a reputation as a 'reactionary' force. A similar ethos and reputation has also surrounded applied psychology in the areas of psychiatry and education.

Through the use of various tests, and an emphasis on 'correcting' behaviour, educational psychology has been used to reinforce social differences, which has naturally been unacceptable to most social workers. Clinical psychology appears on the whole to be used to establish or confirm psychiatric diagnosis, whereas psychology itself has the potential, to show-empirically—that certain psychiatric diagnoses and treatment regimes are unsound. Clinical psychology in Britain is part of the existing culture in psychiatry, and operates very much under the control of the psychiatric consultant. Originally the major part of psychologists' work was to provide information on a person's intellectual ability and mental state, but gradually it has come to include certain forms of therapeutic techniques. The main emphasis is on behaviour modification, the practice of which is sometimes of use in retraining institutionalised psychiatric patients to function in social settings. However, psychologists usually take the role of teacher to help nurses and occupational therapists, and thus are distanced from the patients themselves and become allied with the 'controlling' group in the hospital. In America a branch of clinical practice referred to as 'community psychology' has emerged, whereby psychologists provide a direct service to people with emotional problems in the community, and thus individuals may receive specialised help without being labelled as a 'psychiatric patient' or being prescribed drugs. This concept has been largely unaccepted in this country (with the possible exception of the Borough of Newham in East London) and psychologists remain medically bound (Bender, 1976; Heather, 1976).

Social Work and Psychology History

Social workers, especially those trained for generic work, have not been satisfied with psychodynamic psychology, and have vigorously drawn attention to its limitations. Training courses have tried to respond to this by bringing in psychologists to teach on CQSW courses. However this has led to a certain amount of conflict and confusion. One reason has been that the psychologist's brief has been to teach psychology, but they have been left to their own devices as far as course content goes. This is largely because the non-psychologist requesting the teaching is unlikely to be able to identify the appropriate elements within psychology which are most relevant to CQSW students. Frequently they teach an introductory psychology course, similar to one which might be taught to undergraduate psychologists, and this leaves practically-oriented social workers with a gap between their professional needs and their desire to understand and use the material they are being taught (Herbert, 1981, p.2). Another reason why this situation arises is because social work tutors are torn between the need to establish academic credibility, forced upon them by CCETSW (the Central Council for Education and Training in Social Work) and their own educational institutions, and the need for their students to understand human behaviour on a practical level. The only academically credible option for them is to let an academic psychologist teach their students, and for them to also teach psychodynamic psychology themselves.

Thus students and social workers are even more confused, and the result has frequently been for them to reject psychology altogether, and focus upon other aspects of social work (meeting the practical needs of clients, organising for social change, etc.). The interaction skills they need are learned during the course of their practical placements and their subsequent work experience, and are not seen as part of psychology, nor as the 'psychological' part of social work. This is not particularly satisfactory, either for clients or the profession. Clearly clients do reap benefits from the 'practical help/information giving' approach to social work. They also benefit from the results of community action and change. We would argue though that clients would benefit more from a social worker able to make use of skills and theory in order to formulate an accurate assessment of a client's needs. Psychological skills are also essential for effective intervention in the numerous meetings that social workers attend, and for understanding and mobilising community groups. These skills are *not* to be confused with certain features of the social casework approach which require the social worker to look for the latent component of the interview or meeting and offer an *interpretation.* The skills we advocate will contribute towards an accurate and clear understanding of the social relationship between individuals and allow social workers to make more effective use of the social situations in which they operate.

In this study, the relevant approaches to psychology were summarised. They will be used in subsequent chapters to draw attention to important applications within social work. These are:

- Looking at skills connected with working with individuals and in groups.
- Considering the interpersonal, social and developmental issues between social workers and their clients.
- Making *sense* of the context of social work both on the micro-level (within social work agencies), and on the macro-level (within society).

There are limitations to the extent and depth of the subject a book of this size can cover. Areas of psychology we could have included but did not, or only touched on, are the nature and causes of psychopathology, psychologically-oriented methods of intervention (such as family therapy and behaviour modification), attitude change, personality theory, the whole area of community work, and evaluation and its associated methodology. We consider that these areas are relatively well provided for. Also we preferred to cover some topics in relative depth, and touch on a few others, rather than write a catalogue. The final part of this chapter outlines the areas of applied psychology which we have included.

Skills

This book has concentrated upon two main areas of social work skills: interviewing and group work. Interviewing embraces both the formal kind of social interaction between professional worker and client, in which the interviewer obtains information and helps someone come to a decision about their own problem, and also the process of giving appropriate information and advice. The interview is crucial because it is during this interaction that social work may either be effective or prove a waste of time.

Psychologists have made studies of a whole range of counselling and assessment interviews, and even more important, used the data from these to develop models of good interviewing practice. These have been developed and improved through trials with several professional groups. It is worth clarifying the differences between the *skills* in an interview, and the *knowledge of human development,* both vital ingredients in successful social work interviews. In the case of reported child abuse, for instance, one aim of the interview would be to gain information.

The social worker must establish the *facts* about whether various incidents have occurred, and if so, when and how. He then has to make an assessment of the most suitable intervention for his agency. The perception of the events and judgements about future plans will depend on how a social worker understands the family dynamics and its social problems (i.e. using knowledge of human development). But for the assessment to take place at all, a social worker must obtain the appropriate information both factual and emotional. Good interviewing is partly communicating to the client that you are *really* listening and understanding; without this the client is less likely to express true feelings and relevant details. Similarly, when working with groups it is essential that the group is allowed to develop in such a way as to enable all the members to benefit. The social worker will make sense of and predict the progress of individual members, but must first be skilled enough to allow the group processes to develop.

Interpersonal, Social and Developmental Issues

In order to prescribe and train people in social work skills, a body of knowledge has to be developed. There are three main areas that this book covers:

(1) The area of describing 'what goes on' in a social interaction. This covers the 'here and now' of social work encounteres. For example a social worker may well be faced with a client who on first meeting makes her feel uneasy, or unsympathetic, or determined to put every effort into dealing with that person's requests - but rarely does a social worker feel apathy! It may be argued that it is the 'problem' which precipitates the social worker's reaction, but psychologists have produced evidence that he or she is likely to be influenced by quite different factors - those involved in the way we form impressions of others, including their nonverbal behaviour and how 'attractive' they are.

(2) In addition to interpersonal factors, there are social psychological factors which affect interactions with clients. As discussed in previous chapters each

individual is equipped with a set of attitudes about most objects and events. Some of these sets of attitudes include stereotypes and positive and negative prejudices, of which individuals may frequently be unaware. The importance of prejudice in social work relationships will be explored in previous chapters.

(3) The area of psychological and social development of individuals which has been referred to earlier in this chapter. It is with this area of psychology that social workers are frequently the most concerned, and are most likely to *recognise* as being psychology!

Context of Social Work

Social workers operate both within and between institutions, and within a socio-political structure; clients have experience of institutions and are frequently victims of the socio-political structure. Psychologists have studied institutional life for both workers and their clients, and the applications of some of their findings are covered in depth in previous chapters. It is the one area which pulls together not only social work and psychology, but also the vital area of social policy. This book then, tackles psychological theory, but its main task is to confront the practical application of theory.

The central issue is that although some critics might say that social work is intuitive - a *craft* (Maas, 1980, cited by Herbert, 1981, pp.3-4), and that social work students have been seen to be 'high in sensitivity and concern for others but low in logical thinking and intellectual discrimination'—it cannot advance as a profession or academic discipline until it takes theoretical concepts seriously. This means not only developing theory for its own sake, but also undertaking relevant research which will sharpen up social work 'tools' - the most important one being each social worker's own knowledge, personality and skills! The following chapter presents a guide to interviewing skills which are derived from psychological research. It may be used as an interviewer training manual to enable social workers to monitor their own development.

It also presents a model for interviewing and shows how information may be gathered and used in the most effective way. Most psychologists have now realised that people need training in social skills, even if they have the necessary qualities such as 'warmth' and 'empathy'. This chapter looks specifically at what these skills are, and how a social worker might develop them. We do stress though that good interviewing includes a large element of individual style, and so we are not presenting a blanket formula for interviewing practice. The skills and model of interviewing are *dynamic:* by improving their ability to help other people express themselves more fully and accurately social workers develop their interpersonal capacities rather than restrict them.

SOCIAL WORK, PSYCHOLOGY AND SOCIAL POLICY

We have argued strongly that psychology informs social work practice and that debates between psychologists occur because of different perspectives in the study of psychology. It is however important to consider a further dimension in psychological debate and that is the one by which psychology reflects and affects changes in social policy. Psychologists have been aware of this link since the mid 1970s, when Jack Tizard drew attention to the differences between psychological theory obtained empirically by academics, and the needs of practitioners (applied psychologists) who have to consider 'what kinds of psychological pursuit are most likely to further the human condition'.

By definition the latter involves a subjective process of selection which is at least partially opposed to the aims of academic 'scientific' psychology. Social workers, as practitioners for whom psychological knowledge plays a critical role, are similarly at risk. An example of how this might happen can be illustrated by considering the concept of 'motherhood' and the connected psychological implications. Most of us have an idea of what 'successful' mothering involves, and probably work on the assumption that motherhood and the desire to care for and rear children is a positive attribute in an individual, and something that is socially desirable.

This particular example has important implications for social workers who are frequently charged with supervising people who carry out the mothering role. But as Badinter (1980) has shown in her study of the history of mothering in France, the whole notion of the role of the biological mother overlapping into child rearing, nurturing and socialisation is relatively modern, and a direct result of political and economic incentives - not the result of a 'maternal instinct' in women. The notion of the maternal instinct as being a *psychological fact has* been challenged, and if this is open to question then certain fundamental concepts by which society and its social workers assess what is 'psychologically good' for people need to be reassessed. In this chapter we are going to look at specific examples of how psychology is understood and used according to changes in social policy. First, a detailed account of the relationship between social policy and notions of 'good practice' in professional child-care over the past forty years. Secondly, the often quoted but significant example of the work of John Bowlby and how this has influenced day care provision and family structure since the war. Finally, the most recent influence of social policy upon social work, in the form of pressure to voluntary provision of services and community care, especially in the light of the Barclay Report. This has had an effect on the relevance and use of psychological theory for social workers.

Psychology and Child-care Practice

Modern child-care policy had its origins in the late 1940s with the creation of the children's departments. Over the last thirty to forty years ideas on what is 'best' for children have fluctuated a great deal. Again there is evidence of intervention by 'experts' and their pronouncement for better child-care. There have also been particular incidents which have evoked serious alterations in policy and the consequent psychological theory adopted by the authorities. The most famous recent example was the tragic death of Maria Colwell, a victim of policy which supported the notion that children should be with their natural parent regardless of the cost. Since the 1975 Children Act, it has been necessary to assess children's needs regardless of those of natural parents. In 1948, as a result of the Curtis Report, the children's department came into being. This was eventually incorporated into the social services department after 1970. Jean Packman (1975) has written a detailed account of the social, economic and psychological influences which informed committees of inquiry from Curtis to Houghton (whose recommendation resulted in the 1975 Children Act). She described child-care policy since 1948 as demonstrating:

> The constraints and opportunities of a legal framework; the interaction between central and local government; the influence of practitioners as well as official 'policy makers'; the effect - or lack of it - of research, pressure groups and scandals; the circular relationship between needs and demands and service responses; and the vital, sometimes fraught and sometimes fruitful

partnership between local government officers and their council members.

In this section, the importance of psychological concepts and research will be demonstrated in relation to the framing of this policy; also the ways in which contrasting decisions about priorities in child-care were related to the political climate, but justified in terms of psychological 'fact'. This will be shown by four examples illustrated from evolutionary stages in child-care policy. These are:

- The notion of substitute care will be examined in the context of the choice of foster homes over residential children's homes.
- The justification for maintaining the child's stable relationship with the natural parents will be considered against the benefits of substitute families.
- The case for adoption in preference to preventive casework.
- The delinquent's needs for care and treatment contrasted with the need for strict discipline and the 'short sharp shock' as a deterrent for juvenile crime.

Foster Homes v. Residential Care

From the mid to the late 1940s, several factors indicated that the piecemeal provision for underprivileged children was inadequate. The Monckton Inquiry of 1945, into the death of Dennis O'Neill after mistreatment in a foster home focused on:

- problems in *administering* the 'boarding out' or fostering service.
- the initial selection of suitable foster homes.

The Curtis Committee, whose report resulted in the establishment of an integrated child-care service, focused upon the poor quality of the residential child-care institutions. The main function of the new children's department was to find suitable foster homes for 'deprived' children, with the aim of providing, via the foster family, a better set of social relationships, a good experience of family life and a variety of human contacts for the child. There was also to be an emphasis upon emptying the orphanages of all the children who were unlikely to return to their parents. There were various psychological research reports which suggested that institutional care from infancy was likely to result in retardation of cognitive skills and intellectual development, as well as impaired emotional growth (e.g. Spitz, 1945).

The Curtis Committee itself presented evidence that children in foster homes seemed to be more integrated into society than children in orphanages who experienced the effects of segregation. Curtis reported that children in foster homes were less starved of affection and more independent than those in residential care. These findings were given extra significance by evidence from the work of John Bowlby. He produced a report for the World Health Organisation (1951) apparently demonstrating that children brought up in institutions were much more likely to suffer disturbed emotional and intellectual development than those who were in a family. In addition, fostercare had one great political advantage over residential care - it was very cheap. It was a generally held belief that substitute care for children was provided for love rather than money, and that high rates of pay for foster parents were closely linked with child exploitation, so payments to foster parents were kept low. In the early 1950s there was a great deal of pressure on the newly-formed children's departments to save money on the number of children they had in care in England and Wales, which had increased by 10000 between

1949 and 1953. Therefore an economic solution had to be provided, and this tied in with current psychological evidence that institutional care was damaging. Even so, the rationale for this development of foster care was based mainly on the research evidence related to the *negative effects of residential institutions,* and not so much on the benefits of foster care.

It was also clear that improving residential care would cost much more than increasing the supply of foster homes, and so no evidence on how institutional care might be improved, or even be of ultimate benefit to children, was presented. This resulted in the decline of the children's home: residential staff received less money and training, and recruitment in this area declined in quantity and quality. Some time later, in 1963, the Williams Committee found that only fifteen per cent of staff in local authority children's homes were qualified. Fieldworkers had much higher status, and morale among residential staff dropped. It has remained so with all but a few exceptions. (See below for Barclay's recommendations for residential and day-care staff.) Sociological and psychological research has examined a variety of institutions and demonstrated ways in which a process of 'institutionalisation' occurs for residential workers and inmates. This is characterised by flattened emotional responses, retarded learning, poor memory, and conformity.

Thus, the institutional life is considered undesirable. However, it is within the realms of most social scientist' imaginations to see that a residential experience might provide opportunities that family life cannot, in terms of adaptability to a variety of social relationships, understanding the implications of living with other people, reducing desire to compete and seek attention, and other socially-oriented characteristics. The introduction of these points in this context is to demonstrate that social policy is not value-free in the way it selects psychological evidence to support decisions; and that the major impetus behind the expansion of fostering is more likely to have been economic than a result of psychological research.

Permanent Substitute Care

The link between the natural parents and the child was challenged ten years later in the light of events which once again affected policy development. In 1971, the Seebohm Committee's recommendations resulted in the social services departments being formed from existing welfare services. Shortly afterwards the death of Maria Colwell, who had been returned to her mother from foster parents by social workers, resulted in the Houghton Committee Inquiry. The report expressed concern for children who were suffering because bonds with their natural parents were being preserved at all costs. A report from the National Children's Bureau highlighted the vulnerability of children who were 'born to fail' because of their social and economic background, and contrasted their prospects with those of children from similar backgrounds who had been adopted. Barbara Tizard's work *Adoption: A Second Chance* (1975) presents case studies of children who had overcome earlier deprivations due to the security achieved by living with permanent substitute families. Tizard argues that security and love are more important to children's welfare than being with the natural parent when they cannot provide this. The 1975 Children Act emphasised the need to protect the *child's* interests above all others especially when they are in conflict with the needs and desires of the natural parents.

BASW refers to this as the 'adversary model' and rightly expressed the fear that changes in legislation to this effect could well ignore the subtleties in attachments between parents and children. Parents would be discouraged from requesting voluntary receptions into care because they feared that admitting the need for help with child-care might expose them to the possible permanent loss of their children. The Children Act of course, gave increased powers to social workers to make decisions about what actions would be in the child's best interests. Social workers over the last five years have also evolved a more specialist service for children. This is as a result of the inadequacies highlighted by inquiries into cases of child abuse, and the frustration many social workers have felt in not being able to 'specialise'. The new specialist services have included social workers and social work teams with responsibility for non-accidental injury, and specialist fostering and adoption workers.

Juvenile Delinquency

Children's departments were not primarily concerned with delinquency. This remained the province of the Home Office until the 1960s. In 1956 the report of the Ingleby Inquiry which focused upon the power of the juvenile courts and residential treatment facilities for children, gave evidence that the children who came before the courts did so because they had been exposed to cruelty, neglect and danger. They linked neglect and ill-treatment of children to the incidence of juvenile delinquency, and this gave rise to a series of reports and White Papers during the 1960s. Delinquency had been rising, and although this was previously blamed on wartime upheaval and separation of evacuees from parents, this no longer, held true. The growing body of opinion was that prevention of distress in children would prevent deviant behaviour. It was also clear that the type of institution (the approved school) to which young offenders were sent, was not having the reforming effect that was hoped.

The Children and Young Persons Act (1969) saw the delinquent as a victim of circumstances whose offence was a cry for help, and therefore care and treatment should be provided to meet this need. This was in the form of community homes with education, which were set up to deal with most delinquents committed to care. Under this Act the social worker was able to place a child in care at home. The magistrates were empowered to command the care order, but had no say in the placement. Also, social workers could supervise children at home under a Supervision Order, and there was the possibility of Intermediate Treatment being included in this. This provided a sentencing option for magistrates and a duty was placed on local authorities to make money available for preventive work with young offenders. For many local authorities though, this has only recently been exploited on a large scale.

The liberalism of the 1960s and 1970s declined in the light of the apparent failure of the community homes to curtail delinquency. The present Conservative Government has seen delinquency in terms of criminal behaviour and chosen, as far as possible, to return power to the magistrates and implement more custodial sentences in detention centres and borstals, with the idea that the 'short sharp shock' will solve society's problems. The child's problems are currently of little political interest.

Preventive Casework

Although fostering as a form of substitute care has never been totally neglected, the children's department did find it difficult to match all the children in need to suitable foster homes. The task was becoming a burden, and so they responded by seeking alternatives which were equally cheap. Such alternatives had been discussed as early as 1946 by the Women's Group on Public Welfare (a sub-committee of Curtis) which had looked at 'The Neglected Child and His Family'. They argued that the removal of a child from his family was an easy answer to an unsatisfactory home, but not psychologically sound in terms of the child's emotional life. They proposed the radical suggestion that an 'intensive family casework service' might provide ways of helping families stay together. This of course is well supported by Bowlby's thesis that continuous care, preferably from the child's mother, is best for his future mental health. Thus child-care officers were trained in 'preventive' work, but there was also a need for legislation to enable them to intervene in a family if they were not going to remove a child. This came in the form of the 1952 Children and Young Persons (Amendment) Act, which gave local authorities the right to enter the homes of children who were likely to be at risk of going into care. This was justified by the psychological concept that *separation from the natural parent increases a child's deprivation.* It was also becoming apparent that children suffering from neglect often had parents with similar backgrounds. Local authorities found themselves intervening in families where adequate emotional and physical care could not be provided, and in doing so were likely to reinforce the family's inadequacy, and do nothing to prevent its effects on subsequent generations.

Those who advocated 'preventive casework' were of the opinion that if financial pressures were reduced, then casework might enable families to modify their existing capacities for relationships and provide a suitable environment for child-care. Thus, in 1963 Children Act, the local authorities were empowered to provide material and monetary aid for families, which was important since the National Assistance Board was frequently too inflexible to provide additional help for deprived families. The implementation of this Act meant that more children were supervised at home than were received into care, and it increased the complexity and workload of the children's department once again. The child-care officer was not in a position to weigh the dangers of *separation* for children against the *physical, material or emotional* neglect they might be suffering, and be equipped with a variety of possible solutions. However, statistics show that the emphasis in this period was on *prevention* which reflects the policy of the era rather than a 'value-free' assessment.

Day Nurseries and John Bowlby

Tizard and other writers have drawn attention to Bowlby's work, which has probably been the most influential research on child welfare. It also demonstrates in a variety of ways how effectively research findings can be used by politicians to change people's behaviour. For social workers and their clients the consequences have been a fundamental influence upon a whole generation's (and possibly the subsequent generation's) attitudes, behaviour and provision regarding child-care. Basically, Bowlby (a psychoanalytically-oriented psychiatrist) argued that the mental health of infants and young children was dependent upon the experience of a warm, intimate and continuous relationship with their mother, or a permanent mother substitute. 'Maternal deprivation' resulted in delinquent, psychopathic or at the very least grave, personality disorders. Bowlby's evidence was gained from studies of residential institutions, hospitals and case studies of children who experienced separation due to wartime evacuation.

Some of his work was retrospective, based on work with disturbed children for whom he traced a link with inadequate maternal bonding. His findings were supported by other studies, which looked at emotional deprivation in children in French orphanages. Despite the source of his evidence, derived from institutions which generally made inadequate provision for the emotional development of children in their care, the conclusion drawn by Bowlby and others from his work was the separation *of a young child from its mother was in itself a bad thing.*

Tizard contends that such was the impact of Bowlby's work that this notion almost assumed the status of a *law* in psychology. As such it was not only used in argument against residential care, but for closing day-nurseries, despite the fact that no studies showing deleterious effects of day-nursery placement had been published. It is now common knowledge that Bowlby's work was used after the Second World War to encourage women who had taken essential jobs in factories as part of the war effort to relinquish them to returning men.

They were persuaded of the permanent damage that their children would suffer if they did not offer them fulltime care. A recent American film (*Rosie the Riveter*) illustrated this dramatically by contrasting the pre-war propaganda shown to American mothers about the *benefits* of day-care for their children, with subsequent campaigns telling them of their selfishness, cruelty and maladaptive sexuality if they had not returned to their 'natural' role as fulltime mother. Shortly after the publication of Bowlby's findings and their recommendations being implemented, other studies like those of Schaffer and Emerson showed that children were capable of forming multiple attachments by the age of 6 months. Subsequent work by psychologists has shown that a child will benefit from forming several attachments, and their social skills in this actually improved with practice. It is only in the 1970s that psychologists have concentrated on the *benefits of* multiple attachments and the lack of such research has been a consequence of the massive political impact of the earlier work.

Eckennan and Whatley (1977) have shown the importance of the peer group for emotional and intellectual development. They demonstrated that 10 to 12 month old children will play with each other, and although no *attachment* appears to form, they are not indifferent to their peers. Mueller and Brenner (1977) emphasise the importance of practice in social relationships in 1 to 2 year olds, and Hartup (1970) has shown that 3 year olds and above have 'best friends'. However this whole area has been relatively neglected, and work is currently being encouraged in the USA, where experimental day-nurseries have been set up in conjunction with research projects. Also in the 1970s, work was done to see whether there was evidence that children at day-nurseries do suffer from 'maternal deprivation'.

Willis and Riccuti (1974) studied infants' (4 to 15 months of age) arrivals at day-nursery over a period of 6 months. Most babies greeted the nurses with pleasure, or without distress, and at the end of the day greeted their parents happily. Although Ricutti concluded that children preferred their mother, they had also developed an attachment to the nursery worker. These studies, if taken seriously, go some way to avoiding the blind acceptance of research findings as 'psychological facts'. Other research in the same period has demonstrated that it may well be damaging for some children to have a close and continuous relationship with one person.

It is likely that the child will suffer in some way from the problems that the person experiences, and in the case of depressed mothers the children's accident rate was four times higher than that of children whose mothers were not depressed. Mothers in this study reported loss of interest in their children when they were depressed and anxious. Richman (1976) also found a link between the state of the mother and the child. Mothers who were depressed were most likely to have children with behaviour problems. He asserts that even if they do not exhibit problems, they are less likely to be stimulated by a depressed mother. Despite a wealth of evidence, which has at least equal if not more validity than Bowlby's work, the research on the benefits for children and parents of day-care has not been incorporated into practice. This is likely to be at least partly related to high rates of unemployment among the male population and the fear that if free from fulltime child-care, women will flood the job market. Tizard has said that the situation will not change until psychologists are taught about 'problem-oriented' psychology, and thus understand that their discipline is not value-free but responsive to social and political pressure. Belskey and Steinberg have stressed the need for psychologists working in the area of day-care for children to ask questions about the impact on parents, families and the social structure. Social workers however, are aware of the social and political context of their work, and it is essential that they bring this knowledge into use in any assessment of psychological aspects of their clients' lives and their own role.

Decentralisation of Social Work: The Use of Community Resources

The past forty years has seen the growth and development of the profession of social work. However within this profession various developmental 'sub-phases' have occurred which demanded reorientations of approach among social workers. These have been in reaction to social policy and economic changes, have had an impact on the attitudes of social workers towards the use of psychological theory. The first sub-phase was the professional development with the emphasis on psychodynamic work and social casework. This was followed by the 'sociological' reaction and the growth of community work in the late 1960s and early 1970s, accompanied by a 'flirtation' with the systems approach, requiring that social workers try and make some sense of social institutions as well as of the behaviour of their clients.

More recently, social workers have responded to the limitations in their resources and have stressed task-centred and intake work, and crisis intervention. These are relatively cheap ways of dealing with the more demanding problems, but the emphasis on expediency has frequently meant that a consideration of the social causes of individual or family problems has received less time and attention than it deserved. This sub-phase, occurring at the end of the 1970s, appeared at the stage when voluntary agencies, particularly those concerned with community work and prevention, were on the decline. They were classed as agents of 'radical' social work and certain local authorities put forward strong cases for withdrawing any resources they had invested in such projects. The conservatism of the 1980s has stressed community care, and encouraged the role of volunteers in keeping many people out of institutional care, for economic reasons. Although it was not the overt aim of policy, it set the scene for social workers to think once again in terms of working on a community basis, and many local authorities reorganised their area teams to a patch structure and set up sub-offices. In 1982 the working party set up by the National Institute of Social Work (Barclay Committee) to review the role and tasks of social workers in social services departments and related voluntary agencies, published its report. This report reinforced the trend, stressing the importance of mobilising community resources and informal care.

In addition to an emphasis on caring for people in the community it proposed the idea that community social work could be put into practice by using residential and day-care institutions as community resource centres. There have been several examples of this but as yet no formal research into the psychological effects on residents and their relatives. So, for example, some elderly people's homes have become day-centres and clubs as well, and friendships have developed between residents and club members, breaking down social isolation on both sides. Children's community homes have run clubs for old people and handicapped children, encouraging children with social problems, and often a history of delinquency, to do voluntary work and take an interest in various community activities. Another effect proposed by Barclay is the breaking down of the rigid distinction between field and residential workers, because residential and day-care establishments are proposed as the focus of most of the community-oriented social work, and there is a requirement for all social workers to develop new skills and assess the needs of clients according to very different criteria, which will probably differ from the criteria operated by existing community workers. The brief outline above, which categorised community work with 'radical sociological' social work was deliberately emphasised.

In 1976 the Association of Community Workers stated that 'conventional individual and social psychology offers little help to community workers who work with a range of "normal" individuals ... in a variety of roles'. They criticise social psychology not only for its *content* (e.g. effects of the mass media, effects of collective action) but also because little work has been done in 'natural' settings. That is, they feel that on the one hand psychological knowledge is irrelevant and should be seen as part of 'psychological studies' and not real life, and on the other hand they feel that psychologists should do some research into what actually happens in communities. This typifies the confusion of 'radicals' who operated in a climate where psychology had not been usefully or critically incorporated into social and community work education, but seen as an outmoded and reactionary discipline. More recent writers (e.g. Twelvetrees, 1982) have progressed beyond this stance. He encourages the integration of literature on group behaviour and social groupwork into community work theory, stressing that some understanding of group processes will enable the community workers to know what to look for and how to understand what is going on, and so provide an acceptable basis for intervention. He also emphasises the point made by Goetschius that it is important for the worker to help the community group to evaluate its work, and decide how to alter their behaviour and avoid repeating mistakes. Again, Twelvetrees correctly considers that despite the emphasis on action and social change, individual members of community groups suffer from a variety of emotional and psychological reactions. It is important for workers to make sense of these as part of the helping role. It is no longer 'reactionary' to understand the emotional side of people's lives. So the most recent policy proposals on the future of social work require that social workers extend their practice beyond concern for interpersonal relationships.

Psychological theory incorporated into social work training and practice has to be developed and understood accordingly, taking political and sociological perspectives into account. This means that social workers will need to be familiar with *more* psychology, with an increased critical facility to select and integrate relevant knowledge and skills.

Thus, the psychology and social work are unable to

operate as 'value-free' disciplines. Not only are various groups within society influenced by policy, but researchers and practitioners are greatly affected by the context in which they work. This means that professional practitioners need to reach beyond just the theory; they have to make sense of the origins and context of the whole operation of social work practice. To analyse, understand and continue to practice is often difficult, but it is more problematic in the long term if practitioners attempt to operate in a vacuum.

REFERENCES

Atwood, G. and Stolorow R. (1984). *Structures of Subjectivity*. Hillsdale, NJ: The Analytic Press.

Baker, H. & Baker, M. (1987). Heinz Kohut's self psychology: an overview. *American Journal of Fsychiatry*, 144:1-9.

Basch, M.F. (1976). The concept of affect: A re-examination. *Journal of the American Psychoanalytic Association*, 24:759-777.

Basch, M.F. (1980). *Doing Psychotherapy*. New York: Basic Books, Inc.

Basch, M.F. (1989). *Understanding Psychotherapy*. New York: Basic Books.

Beebe, B. & Lachmann, F.M. (1988). Mother-infant mutual influence and precursors of psychic structure. In *Progress in Self Psychology*, vol. III, ed. A. Goldberg. New York: Guilford Press (pp. 3-25).

Bibring, E. (1941). The development and problems of the theory of instincts. *International Journal of Psychoanalysis*, 21:

Bowlby, J. (1969). *Attachment and loss, Vol. I: Attachment*. New York: Basic Books.

Brandschaft, B. (1983). The negativism of the negative therapeutic reaction and the psychology of the self. In *The Future of Psychoanalysis* (Ed.) A. Goldberg. (pp. 327-359). New York: International Universities Press, Inc.

Breuer, J. and Freud, S. (1893-95). Studies on hysteria. *Standard Edition*, 2:3-305. London: Hogarth Press, 1955.

Coburn, W.J. (1997). The vision in supervision: Transference-countertransference dynamics and disclosure in the supervision relationship. Bulletin of the Menninger Clinic, Vol. 61, No. 4 (Fall).

Coburn, W.J. (1998). Patient unconscious communication and analyst narcissistic vulnerability in the countertransference experience. In *Progress in Self Psychology* (Ed.) A. Goldberg, Vol. 14, 1998.

Coburn, W.J. (2000). The organising forces of contemporary psychoanalysis: Reflections on nonlinear dynamic systems theory. *Psychoanalytic Psychology*, Vol. 17, No. 3.

Coburn, W.J. (2001). Subjectivity, emotional resonance and the sense of the real. *Psychoanalytic Psychology*, Vol. 18, No. 2.

Fosshage, J. (1983). The psychological function of dreams: A revised psychoanalytic perspective. *Psychoanalysis and Contemporary Thought*, 6:641-669. Also published in *Essential Papers on Dreams*, ed. M. Lansky. New York: New York University Press.

Fosshage, J. (1987). New vistas on dream interpretation. In M. Glucksman (Ed.), *Dreams in new perspective: The royal road revisited.* New York: Human Sciences Press.

Fosshage, J. and Loew, C. (1987). *Dream interpretation: A comparative study: Revised edition.* Costa Mesa, CA: PMA Publications. (Also translated into Japanese and published in Japan).

Fosshage, J. (1992). Self psychology: The self and its vicissitudes within a relational matrix. In N. Skolnick and S. Warshaw (Eds.), *Relational perspectives* (pp. 21-42). Hillsdale, NJ: Analytic Press.

Fosshage, J. (1992). Discussion on Morrison's Paper "On Shame". *Psychoanalytic Dialogues*. Vol. 4, l: 37-44, (1994).

Fosshage, J. (1994). Toward reconceptualising transference: Theoretical and clinical considerations. *International Journal of Psycho-Analysis*, 75, 2: 265-280.

Fosshage, J. (1997). Listening/experiencing perspectives and the quest for a facilitative responsiveness. In A. Goldberg (Ed.), *Progress in self psychology* (pp. 33-55), Vol. 13. Hillsdale, NJ: The Analytic Press.

Fosshage, J. (1997). 'Compensatory' or 'primary': An alternative view: Discussion of Marian Tolpin's Compensatory structures: Paths to the restoration of the self. In A. Goldberg (Ed.), *Progress in self psychology* (pp. 21-27), Vol. 13. Hillsdale, NJ: The Analytic Press.

Fosshage, J. and Lichtenberg, J. (1997). Transference: A self and motivational systems perspective. In M. Moskowitz, C. Monk, C.

Kaye, and S. Ellman (Eds.), *The neurobiological and developmental basis for psychotherapeutic intervention*. Livingston, NJ; Jason Aronson.

Fosshage, J. (1998). On aggression: Its forms and functions. *Psychoanalytic Inquiry*. Vol. 18, 1: 45-54.

Fosshage, J. (1998). Discussion of Anna Ornstein's, "The fate of narcissistic rage in psychotherapy." *Psychoanalytic Inquiry*, Vol. 1, 1: 71-81.

Freud, S. (1900). The interpretation of dreams. *Standard Edition*, 4 & 5. London: Hogarth Press, 1953.

Freud, S. (1905). Three essays on the Theory of Sexuality. *Standard Edition*, 7. London: Hogarth Press, 1953.

Freud, S. (1926). Inhibitions, symptoms and anxiety. *Standard Edition*, 20:87-179. London, Hogarth Press, 1959

Freud, S. (1933). New introductory lectures on psychoanalysis. *Standard Edition*, 22:5-182. London: Hogarth Press, 1964.

Gunderson, J.G. (1984). *Borderline personality disorder*. Washington, DC: American Psychiatric Press.

Gunderson, J.G. (1989). Borderline personality disorder. In H. I. Kaplan and B. J. Sadock (Eds.), *Comprehensive textbook of psychiatry / V*. Baltimore, MD: Williams & Wilkins.

Kohut, H. (1979). The Two Analyses of Mr. Z. *International Journal of Psychoanalysis*. 60:3-27.

Kohut, H. (1980). Summarising reflections. In *Advances in Self Psychology*, ed. A. Goldberg, New York: International Universities Press.

Lee, R.& Martin, C. (1991). Psychotherapy after Kohut: A textbook of psychology. Hillsdale, NJ: The Analytic Press.

Leider, R.J. (1983). Analytic neutrality - a historical review. *Psychoanalytic Inquiry*, 3:665-674.

Lichtenberg, J.D. (1983). *Psychoanalysis and Infant Research*. Hillsdale, NJ: The Analytic Press.

Lichtenberg, J.D. (1984). The empathetic mode of perception and alternative vantage points for psychoanalytic work. In: *Empathy II* (ed.) Lichtenberg. Bornstein and Silver. Hillsdale, NJ: The Analytic Press.

Ornstein, A. (1981). Self pathology in childhood: Developmental and clinical considerations. *Psychiatric Clinics of North America* 4:435-453.

Ornstein, A. and Ornstein, P. (1984). Empathy and the therapeutic dialogue. *The Lydia Rapoport Lectures* #11, available from Smith School of Social Work, Northampton, MA. (Ornstein and Lachmann 8/12).

Ornstein, A. and Ornstein, P. (1985). Parenting as a function of the adult self: A psychoanalytic developmental perspective. In: *Parental Influences in Health and Disease*, J. Anthony and G. Polluck (eds.). Boston: Little, Brown Co.

Ornstein, P. & Ornstein, A. (1980). Formulating interpretations in clinical psychoanalysis. *International Journal of Psychoanalysis*, 61:203-211.

Overton, W. (in press). The structure of developmental theory. in P. van Geert and L. P. Mos (eds.). *Annals of Theoretical Psychology*, Volume 6. New York: Plenum.

Palombo, J. (2001). *Learning Disorders and Disorders of the Self in Children and Adolescents*. New York: W. W. Norton.

Papousek, H., & Papousek, M. (1979). Early ontogeny of human social interaction. In M. von Cranach, K. Koppa, W. Lepenies, & P. Ploog, eds. *Human Ethology: Claims and Limits of a New Discipline*. Cambridge: Cambridge University Press.

Parens, H. (1979). *The Development of Aggression in Early Childhood*. New York: Aronson.

Panel (1981). The neutrality of the analyst in the analytic situation, R.J. Leider, reporter. *Journal of the American Psychoanalytic Association*, 32:573-585.

Perlman, Stuart (1999). *The Therapist's Emotional Survival: Dealing with the Pain of Exploring Trauma*. New York: Aronson.

Racker, H. (1968). *Transference and Countertransference*. New York: Int Univ. Press.

Reed, G. (1987). Rules of clinical understanding in classical psychoanalysis and in self psychology: A comparison. *Journal of the American Psychoanalytic Association*, 35:421-446.

Ringstrom, P.A. (1994) "An Intersubjective Approach to Conjoint Therapy," Progress in Self Psychology, Vol. 10, Hillsdale NJ: The Analytic Press.

Ringstrom, P.A. (1995) "Exploring the Model Scene: An Intersubjective Approach to Brief Psychotherapy." Psychoanalytic Inquiry.

Ringstrom, P.A. (1998) "Impasses in Contemporary Psychoanalysis: Revisiting the Double Bind Hypothesis," Psychoanalytic Dialogues Vol. 8, #2.

Ringstrom, P.A. (1998). "The Pursuit of Authenticity and the Plight of Self-Deception - Precursors to Paradoxes, Double Binds, and Therapeutic Impasses: Commentary on Malcolm Slavin and Daniel Kriegman's Article" Psychoanalytic Dialogues Vol.8, #2.

Ringstrom, P.A. (1998). "Metacommunication versus Negotiation - Distinguishing Responses to Paradox versus Conflict: Response to Slavin and Kriegman's Commentary," Psychoanalytic Dialogues Vol. 8, #2.

Ringstrom, P.A. (1998) "Competing Selfobject Functions: The Bane of the Conjoint Therapist," The Bulletin of the Menninger's Clinic.

Ringstrom, P.A. (1998) "An Interview with Bernard Brandchaft" Self Psychology Newsletter (June).

Ringstrom, P.A. (1999) "Exploring the Patient's 'Interiority': A Discussion of Joyce Slochower's Paper," Psychoanalytic Dialogues Vol. 9, #6.

Ringstrom, P.A. (1999) "News from the Western Division" Self Psychology Newsletter (June).

Ringstrom, P.A. (1999) "Self-Psychology Integrating and Evolving Therapeutic Action or, How Does Analysis Cure" Self Psychology Newsletter (June).

Ringstrom, P.A. (in Press) "Psychoanalysis: The Extraordinary Path: to the Ordinary Mind - A Discussion of Barry Magid's Chapter, 'Your Ordinary Mind'" in Buddhism and Psychoanalysis, ed. By Jeremy Saffron, NY.

Ringstrom, P.A. (in press) Cultivating the Improvisational in Psychoanalytic Treatment," Psychoanalytic Dialogues.

Rowe, C. (1992). Development from archaic to mature selfobject transferences. Clinical Social Work Journal, Vol 20, No. 1 (Spring).

Rowe, C. & MacIsaac, D. (1989). Empathic Attunement: The "Technique" of Psychoanalytic Self Psychology. Northvale, NJ: Jason Aronson.

Rubovits-Seitz, R. (1988). Kohut's method of interpretation: A critique. *Journal of the American Psychoanalytic Association*, 36:933-959.

Schafer, R. (1976). *A New Language for Psychoanalysis*. New Haven: Yale University Press.

Schore, A.N. (1994). Affect regulation and the origin of the self: The neurobiology of emotional development. Mahwah, NJ: Lawrence Erlbaum Associates. [Not primarily self psychology, but helpful with understanding affective development of the self. - P. Ornstein.].

Shane, M., & Shane, E. (1980). Psychoanalytic developmental theories of the self: An integration. In *Advances in Self Psychology*., ed. A. Goldberg, New York: International Universities Press, pp. 19-46.

Shane, M., & Shane, E. (1986). Self change and development in the analysis of an adolescent patient. In *Progress in Self Psychology, vol., 2*, ed. A. Goldberg, New York: Guilford Press, pp. 142-160.

Shane, M., & Shane, E. (1988). Pathways to integration: Adding to the self psychology model. In *Progress in Self Psychology, vol., 4*, ed. A. Goldberg, New York: Guilford Press, pp. 71-78.

Shapiro, S. (1995). *Talking with Patients: A Self Psychological View of Creative Intuition and Analytic Discipline*. Northvale, NJ: Jason Aronson Inc.

Socarides, D. and Stolorow, R. (1984/85). Affects and selfobjects. *Annual of Psychoanalysis*. 12/13:105-119. New York: International Universities Press.

Spence, D. (1982). *Narrative Truth and Historical Truth*. New York: Norton.

Steele, R. (1979). Psychoanalysis and hermeneutics. *International Review of Psychoanalysis*, 6:389-411.

Stepansky, P.E. & Goldberg, A., eds. (1984). *Kohut's Legacy: Contributions to Self Psychology*. Hillsdale, NJ: Analytic Press.

Sterba, R. (1934). The fate of the ego in analytic therapy. *International Journal of Psychoanalysis*,15:117-126.

Stern, D. (1985). *The Interpersonal World of the Infant*. New York: Basic Books.

Stolorow, R. et al.,(1987) *Psychoanalytic Treatment: An Intersubjective Approach*. Hillsdale, NJ: The Analytic Press.

Stolorow, R. & Atwood, G. (1992). *Contexts of Being*. Hillsdale, NJ: The Analytic Press.

Stolorow, R. and Lachmann, F. (1980). *Psychoanalysis and Developmental Arrests: Theory and Treatment*. New York: International Universities Press.

Stolorow, R. and Lachmann, F. (1984/85). Transference: The future of an illusion. *The Annual of Psychoanalysis* 12/13:19-38. New York: International Universities Press.

Stolorow, R., Brandchaft, B., and Atwood, G. (1987). *Psychoanalytic Treatment: An Intersubjective Approach*. Hillsdale, NJ: The Analytic Press.

Strozier, Charles B. (1978). Heinz Kohut and the Historical Imagination. *The Psychohistory Review*, Vol. VII, No. 2. Reprinted (1980) in Arnold Goldberg (Ed.), *Advances in Self Psychology* (pp. 397-406). New York: International Universities Press.

Strozier, Charles B. (1983). Fantasy, Self Psychology and the Inner Logic of Cults. In Arnold Goldberg (Ed.), *The Future of Psychoanalysis* (pp. 477-493). New York: International Universities Press.

Strozier, Charles B. (Ed.). (1985). *Heinz Kohut, Self Psychology and The Humanities: Reflections on a New Psychoanalytic Approach*. New York: Norton Publishing Company.

Strozier, Charles B. (1985). Glimpses of a Life: Heinz Kohut (1913-1981). In Arnold Goldberg (Ed.), *Progress in Self Psychology* (Vol. 1, pp. 3-12). New York: The Guilford Press.

Strozier, Charles B. (1987). The Soul of Wit: Kohut and The Psychology of Humor. *The Psychohistory Review, 16*, 47-68.

Strozier, Charles B. (1996). Heinz Kohut and Psychohistory. *The Psychohistory Review, 25*, 1-18.

Strozier, Charles B. (1997). Heinz Kohut's Struggles with Religion, Ethnicity, and God. In Donald Capps and Janet L. Jacobs (Eds.), *Religion, Society, and Psychoanalysis*. San Francisco, CA: Westview Press.

Terman, D. (1975). Aggression and Narcissistic Rage: A Clinical Elaboration. In: *The Annual of Psychoanalysis, 3*:239-255.

Terman, D. (1980). Object Love and the Psychology of the Self. In A. Goldberg (Ed.), *Advances in Self Psychology*, 349-365. New York: International Universities Press.

Terman, D. (1988). Optimal frustration: Structuralisation and the Therapeutic Process. In: *Progress in Self Psychology, vol., 4*, ed. A. Goldberg, New York: Guilford Press, pp. 113- 125.

Terman, D. (1992). Introduction. In: *Progress in Self Psychology*, Vol.8, ed. A. Goldberg. Hillsdale, NJ: The Analytic Press.

Tolpin, M. (1971). On the beginnings of a cohesive self. In: *The Psychoanalytic Study of the Child*, 25:273-305. New Haven: Yale University Press.

Tolpin, P. (1983). Self psychology and the interpretation of dreams. In *The Future of Psychoanalysis* (ed.) A. Goldberg. (pp. 255-271).

Tolpin, P. (1983). A change in the self: The development and transformation of an idealising transference. *International Journal of Psychoanalysis*, 64:461-485.

Wallace, E.R. (1988). What is truth? Some philosophical contributions to psychiatric issues. *American Journal of Psychiatry*, 145:137-147.

Winnicott, D (1949). Hate in the counter-transference. *International. Journal of Psychoanalysis*, 30:69-74.

Wolf, E.S. (1976). Ambience and Abstinence. In: *The Annual of Psychoanalysis*, 4:101-115. New York: International Universities Press.

2

Historical Development of Psychiatric Social Work

The development of psychiatric social work has been largely dependent on the rise of social psychiatry in this country, especially that type represented by such leaders as Dr. Adolf Meyer, Dr. E.E. Southard, and Dr. William A. White. It was admitted, as it had been stressed too exclusively in the prior period, that some mental problems have their origins in biological conditions which are relatively unaffected by social factors and need medical rather than psychological or social treatment. But this early group of psychiatrists also emphasised that many cases of mental instability were basically social in their causation and accordingly needed social treatment. It was not possible, they argued, to think of treatment as solely individual. The patient suffers from a condition which cannot be fully treated without consideration of his environment. The patient may be treated successfully on an individual basis, but still may need counsel on working out an adjustment with his family, with his neighbors, at work, and in other life situations. This kind of social interpretation of the nature of treatment provided the groundwork on which psychiatric social work could build.

Use of Detailed Records

Another important contribution of this school of psychiatrists was record-taking. At the time of Meyer, mental patients were given hasty diagnoses which consisted for the most part of someone's guess about the central psychological manifestation of the patient. At one time this diagnosis might be correct, and at other times it might be wrong, but by any modern standard it was sadly inadequate, since it did not relate the individual to his past and to the real relationships which he had with the community of which he was a part. Meyer believed that classification systems were woefully lacking and sought to encourage securing case records of a fairly detailed character.

Social Work Contribution

These developments (and others) within the field of psychiatry were significant for the origin of psychiatric social work because they early defined the function of the psychiatric social worker. In the first place the psychiatrist had to understand the kinds of social information required by Meyer's views or find someone else who did. Because of the division of labor and the crying need for psychiatrists, among other reasons, it was natural that there should arise a special group of workers who assisted the psychiatrists in using the social evidence of mental cases. The psychiatrists were most proficient in the psychiatric aspects of mental disease, and the psychiatric social workers were most capable in uncovering social causes and implications. Psychiatric social workers were not only called upon to make the diagnostic work of psychiatrists more meaningful; they were also needed to participate in the treatment. The same skill used in gathering and understanding the social experience of a patient was important in the adjustment of the patient to his home and community. Thus psychiatric social workers were needed both for analysis and therapy.

But aside from the need for psychiatric social workers on the part of psychiatrists, social workers generally were interested in the problems of people suffering from mental disorders. As early as 1874 a paper was read at the National Conference of Social Work (now the National Conference on Social Welfare), with the title "The Duty of the States Toward Their Insane Poor." Soon afterwards, a section of the Conference was formed on insanity and feeble-mindedness to give expression to the rising interest of social workers. The rise of the mental hygiene movement also became an important rallying point for social workers interested in the mental aspects of clients' problems.

Professional Training Beginnings

The acceptance of psychiatric social work as a definite part of social work was aided noticeably by the experiences of the Botson Psychopathic Hospital. From the very beginning of the hospital there as some provision for such work. A year after the hospital was established under the leadership of Dr. E. E. Southard (1912), Miss Mary C. Jarrett became the head of its social service department. The psychiatric social work of this hospital has been ably described in *The Kingdom of Evils*, written by Dr. Southard and Miss Jarrett (1922). The book is one of the first detailed and reliable accounts in the new field. While the authors made no claim to the use of revolutionary materials in their work, they did provide a guide for the types of activities which prevailed at the Boston Psychopathic Hospital. In general, the writers saw four kinds of social work activity within their hospital: (1) casework service, (2) executive duties, (3) social research, and (4) public education. While they recognised all these four divisions, they believed and it is now accepted generally, that the major energies of the worker should be utilised in casework service. The other functions have today mostly fallen to specialists in other areas of social work.

As a means of increasing the number of proficient workers in psychiatric social work, Dr. Southard and Miss Jarrett arranged for some students to take their social work training in the social service department of the Boston Psychopathic Hospital. It was principally through this educational device that the first genuine professional training originated. At first the training was related to the professional social work programme of the Simmons College School of Social Work. Four years later, in 1918, under the impact of the war-created needs in the psychiatric field, the Smith College School for Social Work was founded to meet the demand for personnel which the new awareness of mental problems required. Co-operating in this venture was the National Committee for Mental Hygiene. What began as an eight-month experimental Training School for Psychiatric Social Work under the direction of Miss Jarrett and the joint sponsorship of Smith College, the National Committee, and the Boston Psychopathic Hospital, became in time one of the outstanding schools for the training of social workers.

After Care Development

The interest of social workers in psychiatry was further stimulated by their contacts with discharged patients from mental hospitals and institutions.

The experience of the State Charities Aid Association in New York shows the development of such interest on the part of social workers. In 1906, as a result of a study made on the subject, an "aftercare agent" was appointed by the Association to handle those cases in which some change was needed in the home circumstances of patients who no longer had to be hospitalised or institutionalised. It was the job of this "agent" to ease the adjustment problem of the discharged patient as he sought to re-establish normal personal and community relationships. Half a decade later, on the basis of the experience of the State Charities Aid Association, a worker was provided, out of public funds, to perform a similar function under the State Commission on Lunacy at the Manhattan State Hospital. In 1912 an outpatient department was established at the Long Island State Hospital. Similarly, a clinic created for mentally ill persons was established in co-operation with the Manhattan and the Central Islip State Hospitals. In the years immediately following, numerous arrangements were made through the co-operation of social workers and psychiatrists to care for the social and psychological aspects of mentally disturbed people.

Elsewhere the interest of social workers originated other psychiatric social service facilities. In Massachusetts, beginning in 1913, attempts were made to formalise, through the creation of outpatient departments of mental hospitals and institutions the attention which social workers had been giving informally to discharged mental patients. Also in Massachusetts, as early as 1918, a Division of Social Service was inaugurated which had, among other responsibilities, the task of planning and co-ordinating the various social service activities of the state mental hospitals. This was the first example of co-ordination in psychiatric social work on a state level.

Even general hospitals with psychiatric clinics began to see the need for social work. Bellevue Hospital and the Cornell Clinic in New York City, and the Massachusetts General Hospital are excellent illustrations of this movement. It was readily realised that clinics dealing with mental patients on a less permanent and less intense basis than the state hospitals and institutions had need for extended social service work. The desire for concrete data on the life of the patient was felt no less in the clinic of the general hospital than in the state mental hospital. Perhaps the origin of the current co-operative treatment used by psychiatric social workers and psychiatrists can be traced, in part, to their activity in the general hospitals.

Moreover, through the activities of the psychiatric social worker in the general hospital, the social service agencies of the community were reminded rather vividly of the reality and promise of social work applied to psychiatric cases.

Recent Trends

The need for psychiatric social workers has increased in recent years. Psychiatric social workers continue to practice in their traditional settings, as will be explained in detail later in this chapter, but newer demands are being made on them for service.

The psychiatric social worker is gaining wider acceptance in community planning. Since a large part of the mental health need in many communities is for community-wide preventive services, it is natural that the psychiatric social worker be invited to contribute to the indirect assistance of individual persons. The task of educating the general public in strengthening mental health requires that psychiatric social workers take part in various local and state programmes devoted to this end.

Psychiatric social workers are being employed increasingly in programmes for older persons and for juvenile delinquents, in residential treatment homes for children, and in diagnostic and consultation services for the mentally retarded and their families. Psychiatric social workers today are participants in various research studies which are aimed at understanding, preventing, and treating mental illnesses.

In a few instances there are psychiatric social workers who are employed by private psychiatrists. Their work is obviously different from that of the psychiatric social worker who maintains his own private practice without the controlling judgments of a psychiatrist.

National Mental Health Act

The National Mental Health Act, passed by Congress in 1946, resulted from a growing concern on the part of many persons and organisations for the mental welfare of the citizenry. The Act is administered by the National institute of Mental Health of the United States Public Health Service in the Department of Health, Education, and Welfare. The Institute is guided in its activities by the National Mental Health Council, headed by the Surgeon General. Under the terms of the Act, the following programmes have been established: (1) research, (2) training of personnel (psychiatric social workers, psychologists, psychiatric nurses, laboratory technicians, and psychiatrists), and (3) the creation of mental health services for the prevention and treatment of mental illness. Although the National Institute maintains a hospital for clinical observations and research, it does not itself achieve the above-listed purposes, but works through a complex system of grants to states, universities, laboratories, hospitals and individuals.

Treatment of So-called Normal People

Aside from the growing need for psychiatric social workers in hospitals, social workers generally have for a long time been interested in psychiatry because of their constant relationships with so-called normal people in their daily work. While most persons came for many kinds of services other than help with their mental and emotional difficulties, there were many individuals in whom the social workers detected some kinds of conflict, disorganisation, and inability to handle themselves in their life situation. These persons were not so disabled mentally and emotionally that they needed to be placed in a mental hospital, and often they did not require extensive treatment of their psychiatric problems. They were able, by and large, to manage their own affairs in the community, to take part in family life, in work, and in recreation. Yet many of them suffered from such emotional disturbances as excessive moroseness, excitability, guilt, or some other undesirable personality characteristic. These people stimulated a wide interest in psychiatry among social workers.

Thus family casework, child welfare work—in fact, all of the specialties of social work—became psychiatrically oriented. Social workers generally were seeking to understand why and how the people they dealt with behaved as they did—why it was, for example, that an individual who could see the rationality of a certain way of behaviour could not seem to carry through on it. The older, nonpsychiatric theories of human motivation and conduct were not able to satisfy the more inquiring minds among the social workers. It was logical, therefore, for them to turn to psychiatry to learn its contributions to a fuller and more profound understanding of human nature and conduct.

Formation of Professional Organisation

By the second decade of the present century psychiatric social work had been established on a rather firm footing. In 1920 a group of psychiatric social workers met at the Psychopathic Hospital in Boston to discuss the possible formation of a professional body to serve their interests.

The fact that the group felt initially that the time might be ripe for establishing a professional organisation attests to the intensity of sentiment for psychiatric social work which must have been present in that section of the country. But, after due consideration, the group felt it would be unwise to set up such a body and they relinquished the idea of a formal organisation. They did form, however, a Psychiatric Social Workers Club which had as its purpose "to maintain the standard of psychiatric social work throughout the country." Because the American Association of Hospital Social Workers (composed of those social workers employed in hospitals usually not concerned with mental patients) was already in existence, the Psychiatric Social Workers Club decided that it would be suitable to petition that organisation for affiliation.

In 1922 the Club became the Section on Psychiatric Social Work of the American Association of Hospital Social Workers. Under the leadership of this Association, psychiatric social work was encouraged and became an active specialty in the field of social work But because the alliance seemed to imply too exclusive a relationship with one social work service, namely, medical social work, interested psychiatric workers separated from the hospital association and in 1926 formed the American Association of Psychiatric Social Workers. In 1955 this Association became a part of the National Association of Social Workers.

Definition of Psychiatric Social Worker. In recent years there has been some confusion about the exact meaning of the term *psychiatric social worker*. At the present time the psychiatric social worker is thought of as a social worker who deals with mental and emotional problems of clients, either in conjunction with a psychiatrist or with a psychiatrist taking major supervisory responsibility for the cases.

Developments During Two World Wars

There is an impression even among some social workers that the rise of psychiatric social work was the result merely of the needs arising out of the First World War. This is not so. There can be no doubt that the war accented the needs in the psychiatric field and provided fresh and frequent cases for consideration, but the psychiatric social work movement, like the psychiatric movement itself, was on firm ground even before the war. The First World War did, however, create a number of benefits for the rising field of psychiatric social work. It stimulated the development of training facilities and defined the scope and function of the psychiatric social worker. It also brought the subject of mental illness to the attention of the general population.

The Second World War, with its increased stress on the importance of psychiatric treatment, greatly strengthened the possibilities of psychiatric social work by opening for it new and increased responsibilities. The recognition in 1943 of the personnel category S.S.N. 263 by the armed forces, creating military psychiatric social workers, and the establishment in 1945 of the classification M.O.S. 3605, giving officer status to those who could qualify for military psychiatric social work, gave positive and new prestige to psychiatric social work. Following the Second World War additional civilian interest has been shown on the part of informed citizens. The employment of psychiatric social workers in the Veterans Administration under Public Law 390 also is doing much to strengthen the field.

Teamwork

The psychiatric social worker is in most instances part of a team of workers consisting of psychiatrists, psychiatric nurses, laboratory technicians, and occupational and physical therapists. Each member of the team utilises his special training and skills in the joint effort to understand and treat the patient. The role of the psychiatric social worker as a team member is explained in the following account:

The psychiatric social worker's primary contribution to the diagnosis, treatment and disposition of mentally-ill patients and their families is made through casework and group work services. By means of this person-to-person helping relationship through individual interviews or group process the social worker can assist the individual to determine and resolve specific problems in his environment and interpersonal relationships which interfere with adequate functioning. This helping process derives solely from the social worker's professional skills and techniques. The psychiatric social worker works in a collaborative relationship with other members of the psychiatric team, in which the psychiatrist has ultimate medical responsibility. The social worker coordinates his activities and functions with those of other members of the team and contributes his particular competence to the formulation and execution of the team plan, policies and procedures.

Places of Practice

Psychiatric social workers are employed in hospitals and clinics, in public health nursing agencies, and in educational institutions. At the present time the Veterans Administration is the largest employing agency of psychiatric social workers in the country, with over 1,3000 social work personnel, most of whom are psychiatric social workers. These workers are employed in Administration-sponsored hospitals, clinics, and regional offices.

Hospitals

The psychiatric social work movement has always had close association with hospitals. In the light of what is now known about psychosomatic disorders—the sometimes subtle and complex connections between illnesses of the body and conditions of the mind—this association certainly has been fortunate. Medicine and social work are now co-operating on the study and treatment of psychosomatic cases.

The need for social workers in mental hospitals is obvious. Historically, the programme of the Veterans Administration of the federal government, in the wake of the First World War, contributed to the increasing awareness of the possibilities of psychiatric social work care in veterans hospitals for the mentally ill. But the development of social work care in mental hospitals has been uneven. On one extreme some states and individual organisations (the Veterans Administration, for example) have created quite admirable programmes of social service care which have involved a more or less complete service to patients from planned intake, through hospital treatment, and release into the community. These programmes have also been marked with a high spirit of co-operation among the staffs in the mental hospitals. But there are all too many states and organisations which have practically ignored the possibilities of adequate social service for the mentally ill.

Intake. The psychiatric social worker in the mental hospital is first of all concerned with intake. When the patient is referred to the hospital, it is generally the responsibility of this specialist to contact the patient's home and community and to make a preliminary arrangement with the patient himself in order to gather facts which can be used in diagnostic work within the hospital. In some places the nature of this work is informal, though it is recognised as being tremendously important. By means of such work the hospital gains an insight into the patient's background and the special circumstances of his home and community, and thus is better able to initiate treatment appropriate to the case. Moreover, a preliminary survey will indicate the possibilities of further home contact, of visits by relatives and friends, and of the later return of the patient to his home.

Often the intake process involves the social worker in some casework service to the patient's family.

Shortly after her husband had been admitted for attempting suicide, a tearful, distraught Mrs. A. was met in the lobby by the social worker, who introduced herself and then escorted Mrs. A. to her office. On the way to the office, Mrs. A. bombarded the worker with questions about her husband's condition. On several occasions she expressed fear that her husband would die. The social worker telephoned the ward physician and learned that the patient's stomach had been washed out. The worker then made arrangements for Mrs. A. to see the ward physician, who reassured her that everything was being done for her husband. After seeing the doctor, Mrs. A. and the worker returned to the Social Service office where Mrs. A. continued to cry for a few minutes. The worker allowed her to express her concern in this way. When Mrs. A. stopped crying, she then verbalised her concern for her children and herself since she had only 50 in her purse and no other funds were available.

The worker made definite arrangements for a community agency to give financial assistance and transportation. She gave Mrs. A. her card and wrote on it the name of the ward physician in the event Mrs. A. wished to call either of them. She also gave Mrs., A. an appointment to return to see her.

Social Treatment. The second responsibility of the psychiatric social worker in a mental hospital is that of treatment. In one sense treatment begins on the day of the first contact and is involved in everything that the worker does while interacting with the client. In some hospitals the psychiatric social worker has social investigation as his main duty and may have little or no relation with the patient himself. In other situations the worker may have shared and co-operative responsibility for treatment in addition to the task of investigation. In the following case, a psychiatric social worker describes his part in the treatment of a patient:

A patient who was quite characteristic of many seen in the treatment center was a Marine who had gone through a part of the Marshall campaign, had been in the Saipan and Tinian campaigns from beginning to end, and who on D Day went in on Iwo Jima. The final psychic insult came when he and one of his buddies were trying to take what looked like a pillbox. His buddy, who was operating a flame thrower, discovered too late that their objective was not a pillbox but an ammunition dump. The ammunition dump exploded, killing his buddy and burying the patient under several feet of volcanic soil from which he extricated himself and walked back to his outfit in a dazed condition. The patient was given an examination at a mobile hospital unit, was sent back to a base hospital, and nnally came to our hospital.

When I first saw the patient, he was hostile, irritable, suffering from loss of appetite, and showing gross weight loss. He was troubled with insomnia and had marked startle reactions. He related to me, however, rather easily, and I gave him adequate opportunity to recount his experiences and feelings about those experiences. During the seven-week period from the incident on Iwo Jima to the point of the patient's arriving at our treatment center, his symptoms had been getting progressively more severe.

With this case we considered it our goal to attempt to release the patient from his acute anxiety state and possibly to deal superficially with some of his feelings relative to the death of his buddy and his leaving his outfit. The treatment in this case consisted of three one-hour interviews a week during which we discussed his feeling state centering around his symptoms. After eight or nine interviews he seemed to experience considerable relief, particularly as we were able to relate his specific symptoms to the reactions of a normal human being under situations of severe stress. Also, concurrently with these interviews, the patient co-operated fully in participating in aggressive physical and recreational activities—boxing and playing touch football and badminton, combined with work in the photography laboratory where he showed his considerable skill and interest.

At the end of five weeks he was eating well, showed a substantial gain in weight, and was less hostile. His startled reactions had subsided, but he still complained of insomnia and showed considerable irritability. During the sixth and seventh week he was able to discuss these problems rather freely. In discussing these he was enabled to bring forth some of his guilt feelings incidental to the death of his buddy and the leaving of his outfit. As we got into this area he showed a marked reduction in irritability and reported sleeping better. At the end of eight weeks he was able to leave the center with what we considered to be good insight and with a feeling of being quite adequate to meet most situations in civilian life.

The auspices of the hospitals, the availability of psychiatrists, the nature of cases, the skill of psychiatric social workers, the philosophy of treatment held by the staff of hospital—all have a part determining the psychiatric social workers role. Recently, as in the case of the child guidance clinic, psychotherapy has become the responsibility of some psychiatric social workers.

Treatment of the patient may involve the worker not only in direct contact with the patient but also in continuing relationship with the patient's family. An example of the type of work which may be required with the relatives of a mental hospital patient is shown in the problem of gaining consent for treatment. A worker writes about this as follows:

Signing the required consent for shock therapy is in itself a grave responsibility for the relative to take, and when his conflict is heightened by ambivalent feelings, conscious or unconscious guilt, and hostility toward the patient, his indecision and suffering are heightened. Whereas the recommendation for treatment is made by the physician, the responsibility for helping the relative work through his own feelings is more often the responsibility of the social worker. The relative asks innumerable questions which he may have asked the physician previously, or which he has been afraid to ask. About electroconvulsive therapy, for example, he questions whether the memory loss is permanent. Does brain damage occur which affects the higher centers of the brain? What is the voltage? Have there been fatalities? What is the convulsion like? Is it painful? Does the patient remembers it? Is his personality going to be changed? Will he be cured? Will he resent the relative for giving consent? Simple, direct replies may prove sufficiently reassuring to the relative. Often it is evident that deeper anxieties prevent his arriving at a decision.

A daughter unable to sign consent for electroconvulsive therapy for her mother discussed several times with the social worker the doctor's recommendation, including the special involvement of the patient's having a mild arteriosclerotic condition. The daughter's anxiety was not alleviated. Alternative possibilities of removing the patient from the hospital and of additional consultation for confirmation of the recommendation were discussed and discarded. Some further exploration revealed that the daughter had experienced similar anxiety regarding every major decision involving the mother's physical welfare in the past.

It was not until this relative brought out her ambivalent feelings toward the patient, her feeling of having been rejected as a child, and her resentment at being in the position of having the mother-daughter role reversed, that she gained insight into the basis of her indecision. Feelings of hostility against the mother and their defense in fear of "hurting" and thus retaliating for previous injustices stood in the way of her signing the necessary consent papers. With this insight into her own attitudes, the daughter was able to face the problem with greater objectivity and arrive at a decision that involved less guilt and suffering for herself.

Release. The third of the psychiatric social worker's responsibilities is concerned with the release of the mental patient from the hospital or institution. In many hospitals the value of the psychiatric social worker is mainly demonstrated in this third period. Usually, the patient admitted to a mental hospital has left a community situation which has contributed in some measure to his problem. It is only a sign of basic intelligence for a mental hospital to want to make sure that the community into which the patient will return will enable him to overcome his previous difficulties and to make the best possible adjustment. However, it is not always easy for the psychiatric social worker to secure necessary changes in the families and communities in order to assure their acceptance of the patients. Often family members need to rethink their attitudes toward the patient, to settle their own problems, to extend themselves in such ways as will enable the patient to make sure of his complete recovery, if that is possible:

Mr. P. had been hospitalised as a result of an accidental gunshot wound in the head while hunting. History revealed a marital conflict and when he was referred for Trial Visit preparation, the wife was informed of the recommendation and she immediately remembered all of the quarrels and abuse her husband had heaped upon her and how on one occasion, he had attempted to choke her. Throughout his hospitalisation, she had always indicated a willingness to have him home "when the doctors say he is ready" but she had been "skirting" the patient's requests to go home on week-end leaves because she felt that the children didn't miss him as much as he said. Eventually, he did go home for a week-end and the wife complained of his dependence and referred to him as another "messy child." Subsequent week-end visits were planned with the wife. The patient's behaviour was discussed and the wife definitely asked how she handled him in various situations. Meanwhile, her husband's problem and limitations were explained along with due role of the worker when Trial Visit was actually granted. With this protection, the wife agreed to give him a chance to come home.

Henry Freeman suggests that the relatives with whom the psychiatric social worker has to deal may fall into three classes. The first of these is the group which seems capable of meeting the patient's needs. These relatives may need little more than some practical interpretation and suggestions from the hospital. The second are those that have problem attitudes but seem capable of modifying them. The third group is composed of those who present rigid and inflexible patterns. Both the second and third categories may require extensive casework attention from the psychiatric social worker if the full adjustment of the patient is to be achieved.

In planning for the patient's successful community adjustment, the psychiatric social worker must also consider the patient's own attitudes. While he has been in the mental hospital, the patient has learned a new mode of life. He must become accustomed again to economic responsibility for his family. Separation from those who have been greatly involved in his problem will required relearning in order to adjust to these persons. The psychiatric social worker helps the patient establish as normal a life as possible. The tie between the worker and the patient may continue long after the discharge.

Summary of Responsibilities. The responsibilities of the psychiatric social worker in a mental hospital—intake, treatment, and release—are portrayed in the following case summary in the fashion in which they most often occur—as a connected series of events:

The ward physician referred John Smith, twenty-three years old, because "he is depressed and needs someone to talk to" and, as a secondary reason, because additional history was needed for diagnosis. During the first interview the patient responded positively to the worker's suggestion that talking over some of his difficulties might be helpful. He mentioned his physical condition and employment as his two chief problems. He had had surgical treatments for a mastoid condition while in service and had been told that about once a year his ear would become infected and would run. This was very disturbing to him. In addition, he had been hospitalised by the army on several occasions because of a varicocele. He felt that the doctors had disagreed about the need for further treatment for it and about the prognosis. Already, he had spent some money on private medical care and was concerned about future expense. He talked at some length about his failure to achieve his lifelong ambition to become a policeman. Although he knew that his limited education would probably have to be supplemented, his greatest frustration came from the fact that he felt that he had been given the "run around" when he inquired at various places about how he could apply for an appointment to a police force. He told the worker that he had attempted suicide at least four times, and emphasised in this connection worry about his health and about work. At the conclusion of the interview the worker said that she thought that she could help him and that she would be able to talk with the ward physician before seeing him again.

During the second interview the patient was in better spirits. He said that he felt that the worker's talk with him had helped him to see that he was not using his energies constructively in solving his problems. Also being on the ward with so many other patients who were worse off than he had made him look at things differently. At times during this interview he was able to make a realistic approach to his difficulties. For instance, he said that in the first place, suicide was contrary to the teachings of his religion, and secondly, that if he really wanted to do something to help his wife and child, killing himself would certainly not be the answer. Also he felt that he had dwelt too much on the importance of his getting a job as a policeman, and that possibly later on when he had additional preparation he might make further application. At present he would concentrate on supporting his family as best he could.

On the next visiting day the worker talked with the

wife. She was a very small, pale young girl who seemed to be emotionally unstable and showed very little insight into her husband's condition. On the day the patient was admitted to Lyons she had been discharged from a period of hospitalisation resulting from a miscarriage. Although she since had been advised that she needed additional medical care, she refused to consider securing it until the patient left Lyons. She was inclined to be overprotective in her attitude toward her husband and wanted to give the worker the impression that there was nothing wrong with him. The worker interpreted to her that she was not judging the patient but that the staff was interested in his condition and in helping him. Additional history was secured from her which confirmed a particularly poor family background with extreme poverty during the patient's childhood and adolescence and serious delinquency among siblings. Although he later returned it, the patient had picked up a wallet belonging to another soldier during service because he was so distressed over letters received from his wife describing financial difficulties. As a result of this he was reduced in rank to a buck private. His wife continued to write him of difficulties at home and he finally went AWOL, returned home, secured work, and supported his wife and his mother for some time. He was eventually apprehended and court-martialed. While serving the six months guardhouse sentence imposed, he was hospitalised because of somatic symptoms and emotional instability. During this hospitalisation a medical discharge from the Army was granted on the basis of a diagnosis of psychoneurosis. The worker felt that Mrs. Smith had considerable guilt about her part in these two incidents, and that probably this was influencing her present protective attitude. Following his discharge Mr. Smith became discouraged about not getting a promotion on his job, which he felt he deserved. Real misfortunes occurred about housing and finances and he began to quarrel frequently with his wife. They finally separated. Shortly afterwards he was admitted to Lyons.

The worker continued to see the patient who maintained his pleased improved outlook and was able to be very helpful to some of the other patients on the ward. His wife had decided that she wanted him back and they intended to re-establish their home again following his discharge. He said that he was not unhappy in the hospital but that he would like to go out and prove that he could make good. Recognising that there were serious environmental and emotional problems with which Mr. and Mrs. Smith would have to contend, the worker discussed with them the possibility of a referral to a family agency in order that they might have continued professional assistance in working out their plans, and, after some interpretation, they both decided they wanted to follow this suggestion. When the case was considered by the diagnostic staff, the patient's symptoms were considered to be psychoneurotic in origin. The worker was asked to carry out the plan for referral to a community agency since it was felt that continue hospitalisation would not benefit Mr. Smith but that both he and his wife needed additional casework help. The case will be continued as active with social service until the referral has been accomplished.

Use of Foster Home Placement. The possibilities of employing foster home placement for the mentally ill have been demonstrated for a long time, but they have never been so appealing as now to social workers who deal with patients in mental hospitals. The idea that the family is beneficial and even therapeutic and may bring healing to the mentally sick is not new nor is it the special property of any group. Involved in foster home programmes are all of the problems that have been discussed previously under the foster home placement of children, plus other problems as well. The worker, therefore, who has responsibility for the operation of a foster home programme for mental patients must possess a high degree of social work competence in order that the objectives of such a programmemay be achieved. His responsibility lies in the following activities: (1) *selection of suitable patients*—obviously, not all mental patients can benefit from foster home placement; (2) *selection of homes*—because of the intricate and profound meaning which foster home placement may have for mental patients, appropriate skill must be shown in the selection of suitable foster homes; (3) *supervision of patients and homes*—after an arrangement has been made to place a patient in a foster home, the social worker has continuing obligations to see that the most is made of the situation.

The following is a case summary which shows the social worker's task in foster home placement of a mental patient:

> George's case is presented as an example of the adjustment of a continuous-treatment patient for whom many factors had to be considered in finding a home. First of all, the caretaker had to have enough understanding of venereal disease to know that there was no danger whatsoever of infection from the patient, for George was a general paretic. A second thing of importance was to have someone in the home to whom George could talk freely in Italian, for he had been born in Italy and his English was limited and third, the caretaker had to be a person who could handle George sufficiently firmly to see that he looked after himself adequately and that he did not annoy others. Finally, since George was somewhat infirm physically, he had to be helped up and down steps and watched to see that he did not fall as he walked around the house and yard. A home which answered all these needs and

offered many other possibilities for satisfaction was finally found.

Not much was known about George's early life in Italy. During the First World War George served three years in the Italian army. During this time he contracted syphilis, which many years later caused his mental illness. He was a skilled workman who had made a comfortable living for himself for many years. His marital adjustment had been unsatisfactory and terminated in a divorce, but his relationship with his daughter born before he entered the army, had been pleasant enough until he became mentally ill. He was admitted to a state hospital when he was forty-two years old. As the result of malarial treatment, he improved somewhat and was given parole, although he was far from well both physically and mentally. His daughter tried at this time and on many occasions subsequently to give him care in her home, but she could do nothing with him. She continued to show her interest, however, after he was committed, by providing him with clothing and spending money.

In spite of George's difficulty in adjusting, even for a short visit, at his daughter's, he wa placed in a family care home. it was thought that his daughter had always expected too much of him and that perhaps he would respond better to the care of a stranger who would not be upset by the annoying things he did. The home in which George was placed was a most unusual one. Mrs. Van, a widow, her sons and their wives, and her daughters and their husbands, all lived gaily and harmoniously in a large, rambling, old house with a fine garden. All the young people went out to work, which would leave Mrs. Van knew what had caused George's illness and understood that the infectious stage had long since passed and that he no longer needed any treatment. The social worker had also told her that George had been found very difficult for his daughter to handle. However, with the suggestions which the social worker gave Mrs. Van as to how to help George to do what was expected of him, she said she thought she would like to try caring for him. Mrs. Van had one other patient, a well-educated man who spoke Italian fluently, and she felt that interpreting for George would give this patient something to do that he would enjoy.

When George was first placed in Mrs. Van's home, he behaved exactly as he did at his daughter's—he was untidy, his table manners were terrible, and he was selfish and inconsiderate of everyone. However, Mrs. Van was not daunted. On the advice of the social worker she explained to George that he would have to room alone and eat alone until he had learned to keep himself tidy and to eat sufficiently well to sit at the table with people. She showed him how to handle his knife and fork and make suggestions as to how to eat in a way that was acceptable to others. Mrs. Van gave him this training in much the same way that one would train a child of two. He complained a little and at first there was some question whether he wanted to stay in the home. However, the social worker, in discussing the matter with him, urged him to wait for a few weeks to decide this question, and he consented.

In four months the patient, under the highly individualised care which he received in this home, became neat and tidy and many of his former objectionable habits disappeared. His table manners improved so there was no objection to his eating at the table with the family. He began to keep himself and his clothing clean. Today, while he still rooms alone, he keeps his room clean and attractive and no one would hesitate to share it with him if it were necessary. With the patient's improvement, it became easier to understand his English. He talks with the social worker now in English, confining his remarks chiefly to the statement that it is a nice home and he likes it there, or he may have some little episode to tell about the family, and, while he is not the kind of person who takes part in family activities, it is plain that he observes and takes an interest in what the family is doing. He now is content to listen to the radio and sit quietly looking at the pictures in magazines.

It has been interesting to notice the effect that George has had on the highly educated patient who is also in this home. Apparently, it has given him great satisfaction to feel that he has been important factor in George's improvement. He himself is an elderly man, and he shows George off and brags about him as if he were his grandchild. The relationship of these two patients, which has been considered so carefully when placement was made, has been mutually beneficial and has resulted in satisfactions to both.

While it is not expected that George will show much further improvement, he is comfortable and happy in family care. His daughter's interest in him is much greater than it was formerly. She is much pleased with his improved manners and his attitude of contentment. She says that now it is a pleasure to come to see him when before it was a duty. George has found a life which offers interests in keeping with his mental and physical limitations. There will, of course, be lapses in George's good behaviour, but they will probably not be frequent or prolonged.

With this patient there was little that the social worker could do directly but she was able to help Mrs. Van in training him to be a more socially acceptable human being. Mrs. Van's usually successful method of jollying the other patients under her care into doing things did not work with George. He had to be handled firmly but kindly. He had to be told over and over again what to do and how to do it. At times Mrs. Van called the social worker to come over and support her handling of George. Both Mrs. Van and the social worker had to learn a few Italian words to make George understand them and even then the other patient often had to be called in to explain things (he too had to be cautioned as to how he should speak to the patient). The first weeks were difficult, but as Mrs. Van says, George's improvement is ample reward. George now understands what is expected of him and he is living up to these expectations and derives satisfaction from doing so.

Clinics

Child Guidance Clinic

the child guidance movement presents wide opportunity for psychiatric social workers. The nature and functions of child guidance clinics and the role of the psychiatric social worker.

Outpatient Departments of General Hospitals

At the present time many adults with mental and emotional problems are treated in the clinics of general hospitals. The patients in these clinics may be those who come directly for help with their emotional problems, or they may be those who, having entered the hospital with some physical disability, upon analysis are discovered to be suffering from an emotional upset.

Mental Hospital Clinics

The mental hospital may also have a psychiatric clinic, but its function will differ somewhat from the clinics of general hospitals. It will be used to large part, especially in or near a large city, for the aftercare of discharged patients, thus permitting the continuing contacts of the mental hospital with patients after they have been restored to their families or placed with foster families. The clinics in a mental hospital may be able to offer more intensive and extended treatment for patients who do not need to be hospitalised but who are in need of continuing treatment. It may also facilitate the transfer of more serious mental cases from the community to the hospital.

Independent Clinics

There are some psychiatric clinics which are not associated with hospitals, or which have working relations with hospitals without coming under their direction supervision.

Other Places of Practice

Psychiatric social workers have been employed by public health nursing agencies to help nursing staffs understand the mental hygiene implications of their activities, to detect more readily those cases which need special psychiatric care, and to participate more intelligently in the community aspects of their work. The responsibilities of the psychiatric social worker in public health differ from those of a similar worker in another setting in that the public health organisation usually provides a course or courses for its staff. These courses regularly contain a basic introduction to the field of psychiatry, methods of detecting serious psychiatric ailments, the use of community facilities the basis on which referrals may and should be made by nurses to psychiatrists and psychiatric clinics, and other topics. In addition to giving the course the worker often engages at appointed times in informal discussions with nurses. The psychiatric social worker also may accompany those nurses who make home visits, in order to become more fully acquainted with the types of cases found in the field and to assist the nurse wherever possible in her approach to the patients. As was suggested in the preceding chapter, this type of work may also be performed by medical social workers.

Educational institutions also are currently employing psychiatric social workers in a limited way. The activities of the social worker in the general school setting have been previously described. Here it may be appropriate to mention three special types of situations in which the psychiatric social worker is being used increasingly. Private schools are more and more availing themselves of the services of psychiatric social workers. Undoubtedly, a further increase in the numbers of fully trained workers available will see an increase in the number of workers employed by private schools. So too, nursery schools are more and more interested in securing psychiatric social workers. It is seen that through the sue of such workers the nursery school is better able to serve the needs of its children. Both the child within the nursery school as well as the child's home relationships are considered. Colleges also are more interested in the possibilities of psychiatric social service than ever before. For many colleges an extended social service department considered as an intrinsic part of the educational programmeis seen as the next important step in curriculum advancement.

In addition there are a small number of psychiatric social workers who are employed by mental hygiene societies. These workers do chiefly community organisation works rather than casework and are used in preparing public relations materials, in co-ordinating the work of community agencies in the field, in planning conferences, and in assisting in community surveys.

REFERENCES

Deutsch, Albert, *The Mentally Ill in America*, rev. (Columbia University Press, New York, 1949).

Freeman, Lucy, *Hope for the Troubled* (King's Crown Press, New York, 1953).

Fromm, Erich, *The Sane Society* (Rinehart & Company, Inc., New York, 1955).

Kotinsky Ruth, and Witmer, Helen, eds., *Community Programmes for Mental Health* (Harvard University Press, Cambridge, 1955).

Lowrey, Lawson, *Psychiatry for Social Workers,* 2nd. ed. (Columbia University Press, New York, 1950).

Scheidlinger, Saul, *Psychoanalysis and Group Behaviour* (W.W. Norton & Company, Inc., New York, 1952).

3

Mental Health and Social Work: Co-operation & Contention

Social workers do not of course have a monopoly of sensitivity to social and ethical issues, of healthy scepticism about the medicalisation of problems of living, or of concern as to whether psychiatric intervention may not sometimes be more noxious than what it seeks to cure. But it does seem that social workers bring to their work a special awareness of these issues, which can do much to enrich or temper the deliberations of all those who are professionally involved with the individual who is described as 'mentally disordered', and this client group as a whole. This chapter begins with an overview of some key issues which often arise as opposite sides in a pro-versus anti-psychiatry debate.

However, mental disorder and its treatment is too multifaceted a topic for black-and-white notions. At the centre of the debate are two main questions: (1) Is it harmful to be classified as 'mentally ill'? (2) Is it logical to use the term 'mental illness'? The sociological literature on labelling (for example, Scheff, 1974) highlights the importance of societal reaction to deviant behaviour. Certain people are designated 'mentally ill' by those whom society has authorised to do so, or by other people who can find no better explanation for their deviant behaviour. They may then react by producing more 'illness behaviour'. They may feel stigmatised and see themselves as second-class citizens and withdraw from others, or occasionally try to fight back; and whatever true disability they may have will interact with the negative expectations of others to produce further disability. They may become chronic 'patients' inside or outside hospital.

Even if this does not happen, a record of psychiatric treatment and especially of involuntary hospitalisation can lead to a permanent change of status, with problems arising not only in informal relationships with other people but also in such areas as employment, emigration and relations with the legal system. Further, the use of the term 'mental illness' can deter not only the patient, but also the family and society at large from taking responsibility for helping in treatment and rehabilitation and for the prevention of psychiatric disorder: 'If it's an illness it's the doctors' job.' Alcoholism provides an illustration of this problem.

The notion that this is a disease can encourage the belief that individual effort has no part to play, and that social measures to limit alcohol consumption are irrelevant in the control of problem-drinking rates in the population. A diagnosis of 'depressive illness' can be taken as a signal to expect to be the passive recipient of pills or magic insights given out by a doctor; and the rest of society will regard proposals that social change might reduce the incidence of depression with considerable scepticism. Some of these consequences of the 'mental illness' label relate to the logical issues surrounding the use of the term. This is to some extent, of course, a debate about the use of language. Does 'illness' mean the signs and symptoms of a known bodily dysfunction that can be treated by physical means, without reference to the person's beliefs and feelings, and to which his behaviour and his social environment are irrelevant? If that is what is implied, then many other 'illnesses' would have to be given another name. The vast range of physical disorders with causes and remedies that involve a complex interaction of psyche and soma and environment give the lie to any simplistic notion of what we mean by 'illness' and 'treatment'.

We are being unfair to the general physician as well as to the psychiatrist if we assume that their so-called 'medical model' is a model of man as a machine with a mechanical fault, which can be mended by a technical expert who asks only that the machine be passive while he mends the broken part. 'Illness', then, is rarely a simple matter. It might be more valid to try to combat the notion held by patients, society and doctors alike that it is so, than to look for other language to describe the range of phenomena we now call 'mental illness'. The field of psychiatry encompasses a very wide variety of conditions, from the dementias with known physical damage to the brain, through schizophrenia with known hereditary as well as environmental components and suspected biochemical causes, to hysteria which mimicks physical malfunction without physical pathology. It is essential to recognise that mental illness is not a unitary phenomenon.

There are degrees of potential self-help in its prevention and cure, degrees of environmental influence, and degrees of need for medical, psychological and social intervention. Not only does each diagnostic group differ from every other on all these dimensions, but each individual client or patient differs from every other. For some, the use of the term 'illness' can have benign effects: it can reduce feelings of guilt and anxiety for both the patient and his family. It allows care instead of control, or even punishment, for those whose behaviour has caused alarm or harm to other people. Although we usually wish to emphasise the need for partnership between client and helper, and the need for shared responsibility in putting matters right, we also want to put across a message of compassion. The attitude of the person concerned, and the nature of the disorder, interact to determine the most appropriate balance of responsibility to be placed on the client. Those who would want to insist that mental disorder is never 'illness', and would require everyone to take complete responsibility, should note where such extreme lines of argument can take us: Szasz (1974) describes schizophrenics as people who are inconsiderate of others, and recommends that their behaviour be controlled like that of other deviants-rather than 'treated', and all those who have suicidal impulses, he believes, should be allowed to 'take their lives' without interference. Diagnosis is another form of labelling.

Diagnosis in psychiatry is much less reliable than in other branches of medicine. Temerlin (1968) has demonstrated how readily psychiatrists can be swayed by suggestion, to the extent of diagnosing sanity or mental illness depending on how the 'patient' is presented to them. Rosenhan (1973) and seven volunteers were admitted to mental hospitals and complained only of one symptom: hearing voices saying 'thud' and 'hollow' and 'empty'. All were admitted. Although they then ceased to complain of their 'symptoms', all but one were diagnosed as schizophrenic. Upon release, the seven were described as 'schizophrenic in remission'. These experiments and others like them have no doubt contributed to the vigour with which the goal of more reliable diagnostic practices has been pursued in recent years, and there are certainly still no grounds for complacency.

But as Wing (1978) points out, bad practice does not invalidate the practice itself. Wing and his co-workers have demonstrated that diagnostic practice can be improved. Clare (1976) also argues that abuse of psychiatry in both the East and the West is facilitated by loose and unreliable diagnostic systems, and is less likely when psychiatrists are obliged to follow strict criteria for the recognition of mental disorder and the classification of the various syndromes. Some diagnostic labels, however, remain little more than subjective comments by a psychiatrist: for example, 'psychopath' often means 'no other diagnoses fits (but I've got to classify him somehow)' and 'I don't like him' and 'I can't help him'. 'Psychopath' is, in addition, an example of a stigmatising label, which can colour the perceptions of all who get to know of it.

In this case the stigma is more severe in psychiatrically 'sophisticated' circles. On the other hand, a diagnosis of schizophrenia is more disturbing to the lay person, as a result of public ignorance and bad publicity: it conjures up images of Dr Jekyll and Mr Hyde (the mistaken notion of schizophrenia as split personality), or of the very rare cases of violence that are widely reported in the newspapers. Diagnosis can also have the effect of de-individualising—invalidating—the person who is diagnosed; all his qualities, except those that are subsumed under the diagnostic label, may be disregarded.

Attempts to avoid this have led to the introduction of such terms as 'the person with schizophrenia' instead of 'the schizophrenic' in order to stress that this person is in very many respects like no other person and in very many respects like all other people. Social workers make a valuable contribution in emphasising the individual and the universal; doctors risk concerning themselves too narrowly with the diagnostic category. While narrowness of view is a danger in all branches of medicine (for example, on maternity wards) it is of particular importance for psychiatric patients who are especially vulnerable to feeling devalued. If the person is living in an institution and depends very heavily on professional workers for his sense of worth, the hurt will be even more pronounced. A further problem with diagnostic labels is that they can lead to inappropriate and possibly damaging generalisations, and to premature decisions about the person's prognosis and ability to respond which may turn into self-fulfilling prophecies The person with senile dementia may be deprived of stimulation, medical care, ordinary respect.

The psychopath is assumed to be always 'manipulative' and never depressed, and is denied even the assistance that the rest of our clients can expect from the social and medical services. The schizophrenic is no longer listened to, and his abilities and strengths are forgotten. Once again, these are examples of bad practice, rather than inevitable consequences of diagnosis.

Watson (1979) argues that diagnostic enthusiasts are less often guilty of de-individualising psychiatric patients than are the sociologists who write of mental illness as if it were a unitary concept, and the anti-diagnosis workers in settings such as the therapeutic community, where all the patients are often treated alike regardless of diagnosis. Even writers who have drawn attention to the failings of psychiatry, such as Temerlin and Rosenhan, have not denied the possibility that there may exist clusters of symptoms that regularly occur together and have different causes and different cures, even if these have not to date been identified. A group of symptoms can turn out to have a particular organic basis (as in the case of general paralysis of the insane, now known to be caused by the syphilitic spirochaete), or to show a particular pattern of inheritance (for example, Huntington's Chorea), or to respond to a specific form of medication (for example, schizophrenia). Knowledge advances by a process that begins with categorisation according to specific, repeatable observations; this is followed by the formation of hypotheses concerning the categories, and then the testing of the hypotheses.

In other words, research is impossible without categorisation. This is as true of psychiatry as of any other field of study. For certain diagnostic groups, some compelling evidence about cause, course, and treatment has been obtained; the diagnostic categorisation has already proved its worth. In the chapters that follow there will be many examples of what has been achieved — for instance, the evidence concerning family relationships in schizophrenia and in depression, the effects of medication on these two major disorders, the effectiveness of behaviour therapy in the treatment of phobias. It is not possible, of course, to produce universal laws, only statements of probability. For example, it is probable that a certain kind of family interaction will be associated with relapse in schizophrenia; it is probable that a person who suffers recurrent attacks of hypomania will have fewer relapses if he receives lithium carbonate.

Such statements of probability are of immense value in planning for the patients involved. Practice needs to be anchored in knowledge: the knowledge base of psychiatry is limited but it is growing. Although accumulated practice wisdom must not be devalued, it has to be supplemented and often supplanted by knowledge derived from meticulous research. Research has already provided generalisations that offer a good starting point in individual cases. This body of knowledge would not exist were it not for the efforts of workers who have focused on reliable diagnosis. Despite these advances, there remains the argument that it is better not to fall into the hands of psychiatrists, not only because of their damaging labels and the harmful psychological and social processes that can be set in train, but for the straightforward reason that psychiatric patients are maltreated and unjustly deprived of freedom and human dignity, by psychiatrists themselves or by other staff in the psychiatric services, sometimes out of deliberate cruelty, more often through neglect, or well-meant but ignorant enthusiasm for the "treatment' being given.

Reports of the conditions in psychiatric hospitals, the results of public enquiries, and well-documented accounts of individual cases of mistreatment and injustice have highlighted the need for far stronger safeguards than are currently in operation. In order to stamp out abuses, much greater public awareness and sympathy need to be created; and the power of strong professions to protect their activities from outside scrutiny and debate, and their members from the consequences of malpractice, needs to be curtailed. Large institutions, isolated from the rest of society, need to be opened to the outside world, or, better still, abolished altogether. However, the abolition of psychiatry itself is hardly likely to bring an end to the ill-treatment of those whom we describe as mentally ill: history, and an examination of the practices in countries where psychiatry is less influential, provide clear evidence of this.

History provides numerous instances of the cruelty that can result if mental illness does not figure in explanations of bizarre or deviant behaviour. It is true that these evils did not disappear when asylums replaced prisons and workhouses, and doctors and nurses replaced witch-finders and gaolers. The asylums came to resemble the prisons, and some of the "treatments' were little better than chains or outright assault. However, the cruelties of psychiatry, and its harmful 'treatments', and the continuing indifference or worse of the public at large, are not a function of psychiatry and the psychiatric services *per se:* they are due to ignorance, insensitivity, or lack of resources, and they implicate not only the medical services but the society that employs them. Many of the real advances that have occurred over the last thirty years owe much to enlightened doctors and to medical researchers.

The drugs that maintain so many patients in the community who would otherwise be kept in institutions, and the physical treatments that bring the severely depressed back into contact with their world, are the inventions of psychiatrists. Looking back further, it was Pinel, a physician, who insisted on unchaining the Bicetre Asylum inmates, and Connolly, also a physician, who introduced 'moral treatment' at Hanwell Asylum. It is mischievous to equate bad hospitals and bad treatment with the institution of psychiatry. Attacks have to be aimed at those who are guilty of malpractice and the systems that shield them from outside scrutiny, and not indiscriminately. It is unfortunate, both for the relationship between the professions, and also for the fate of the mentally disordered patient or client, that so many social workers have been influenced by one side only in the anti-psychiatry debate.

Psychiatrists such as Wing (1978), Clare (1976) and Eisenberg (1977) have considered these issues without hysterical counter-attack and without denying the abuses that exist. Social workers need to become more aware of the achievements of modern psychiatry, and, without becoming uncritical psychiatrists' aides, they need to work alongside them in order to achieve more humane and better services. As research continues and empirical data accumulate, some questions that at present are matters of ideology become questions of fact.

For example, the long-term consequences of being labelled 'mentally disordered' are being assessed (for a brief review of the somewhat equivocal findings to date, see Fitzgerald, 1982). The feasibility of shorter hospital stays, and the possibility of overcoming the obstacles to returning to work, are being methodically explored (Hirsch *et al.,* 1979; Wansbrough and Cooper, 1980). And, as mentioned earlier, the fact that diagnostic reliability can be improved, and the value of grouping psychiatric symptoms under diagnoses, are being demonstrated for several diagnostic categories. In so far as empirically based knowledge is absorbed by both social workers and psychiatrists, so the two groups will find it easier to join together in a productive working relationship.

Value questions will remain, of course, and social workers will continue to ask them (so will many doctors, psychologists and nurses). But at the same time, we have to accept that if we are to have the maximum opportunity to bring our skills to the people who need them, we have to work alongside the medical profession: psychiatrists are entrusted with the major responsibility for those whom society calls mentally ill, and their authority is accepted by patients and their families. We need to be able to communicate and fit in with the rest of the team. This does not, of course, mean that we should become obedient technicians, carrying out orders without reference to the intangible but real and far-reaching issues of human rights and dignity.

The concept of teamwork in psychiatry is a problematic one—and the problems are certainly not all of the social worker's making! Teamwork does not mean a single thinker and decision-maker with a staff of subordinates to do his bidding (a view held, it would appear, by a number of consultant psychiatrists). It is a group of professionals who share in assessment, planning and treatment, cooperating to provide a comprehensive and well co-ordinated service. Each member contributes according to his skills and the client's or family's needs, and the contribution of each will vary from case to case.

The recipients of the service do not feel confused or embarrassed at the variety of professionals intervening in their lives, but reassured that a group of people will help them in variety of ways. A number of research studies have shown us a rather different reality: lack of mutual respect, power struggles, poor co-ordination, and some members—especially social workers, but often also nurses and psychologists—feeling undervalued and under-used (Hunt, 1979; Miles, 1977; Sanson-Fisher *et al.,* 1979). Patients who have been persuaded to appear before a roomful of strangers at a case conference may be justified in feeling that this is an audience rather than a team of helpers, and they are often given the message that unless a doctor is seeing them they are being fobbed off with second-best. It would be fanciful to suggest that with more goodwill, status rivalry and bad teamwork will just go away. It is important that members of the team clarify their potential contributions for one another, and learn about each other's background knowledge and range of skills.

This cannot be a once-and-for-all exercise, since individual workers add to their competencies and sometimes change direction over time. Generally speaking, there are areas of exclusive competence, such as pharmacotherapy or psychological testing; areas of exclusive responsibility, such as duties under the mental-health or child-protection legislation; and areas of overlap, such as psychotherapy, groupwork, family therapy, behaviour therapy. We should acknowledge that some members of a profession may lack skills usually expected of that profession: some psychiatrists (in Britain, perhaps most) have had no training in psychotherapy, and there are some psychologists who have not trained in behaviour therapy.

On the other hand, some members of professions have skills not usually associated with those professions; some nurses are highly skilled in behaviour therapy; some occupational therapists have trained in group therapy. The social worker is often the best qualified person to undertake family therapy and other forms of 'talking treatment'.

Social workers are the least predictable occupational group with regard to what they are able to offer, and have—perhaps deservedly—been much criticised on this account. Generally speaking, their particular spheres of interest are the social factors that exacerbate the plight of people with mental disorder, such as poverty, unemployment and poor housing, interpersonal relationships, and the welfare of the family as a whole. They tend to have a good knowledge of social norms, and, as we noted earlier, an awareness of the dangers inherent in entry into the 'sick role' and of the negative consequences of psychiatric intervention.

However, the range of skill and knowledge to be found within social work is extremely wide. Some social workers offer treatment that is scarcely distinguishable from psychotherapy; others specialise in welfare rights; in the USA, social workers can be found in charge of a community crisis intervention centre or a behavioural in-patient treatment ward. Because of the bewildering array of possible competencies it is essential that other professionals do not have to try to co-operate with a large number of unfamiliar social workers, who are prevented by their allegiance to a different agency from taking a full part in the psychiatric service.

As the social worker becomes known to the rest of the team, so the requests made to him will become more appropriate to his skills; at the same time, he will become better able to respond to the requirements of the team's clientele. The social worker can play a useful role at all stages of psychiatric care: diagnosis, treatment and rehabilitation. Diagnosis is traditionally a closely guarded prerogative of the medically qualified, and certainly the psychiatrist's training in this part of the work is unlikely to be surpassed by that of any other profession. The British Association of Social Workers Working Party (1974) suggests that social workers can contribute on two levels: (a) screening as to need for a psychiatric opinion, and (b) contribution to psychiatric diagnosis, and use of psychiatric knowledge in social assessment. For the screening task the social worker needs to be familiar with the kinds of behaviour and complaints that are considered in making a psychiatric diagnosis.

For the second and more specialised level of contribution, he needs knowledge and experience of particular symptoms and the sense that is likely to be made of them by a psychiatrist. Although perhaps beyond the call of duty, the specialist knowledge that some social workers possess can have far-reaching results. An example of this was a probation officer's report on a client who had been detained in a mental hospital following a minor assault. This report, without suggesting a formal diagnosis, commented on the absence of various symptoms that might have attracted a diagnosis of severe mental illness. The probation officer also noted the client's lack of fluency in English, his intense anxiety, and his fear of 'the authorities', and linked these to his status as a recent immigrant. She went on to mention that his conversation, although disjointed was not muddled; his beliefs fitted in with his cultural background, and his history and current life-style were typical of his subculture: he was not confused, and he had coped satisfactorily with work and social relationships in the past.

In this case the probation officer's report helped the defence psychiatrist to exclude the possibility of mental illness, whereas previous psychiatrists without her report had given the man a diagnosis of paranoid schizophrenia. The author, on interviewing a woman complaining of sexual problems, elicited information that suggested that she was suffering from a 'classical' depressive illness. On referral to a psychiatrist this was confirmed, and she responded rapidly to treatment for the depression, and had no need of sex therapy. Systematic evidence of the potential of social workers in assessment (very heartening at a time when doubt is being cast on our competence from so many quarters!) is given by Newson-Smith and Hirsch (1979), whose research on the assessment of overdose patients demonstrated that the social workers in the study were at least as good at detecting illness as the psychiatrists. The social worker's varying contributions to treatment and rehabilitation, as well as to assessment and diagnosis, are discussed in the ensuing chapters.

The greater the social worker's sophistication in psychiatry, the more he can contribute. And this is no sell-out to the so-called medical model— this kind of sophistication can coexist with the generic principles, knowledge and methods that basic social work training has provided.

Mental Health and Hygiene Concept

"Mental health is regarded as a condition which permits the optimal development, physical, intellectual and emotional, of the individual, so far as this is compatible with that of other individuals." 15. Echoing concerns about the absence, or rather limited number of, participants from places such as Far East, South America and the Soviet Union, the hope was expressed that "mental health as understood in Western countries [is not] necessarily at variance with the sense in which it is understood in other countries"

—J.C. Flugel, Chairman of the Conference's Programme Committee

Mental health is a term used to describe either a level of cognitive or emotional well-being or an absence of a mental disorder. From perspectives of the discipline of positive psychology or holism mental health may include an individual's ability to enjoy life and procure a balance between life activities and efforts to achieve psychological resilience. The World Health Organisation defines mental health as ""a state of well-being in which the individual realises his or her own abilities, can cope with the normal stresses of life, can work productively and fruitfully, and is able to make a contribution to his or her community." It was previously stated that there was no one "official" definition of mental health. Cultural differences, subjective assessments, and competing professional theories all affect how "mental health" is defined. In the mid-19th century, William Sweetzer was the first to clearly define the term "mental hygiene", which can be seen as the precurser to contemporary approaches to work on promoting positive mental health. Isaac Ray, one of thirteen founders of the American Psychiatric Association, further defined mental hygiene as an art to preserve the mind against incidents and influences which would inhibit or destroy its energy, quality or development.

At the beginning of the 20th century, Clifford Beers

founded the National Committee for Mental Hygiene and opened the first outpatient mental health clinic in the United States. Mental health can be seen as a continuum, where an individual's mental health may have many different possible values. Mental wellness is generally viewed as a positive attribute, such that a person can reach enhanced levels of mental health, even if they do not have any diagnosable mental health condition. This definition of mental health highlights emotional well-being, the capacity to live a full and creative life, and the flexibility to deal with life's inevitable challenges.

Many therapeutic systems and self-help books offer methods and philosophies espousing strategies and techniques vaunted as effective for further improving the mental wellness of otherwise healthy people. Positive psychology is increasingly prominent in mental health. A holistic model of mental health generally includes concepts based upon anthropological, educational, psychological, religious and sociological perspectives, as well as theoretical perspectives from personality, social, clinical, health and developmental psychology.

An example of a wellness model includes one developed by Myers, Sweeny and Witmer. It includes five life tasks — essence or spirituality, work and leisure, friendship, love and self-direction—and twelve sub tasks—sense of worth, sense of control, realistic beliefs, emotional awareness and coping, problem solving and creativity, sense of humour, nutrition, exercise, self care, stress management, gender identity, and cultural identity—are identified as characteristics of healthy functioning and a major component of wellness. The components provide a means of responding to the circumstances of life in a manner that promotes healthy functioning. Most of the US Population is not educated on Mental Health.

Lack of a Mental Disorder

Mental health can also be defined as an absence of a major mental health condition (for example, one of the diagnoses in the Diagnostic and Statistical Manual, IV) though recent evidence stemming from positive psychology suggests mental health is more than the mere absence of a mental disorder or illness. Therefore the impact of social, cultural, physical and education can all affect someone's mental health.

Mental Hygiene

The science of maintaining mental health and preventing the development of psychosis, neurosis, or other mental disorders. Since the founding of the United Nations the concepts of mental health and hygiene have achieved international acceptance. As defined in the 1946 constitution of the World Health Organisation, "health is a state of complete physical, mental, and social well-being, and not merely the absence of disease or infirmity." The term mental health represents a variety of human aspirations: rehabilitation of the mentally disturbed, prevention of mental disorder, reduction of tension in a stressful world, and attainment of a state of well-being in which the individual functions at a level consistent with his or her mental potential. As noted by the World Federation for Mental Health, the concept of optimum mental health refers not to an absolute or ideal state but to the best possible state insofar as circumstances are alterable. Mental health is regarded as a condition of the individual, relative to the capacities and social-environmental context of that person. Mental hygiene includes all measures taken to promote and to preserve mental health. Community mental health refers to the extent to which the organisation and functioning of the community determines, or is conducive to, the mental health of its members. Throughout the ages the mentally disturbed have been viewed with a mixture of fear and revulsion. Their fate generally has been one of rejection, neglect, and ill treatment.

Though in ancient medical writings there are references to mental disturbance that display views very similar to modern humane attitudes, interspersed in the same literature are instances of socially sanctioned cruelty based upon the belief that mental disorders have supernatural origins such as demonic possession. Even reformers sometimes used harsh methods of treatment; for example, the 18th-century American physician Benjamin Rush endorsed the practice of restraining mental patients with his notorious "tranquilising chair."

The concept of mental health, given its polysemic nature and its imprecise borders, benefits from a historical perspective to be better understood. What today is broadly understood by "mental health" can have its origins tracked back to developments in public health, in clinical psychiatry and in other branches of knowledge. Although references to mental health as a state can be found in the English language well before the 20th century, technical references to mental health as a field or discipline are not found before 1946. During that year, the International Health Conference, held in New York, decided to establish the World Health Organisation (WHO) and a Mental Health Association was founded in London. Before that date, found are references to the corresponding concept of "mental hygiene", which first appeared in the English literature in 1843, in a book entitled Mental hygiene or an examination of the intellect and passions designed to illustrate their influence on health and duration of life (1) Moreover, in 1849, "healthy mental and physical development of the citizen" had already been included as the first objective of public health in a draft law submitted to the Berlin Society of Physicians and Surgeons (2) In 1948, the WHO was created and in the same year the first International Congress on Mental Health took place in London. At the second session of the WHO's Expert Committee on Mental Health (September 11-16, 1950), "mental health" and "mental hygiene" were defined as follows "Mental hygiene refers to all the activities and techniques which encourage and maintain mental health.

Mental health is a condition, subject to fluctuations due to biological and social factors, which enables the individual to achieve a satisfactory synthesis of his own potentially conflicting, instinctive drives; to form and maintain harmonious relations with others; and to participate in constructive changes in his social and physical environment." However, a clear and widely accepted definition of mental health as a discipline was (and is) still missing. Significantly, the Dorland's Medical Dictionary does not carry an entry on mental health, whereas the Campbell's Dictionary of Psychiatry gives it two meanings: first, as a synonym of mental hygiene and second, as a state of psychological wellbeing.

The Oxford English Dictionary defines mental hygiene as a set of measures to preserve mental health, and later refers to mental health as a state. These lexicographic concepts nonetheless, more and more mental health is employed in the sense of a discipline (e.g., sections/divisions in health ministries or secretaries, or departments in universities), with an almost perfect replacement of mental hygiene. In addition, given this polysemic nature of mental health, its delimitation in relation to psychiatry (understood as the medical specialty concerned with the study, prevention, diagnosis and treatment of mental disorders or diseases) is not always clear. There is a more or less widespread effort to set mental health at least aside from psychiatry and at most as an overarching concept with encompasses psychiatry.

Cultural and Religious Considerations

Mental health can be socially constructed and socially defined; that is, different professions, communities, societies and cultures have very different ways of conceptualising its nature and causes, determining what is mentally healthy, and deciding what interventions are appropriate. Thus, different professionals will have different cultural and religious backgrounds and experiences, which may impact the methodology applied during treatment. Many mental health professionals are beginning to, or already understand, the importance of competency in religious diversity and spirituality. The American Psychological Association explicitly states that religion must be respected. Education in spiritual and religious matters is also required by the American Psychiatric Association.

Mental Hygiene Movement

The origin of the mental hygiene movement can be attributed to the work of Clifford Beers in the USA. In 1908 he published A mind that found itself 4, a book based on his personal experience of admissions to three mental hospitals. The book had a great repercussion and in the same year a Mental Hygiene Society was established in Connecticut. The term "mental hygiene" had been suggested to Beers by Adolf Meyer and enjoyed a quick popularity thanks to the creation in 1909 of the National Commission of Mental Hygiene. From 1919 onwards, the internationalisation of activities of this Commission led to the establishment of some national associations concerned with mental hygiene: in France and South Africa in 1920, in Italy 8 and Hungary 9 in 1924.

From these national associations the International Committee on Mental Hygiene was created and later superseded by the World Federation of Mental Health. The mental hygiene movement, in its origins and reflecting Beers' experience in mental hospitals, was primarily and basically concerned with the improvement of the care of people with mental disorders. In Beers' own words: "When the National Committee was organised, in 1909, its chief concern was to humanize the care of the insane: to eradicate the abuses, brutalities and neglect from which the mentally sick have traditionally suffered."

It was at a later stage that the Committee enlarged its programme to include the "milder forms of mental disability" and a greater concern with preventive work. The rationale behind this shift was the belief that "mental disorders frequently have their beginnings in childhood and youth and that preventive measures are most effective in early life", and that environmental conditions and modes of living produce mental ill health.

By 1937, the US National Committee for Mental Hygiene stated that it sought to achieve its purposes by: a) promoting early diagnosis and treatment; b) developing adequate hospitalisation; c) stimulating research; d) securing public understanding and support of psychiatric and mental hygiene activities; e) instructing individuals and groups in the personal application of mental hygiene principles; and f) cooperating with governmental and private agencies whose work touches at any point the field of mental hygiene.

Thus, the mental hygiene movement had initially a para-psychiatric nature, directing its efforts towards the improvement of psychiatric care. The inclusion of preventive activities among its interests did not distinguish it from psychiatry: the movement aimed at maximising what was accepted and proposed by the most advanced psychiatrists of the epoch in the USA, most of whom followed a psychoanalytical orientation.

According to the group which launched it, the mental hygiene movement "visualized, not a single patient, but a whole community; and it considered each member of that community as an individual whose mental and emotional status was determined by definite causative factors and whose compelling need was for prevention rather than cure. The Mental Hygiene Movement, then, bears the same relation to psychiatry that the public-health movement, of which it forms a part, bears to medicine in general. It is an organised community response to a recognized community need." On the other hand, it was also stated that: "At the present time both psychiatrists and mental hygienists are more than ever conscious that their objectives are in fact identical and that each group needs the other for the fulfilment of their common task."

World Health Organisation (WHO)

From its very beginning, the WHO has always had an administrative section specially dedicated to mental health, as an answer to requests from its Member States. The first Report of the WHO's Director General 10, in its English version, refers to an administrative section called "Mental Health". However, the French version of the same report calls it "Hygiene Mentale". Well until the 1960s we find hygiene as the French translation of health in some WHO publications and in some instances we find also mental hygiene used interchangeably with mental health in the English version of some documents.

In the preamble to the WHO Constitutions, it was stated that "health is a state of complete physical, mental and social wellbeing and not merely the absence of disease or infirmity", a now widely quoted definition. This definition is clearly a holistic one, intended to overcome the old dichotomies of body vs. mind and physical vs. psychic. It is also a pragmatic one, insofar as it incorporates into medicine a social dimension, gradually developed in Europe during the 19th century. It should be noted that mental, in WHO's definition of health (as well as physical and social) refers to dimensions of a state and not to a specific domain or discipline. Therefore, according to this concept, it is incongruous to refer to physical health, mental health or social health. Should one wish to specify a particular dimension, the most appropriate noun to designate it should be wellbeing and not health (e.g., mental wellbeing or social wellbeing). This negligent use of the word health seems to have been also in operation when mental hygiene (a social movement, or a domain of activity) was replaced by mental health (originally intended to designate a state and later transformed in a particular domain or field of activity).

Recent Developments

After half a century of the mental health, and almost a century of the mental hygiene movements, some developments can be perceived. On a more general level, the WHO's very concept of health has been recently questioned; formulated half a century ago, it is no longer felt by some as much appropriate to the current situation 16,17. On the whole, mental health continues to be used both to designate a state, a dimension of health – an essential element in the definition of health – and to refer to the movement derived from the mental hygiene movement, corresponding to the application of psychiatry to groups, communities and societies, rather than on an individual basis, as is the case with clinical psychiatry.

However, mental health is, quite unfortunately, still viewed by many as a discipline, either as a synonym of psychiatry, or as one of its complementary fields. A recent trend has been the addition of the qualifier public to either mental health or to psychiatry, as it can be seen in a WHO document entitled Public mental health 18, or in a journal named Psiquiatria Publica, published in Spain since 1989. This is very much in line with the concept of mental health as a movement rather than a discipline. In 2001, the WHO dedicated its annual report (The World Health Report-Mental health: new knowledge, new hope) to mental health 19.

In that same year, the theme of the World Health Day was Stop Exclusion – Dare to Care, a quite clear political statement, that I am sure would have immensely pleased Clifford Beers. In the message from the WHO Director-General that opens that report, Gro H. Brundtland summarizes the three main knowledge areas covered by the document: a) effectiveness of prevention and treatment, b) service planning and provision, and c) policies to break down stigma and discrimination and adequate funds for prevention and treatment. If one allows for the semantic variations between the beginnings of the 20th and the 21st centuries, the same concerns of the origins of the mental hygiene movement, discussed earlier on, can be found in the mental health content of the World Health Report. Perhaps the biggest difference between these two political platforms is the emphasis on the improvement of hospital care in the former (the only form of treatment available by then), and the contemporary emphasis on distancing mental health from psychiatric hospitals and placing it in the community.

However, one must admit that, unfortunately, what was high in Beers' agenda in 1909, namely, an improvement in the standards of mental health care and an eradication of the abuses to which people with mental disorders are usually subject, is still a major concern of the most progressive and advanced agenda of people interested in the promotion of mental health around the world.

International Congress of Mental Health

The First International Congress of Mental Health was organised in London by the British National Association for Mental Hygiene from 16 to 21 August, 1948. Starting as an International Conference on Mental Hygiene, it ended with a series of recommendations on mental health. Throughout the proceedings of the conference, hygiene and health, qualifying mental, are used interchangeably, sometimes in the same paragraph, without any clear conceptual distinction. In addition to the wording employed in the proceedings of that congress, gradually replacing hygiene by health, some of its recommendations were also influential at other levels. An example is recommendation to the WHO that "as soon as practicable, an advisory expert committee be established, composed of professional personnel in the field of mental health and human relations". The conference had been convened under the theme "Mental Health and World Citizenship".

From a conceptual point of view, nevertheless, and perhaps reflecting an immediately post-war situation, discussions over world citizenship prevailed over those on mental health.

In a more detailed way, some delegates elaborated on what was summarized as the "four levels of mental health work: custodial, therapeutic, preventive and positive" 15. It is not difficult to see a considerable overlapping between this proposal and the one already implemented by the mental hygiene movement.

At the closing session, O.L. Forel, Lecturer in Psychiatry at the University of Geneva, answering to criticisms that mental hygiene, as understood in that conference, went beyond the medical and scientific framework, made a clearly political (in Plato's sense) statement by saying that: "I dare hope to be your interpreter in expressing our pride that so many scientists came here not at all to develop their respective sciences, but to have them at men's service" 15.

Reading through the proceedings of this congress gives one a feeling of the tensions between a pragmatic approach, developed by the mental hygiene movement (basically defended by delegates from the USA), and a more politically-oriented approach, proposed by other participants, perhaps translating the experiences of some delegates from European countries, which had severely suffered from the war. In the end this latter approach prevailed, with the transformation of the mental hygiene movement into the mental health movement. Perhaps as a reflection of this basically political movement, in 1949 the National Institute of Mental Health started its activities in the USA.

Frustration and Conflict

Frustration

We strive to gratify our wants and desires, our goals, aims, and ambitions. Introspection and self-knowledge make this much self-evident; experience with others confirms the generalisation. Moreover, we are often unable to satisfy our desires or accomplish our goals. Sometimes our ambitions exceed our abilities, or we misperceive the possibilities. But sometimes we are blocked by an external barrier that precludes gratification. This may be a traffic jam preventing us from reaching an appointment, a college rule prohibiting us from taking a particular course, an amorous neighbourhood tom cat interrupting our sleep, or our race restricting professional advancement.

Whatever the barrier, we are frustrated. All of us are so frustrated from time to time. In addition, we all have experienced irritation and anger at some frustrations. A long line preventing us from seeing an eagerly awaited movie, a crush of shoppers hindering the purchase of some simple necessities, a slow driver obstructing a narrow road, probably have aroused in all of us that familiar flush of annoyance, even anger. That frustration of our desires and goals occasionally leads to anger is a commonplace. It is subjectively unquestionable—a fact of our existence. Of course, not all frustrations lead to anger. Indeed, it is more common to accept frustration—the blockage of our wants or goals—as feedback suggesting that we adjust or alter our aims. We do this automatically, hour by hour, day by day. Frustration signals the error in the trial-and-error process by which we dialectically adjust our perspectives to external powers and potentialities.

To live, to assert oneself, is to be hindered, to face difficulties, to be *opposed*. My desire to write this section uninterruptedly is hindered by construction noise in the background; my desire for physical comfort is defeated by the summer heat; my search for the right words to cxpress my "understanding" is blocked by the barrier between structured language and unstructured "insight" and feelings. Moreover, when I let my consciousness stroll through the nested levels of my existence, I am also aware of a multitude of frustrations that reach consciousness like a flock of pheasants startled out of tall grass.

Frustrations associated with family, research, teaching, politics, and the growing structure of coercive rules and laws. As I write, my life is within a matrix of such frustrations, high and low, large and small, significant and trivial. Yet at the moment I am content, relatively happy, and feel no irritation, no anger. Besides our desires and goals, our frustrations and anger, there are two other commonplace facts of life. We sometimes desire or aim to injure or hurt others, and behave in such a manner, sometimes because of our frustrations. Again, in our subjective world, these two facts are incontestable. Our awareness of them enables us to better perceive others to adjust our interests and interactions, and to develop predictive expectations. We can then understand why on a hot day in slow city traffic, one motorist will attack another for blocking his path, why a parent whose losing bridge game is interrupted for the fifth time by a child will vigorously spank him, and why a mistress cast off by her lover will send poison pen letters to his wife. In the late 1930s, the commonplace enabling us to understand such behaviour in certain contexts was erected into an invariant law of nature by a group of Yale psychologists (et al., 1939). First, they equated aggression with the desire to hurt or injure others. This effectively confused the various forms of aggression with one overt manifestation and confounded the bases of aiming to harm another, which may be instrumental (as in spanking a child), defensive (as in kicking an attacker), or hostile (as in spreading malicious gossip). Were one to equate love with kissing, the conceptual, cognitive confusion would be no less. Second, frustration was defined as interference with a goal *response,* thus keying frustration to an objective barrier or difficulty, and to manifest behaviour. Interference was felt to be through punishment or goal inaccessibility, further confusing frustration as blockage with frustration as deprivation.

Conflict

Some scientific studies clearly indicated that the feelings

of continual conflict and frustration will have a negative effect upon our well-being. The chronic inability to be successful, meet one's goals, or even know one's goals is weakened. Unhappiness, frustration and unresolved needs and desires cause great emotional unhappiness.

The conflict and frustration may be on a conscious level or subconscious level. There may often be conflict in our emotions and attitudes between the conscious and the subconscious mind. For example, an individual may appear to be calm and happy, yet underneath that mask of calmness could be repressed anger and hurt that is hidden. A shy person may actually be full of rage.

The individual tries to maintain his or her life in a way that keeps the mask of the calm person or shy person in place. When there is conflict, and the person cannot predict and be secure in his or her world, then there may be fear and pain for the individual. He or she may not be able to cope. When there is too much conflict between the conscious and subconscious mind, disease may occur, and other emotional problems may appear. Therefore, always be calm and collective in most problems of life and try to face them head on with full determination.

The relationship of relative deprivation-turned-injustice vector to the process of conflict is easily clarified. Injustice vectors—the moral sense of deprivation relative to others—are part of the conflict situation. These are vectors of interest, the opposition of which creates the conflict situation. Here, awareness (or perception) and the situation give context and meaning to the opposing interests; expectations of Behavioural outcomes interrelate the injustice vector and its drive to action with the capability of the other and our expectation of his behaviour.

In other words, the situation of conflict involves our

interests and their justness; our perception of others and our sense of injustice by comparison; and our beliefs about the capabilities of others and the outcomes of our actions. Within the framework of the helix, the conflict situation comprises the variables important to transforming the potential for collective violence into the potential for class violence and, finally, into manifest violence. At the collective level, the injustice vector fundamentally defines the class consciousness necessary to the class struggle within all organisations, including the state. The initiation phase of manifest conflict involves a trigger provoking the will to action, and the occurrence of such a mechanism depends on the balance of powers an individual perceives between himself and others.

Consequently a sense of injustice is no guarantee of action. This is also true of Gurr's model, in which the transformation of potential to manifestation depends on a balance of powers. But deprivation theory does not explain what happens after the manifest conflict or violence ensues, while the conflict helix is in mid-ascent. Out of manifest conflict a balance is formed among the diverse interests held by people on the basis of their capability and wills.

There ensues adjustment among the diverse vectors of injustice, an adjustment based on subjective perception and expectations honed by the reality of others. Conflict and the resulting balance form a structure of expectations that enables different views of injustice and different classes to live together. In time these expectations may become incongruent with the underlying balance; a person may develop new reference groups, have new experiences, be the object of an ideological campaign ("workers are oppressed").

The sense of injustice may change such that the previous

class balance (between workers and management in a factory) no longer reflects the parties' interests, or the underlying capabilities or wills of the parties may alter (bureaucratic dissension may weaken governmental control over dissidents). Then a trigger, such as an event provoking a rearoused or newly inflamed sense of injustice may provoke a turn of the conflict helix, a new balancing of powers and injustices, of classes. At the *ontological and empirical levels* the nature of the psychological field and the conflict helix seems to answer the question, What is social justice? Just wants and injustice vectors vary considerably among people. Such interests and feelings are diverse, multidimensional, and *personal*.

Moreover, the amount willingly sacrificed to satisfy just wants or to right a sense of injustice varies across individuals. People have different expectations, capabilities, interests, and wills. And the overriding superordinate goal, self-esteem, is intrinsic to the individual. Then how, apparently, do we determine what is just? How do we balance different views of what is just? Given the diversity of human beings, this question can only imply two alternatives: we force our view of social justice on someone else (say, through governmental coercion), or people settle for themselves and among themselves their own balance.

If the conflict helix as a field process operates at all levels without the imposition of an antifield on it, the diverse views of social justice will compromise and balance in terms of interests, capabilities, and wills. This seems to argue for the maximum freedom, for a precondition of the conflict helix is that each is free to pursue his just wants and to square his sense of injustice against others. The precondition of social justice is therefore freedom. Or, so it seems. But this is a factual conclusion about an ethical question, which is not logically possible. Facts can be heuristic, they can provide some guidelines to thought, but they cannot make the argument themselves. To fully and logically answer the question we must consider the nature of ethics and then the ethical nature of social justice.

Ultimately, we will have to use ethical arguments to determine what is socially just. And this I will do in the concluding volume of this series, *Vol. 5: The Just Peace.* There we will find that at the level of ethics we arrive at a conclusion similar to that we found ontologically and empirically: as a matter of ethics, social justice is the maximisation of the freedom of individuals to choose the principles that govern them, even if they choose to be unfree.

Mental Illness

A mental disorder or mental illness is a psychological or Behavioural pattern that occurs in an individual and is thought to cause distress or disability that is not expected as part of normal development or culture. The recognition and understanding of mental disorders has changed over time and across cultures. Definitions, assessments, and classifications of mental disorders can vary, but guideline criteria listed in the ICD, DSM and other manuals are widely accepted by mental health professionals. Categories of diagnoses in these schemes may include dissociative disorders, mood disorders, anxiety disorders, psychotic disorders, eating disorders, developmental disorders, personality disorders, and many other categories. In many cases there is no single accepted or consistent cause of mental disorders, although they are often explained in terms of a diathesis-stress model and biopsychosocial model. Mental disorders have been found to be common, with over a third of people in most countries reporting sufficient criteria at some point in their life. Services for mental disorders may be based in hospitals or in the community. Mental health professionals diagnose individuals using different methodologies, often relying on case history and interview. Psychotherapy and psychiatric medication are two major treatment options, as well as supportive interventions and self-help. Treatment may be involuntary where legislation allows. Several movements campaign for changes to services and attitudes.

Teachers are among the most important influences in the lives of school-aged children, yet relatively little emphasis has been placed on examining the potential role general academic teachers may play in facilitating adolescent health promotion efforts, according to a study conducted by researchers at Columbia University's Mailman School of Public Health and published in the *Journal of School Health*. The study results indicate that teachers provide valuable information to school personnel about what health issues are important to adolescents, in particular, because they hear feedback from adolescents on a daily basis.

Unrest

The general condition of the community in which milling is both frequent and widespread and in which rumour is recurrent is the crucible in which the more highly organised forms of collective behaviour develop. This condition, known as social unrest, can lead to outbursts of violence. The American urban black uprisings of the 1960s were preceded and accompanied by social unrest in the form of a rise in tensions in black communities throughout the country; the Russian Revolution was preceded by several years of constant unrest and turmoil, involving random assassinations, strikes, and riots. There are several distinguishing characteristics to social unrest.

First, there is a general impairment of collective life

routines. People find it difficult to concentrate on their work or even to adhere to rules in playing games. Any occasion to abandon routines is welcomed.

Second, people are hyperreactive. The magnitude of the response is out of proportion to the usual meaning of any stimulating incident. A small police provocation elicits a major outcry of police brutality; a trivial success is the occasion for large-scale celebration. Milling and rumour abound because incidents that would normally pass with little notice become occasions for both.

Third, social unrest is marked by contagiousness. When restlessness is strictly individual, one person's restlessness merely annoys another. But when restlessness becomes a shared experience, people are highly suggestible to one another. Questioning and exploring alternative courses of action are reduced to a minimum.

Fourth, social unrest is not specific with respect to grievances or activities. When there is social unrest in a school, students complain of both restrictions on their behaviour and the lack of clearly defined rules; they find fault both with school administrators and with their fellow students.

Finally, social unrest is perhaps the most volatile of collective states. Unlike rumour or milling, it does not remain focused on an issue or problem. Unlike crowd behaviour or fads, it has not yet been channelled into one main direction. Although social unrest may eventually die down without any serious aftermath, it is a condition in which people can be easily aroused.

In psychology, the Behavioural process by which humans and other animals maintain an equilibrium among their various needs or between their needs and the obstacles of their environments. A sequence of adjustment begins when a need is felt and ends when it is satisfied. Hungry people, for example, are stimulated by their physiological state to seek food. When they eat, they reduce the stimulating condition that impelled them to activity, and they are thereby adjusted to this particular need. In general, the adjustment process involves four parts: (1) a need or motive in the form of a strong persistent stimulus, (2) the thwarting or nonfulfillment of this need, (3) varied activity, or exploratory behaviour accompanied by problem solving, and (4) some response that removes or at least reduces the initiating stimulus and completes the adjustment. Social and cultural adjustments are similar to physiological adjustments. People strive to be comfortable in their surroundings and to have their psychological needs (such as love or affirmation) met through the social networks they inhabit. When needs arise, especially in new or changed surroundings, they impel interpersonal activity meant to satisfy those needs. In this way, people increase their familiarity and comfort with their environments, and they come to expect that their needs will be met in the future through their social networks. Ongoing difficulties in social and cultural adjustment may be accompanied by anxiety or depression.

Juvenile Delinquency

Juvenile delinquency refers to criminal acts performed by juveniles. Most legal systems prescribe specific procedures for dealing with juveniles, such as juvenile detention centers. There are a multitude of different theories on the causes of crime, most if not all of which can be applied to the causes of youth crime. Youth crime is an aspect of crime which receives great attention from the news media and politicians. Crime committed by young people has risen since the mid-twentieth century, as has most types of crime. The level and types of youth crime can be used by commentators as an indicator of the general state of morality and law and order in a country, and consequently youth crime can be the source of 'moral panics' Theories on the causes of youth crime can be viewed as particularly important within criminology. This is firstly because crime is committed disproportionately by those aged between fifteen and twenty-five. Secondly, by definition any theories on the causes of crime will focus on youth crime, as adult criminals will have likely started offending when they were young. A Juvenile Delinquent is one who repeatedly commits crime, however these juvenile delinquents could most likely have mental disorders/Behavioural issues such as schizophrenia, post traumatic stress disorder or bipolar disorder.

Theoretical Perspectives on Juvenile Delinquency

Rational Choice Theory

Classical criminology stresses that causes of crime lie within the individual offender, rather than in their external environment. For classicists, offenders are motivated by rational self-interest, and the importance of free will and personal responsibility is emphasised.

Rational choice theory is the clearest example of this approach. It states that people weigh the pros and cons of committing a crime, and offend when the former outweigh the latter. A central deficiency of rational choice theory is that while it may explain when and where people commit crime, it can't explain very well why people choose to commit crimes in the first place.

Neither can it explain differences between individuals and groups in their propensity to commit crimes. James Q. Wilson said the conscience and self-control of a potential young offender must be taken into account, and that these attributes are formed by parental and societal conditioning.

Rational choice does not explain why crime should be committed disproportionately by young people, males, city dwellers, and the poor. (Walklate: 2003 p.2)

It also ignores the influence a young choice theory does not take into account the proven correlations between certain social circumstances and individuals' personalities, and the propensity to commit crime.

Social Disorganisation Theory

Current positivist approaches generally focus on the Culture, which would produce the breakdown of family relationships and community, competing values, and increasing Individualism.

Studies also show only 16 in every 100 kids will do something bad opposed to adult 26 in 100 will do something bad or illegal.

Strain Theory

Strain Theory is associated mainly with the work of Robert Merton. He felt that there are institutionalized paths to success in society. Strain theory holds that crime is caused by the difficulty those in poverty have in achieving socially valued goals by legitimate means.

As those with, for instance, poor educational attainment have difficulty achieving wealth and status by securing well paid employment, they are more likely to use criminal means to obtain these goals. Merton's suggests five adaptations to this dilemma:

1. *Innovation*: individuals who accept socially approved goals, but not necessarily the socially approved means.
2. *Retreatism*: those who reject socially approved goals and the means for acquiring them.

3. *Ritualism*: those who buy into a system of socially approved means, but lose sight of the goals. Merton believed that drug users are in this category.
4. *Conformity*: those who conform to the system's means and goals.
5. *Rebellion*: people who negate socially approved goals and means by creating a new system of acceptable goals and means.

A difficulty with strain theory is that it does not explore why children of low-income families would have poor educational attainment in the first place. More importantly is the fact that much youth crime does not have an economic motivation. Strain theory fails to explain violent crime, the type of youth crime which causes most anxiety to the public.

Subcultural Theory

Related to strain theory is subcultural theory. The inability of youths to achieve socially valued status and goals results in groups of young people forming deviant or delinquent subcultures, which have their own values and norms. (Eadie & Morley: 2003 p.552) Within these groups criminal behaviour may actually be valued, and increase a youth's status. (Walklate: 2003 p.22) The notion of delinquent subcultures is relevant for crimes that are not economically motivated. Male gang members could be argued to have their own values, such as respect for fighting ability and daring. However it is not clear how different this makes them from 'ordinary' non-lawbreaking young men.

Furthermore there is no explanation of why people unable to achieve socially valued goals should necessarily choose criminal substitutes. Subcultural theories have been criticised for making too sharp a distinction between what is deviant and what is 'normal'. (Brown: 1998 p.23) There are also doubts about whether young people consciously reject mainstream values. (Brown: 1998 p.23)

Differential Association

The theory of Differential association also deals with young people in a group context, and looks at how peer pressure and the existence of gangs could lead them into crime. It suggests young people are motivated to commit crimes by delinquent peers, and learn criminal skills from them. The diminished influence of peers after men marry has also been cited as a factor in desisting from offending. There is strong evidence that young people with criminal friends are more likely to commit crimes themselves. However it may be the case that offenders prefer to associate with one another, rather than delinquent peers causing someone to start offending. Furthermore there is the question of how the delinquent peer group became delinquent initially.

Juvenile Delinquency as a Male Phenomenon

Youth crime is disproportionately committed by young men. Feminist theorists and others have examined why this is the case. (Eadie & Morley: 2003 p.553) One suggestion is that ideas of masculinity may make young men more likely to offend. Being tough, powerful, aggressive, daring and competitive may be a way of young men expressing their masculinity. (Brown: 1998 p.109) Acting out these ideals may make young men more likely to engage in antisocial and criminal behaviour. (Walklate: 2003 p. 83) Alternatively, rather than young men acting as they do because of societal pressure to conform to masculine ideals; young men may actually be naturally more aggressive, daring etc. As well as biological or psychological factors, the way young men are treated by their parents may make them more susceptible to offending. (Walklate: 2003 p. 35)

According to a study led by Florida State University criminologist Kevin M. Beaver, adolescent males who possess a certain type of variation in a specific gene are more likely to flock to delinquent peers. The study, which appears in the September 2008 issue of the Journal of Genetic Psychology, is the first to establish a statistically significant association between an affinity for antisocial peer groups and a particular variation (called the 10-repeat allele) of the dopamine transporter gene (DAT1).

Labelling Theory

Labelling theory states that once young people have been libelled as criminal they are more likely to offend. (Eadie & Morley: 2003 p.552) The idea is that once labelled as deviant a young person may accept that role, and be more likely to associate with others who have been similarly labelled. (Eadie & Morley: 2003 p.552) Labelling theorists say that male children from poor families are more likely to be labelled deviant, and that this may partially explain why there are more lower-class young male offenders. (Walklate: 2003 p. 24)

REFERENCES

Kadushin, A. (1976). *Supervision in Social Work*. New York: Columbia University Press.

Kindler, J. (1995). Helping the Helpers: Mental Health Professional on Site of Disasters. *Disaster Response News*. Washington, DC: *APA Practice Directorate, 4,* 1, p. 3.

Kindler, J., Duncan, J., & Knapp, S. (1991). The process of helping. *The Pennsylvania Psychologist, 51,* 15-17.

Kirk, U. (1993). *Psychological First Aid and Other Human Support, A Guide for the Non-Professional Therapist*. Danish Red Cross.

Knudsen, L., Hogsted, R., & Berliner, P. (1997). *Psychological First Aid and Human Support*. Danish Red Cross.

Krug, E. G., Kresnow, M., Peddicord, J. P., Dahlberg, L. L., Powell, K. E., Crosby, A. E., & Annest, J. L. (1998). Suicide After Natural

Disasters. *The New England Journal of Medicine, 338,* 6, 373-378.

Lee, K., Furukawa, P., Malinoski, G., Kaplan, K., & Furuto, S. (1993, November). *Between Crisis and Chronicity: The Crucial Phase of Disaster Response*. Workshop presented at the National Association of Social Workers Annual Meeting, Orlando, FL.

Ornstein, A. and Ornstein, P. (1984). Empathy and the therapeutic dialogue. The Lydia Rapoport Lectures #11, available from Smith School of Social Work, Northampton, MA. (Ornstein and Lachmann 8/12)

Rowe, C. (1992). Development from archaic to mature selfobject transferences. Clinical Social Work Journal, Vol 20, No. 1.

4

Role of Social Work in Health Care

Social work in health care settings is practiced in collaboration with medicine and also with public health programmes. It is the application of social work knowledge, skills, attitudes, and values to health care. Social work addresses itself to illness brought about by or related to social and environmental stresses that result in failures in social functioning and social relationships. It intervenes with medicine and related professions in the study, diagnosis, and treatment of illness at the point where social, psychological, and environmental forces impinge on role effectiveness. Social work relates itself to the goals set by official health agencies, voluntary health agencies, rehabilitation centers, and medical care divisions of public welfare agencies.

Social workers practice in public health at the local, state, federal, and international levels; general medical hospitals; county and state health departments; crippled children's hospitals; outpatient clinics; university teaching hospitals; nursing homes; neighborhood health centers; and private disease centers supported by such funding sources as March of Dimes, and the heart and cancer associations. In addition, social workers are employed in the offices of private physicians and are meeting the challenge of showing that their skills can be cost-effective for private practice. In the past, because of the nature of the practice of medicine, social work in health services emphasized understanding illness. Practice was focused on work with sick people and members of their families. Because of newer emphases in medical care, the scope of social work has been broadened and now encompasses the preservation and promotion of health and the prevention as well as cure of disease.

Consideration is given to psychological factors in prevention of disability as well as in diagnosis and treatment. Using the team approach, medical social workers collaborate with physicians, nurses, and other health professionals for reciprocal sharing of ideas so that the skills of each are employed in the total care of the patients. One of the most important developments for social workers in health care was the Health Maintenance Organisation (HMO) Act of 1973. The Act required provision of social services in HMOs. Several consequent Congressional actions blunted the effects of the original act and the mandates for social workers were eliminated. There has been a positive social work thrust in new home health care and rehabilitation laws which allow Medicaid funds to enhance the ability of handicapped persons to live independently as family and community members.

The most recent development of DRG's (diagnostic related group) is still controversial in its effects on social work. This new national policy seeks to constrain rising health costs by replacing retrospective cost-based reimbursements with set prices for each diagnosis-related group. In nonprofit hospitals, social workers have been asked to do more work in the areas of preadmission and admission screening, but some proprietary hospitals have been cutting social workers in an attempt to maintain their profitability. Regardless of the ebb and flow of federal legislation, social workers will continue to be considered an important health care member because of their special knowledge and skill in the psychosocial aspects of illness. Social work in the health services accepts the World Health Organisation's (WHO) definition of health as "a state of complete physical. mental, and social well-being and not merely the absence of disease or infirmity."

Social workers in health care services use the problem-solving method in assisting individuals, groups, and communities in solving personal and family health problems. Social work is involved at various levels of prevention:

(i) *Primary*—health education, encouraging immunisations, good mental health practice in families, prenatal and postnatal care.
(ii) *Secondary*—early screening programmes for detection of disease, checkups, encouraging treatment.
(iii) *Tertiary or rehabilitation*—preventing further deterioration of a disease or problem.

Social workers engage in research and add to a professional body of scientific knowledge. Through supervision and teaching, they assist par-aprofessionals to develop scholarship and skill. They teach in schools of social work and serve in student-training units as field instructors. What are the distinguishing knowledge and skill characteristics of medical social work practice? It is practice in responsible relation to medicine. Its concern is with the welfare of patients and the causal, contributing interrelation-ships of illness, family failures and break-down, social stresses, and environmental pressures and influences.

Medical social work is shaped and guided by the attitudes, beliefs, knowledge, and acceptable ways of doing things by professionals serving in health care institutions and by the philosophy and practice of modern medicine. It requires a knowledge of illness and of the psychological and social impact of disease on the individual, the family, and the family interrelationships; it calls for the application and adaptation of social work concepts, principles, and ideas to the special needs of hospital and clinic clientele.

In the hospital social workers collaborate with medicine and a broad range of specialists, including nurses, dieticians, physical therapists, speech and hearing specialists, recreationists, and pharmacists. Outside the hospital they work with public health nurses and health educators.

As medicine has become highly technical and specialized, especially as practiced in the university hospital or complex rehabilitation setting, the social worker sometimes holds the process together, explaining the personnel and their functions to patients. If the patient moves from medicine to surgery, and back again, and changes in physicians occur, the social worker is the constant person.

Social work has a coordinate, rather than subordinate or ancillary, role to medicine and is responsible to the institution and the supporting public. The doctor is the clinical and medical authority and is held responsible under the law for medical practice. However, the doctor is only one member of the team in modern medical practice to whom the social worker relates.

What is Illness?

Illness encompasses medical, social, economic, and even spiritual components. Illness affects people in many ways, directly and indirectly, and is of particular consequence to individuals, families, and communities. The social worker plays a major role in interpreting illness to people and in helping them to muster their personal and social resources toward physical and mental well-being.

Webster's *International Dictionary* defines illness as a state of being ill or sick, bodily indisposition disease. An ill person is one of "inferior quality, bad in condition, wretched, impolite, improper, incorrect, bad morally, evil in nature or character, malevolent, wicked, vicious, wrong." The word *disease* literally means want of ease, uneasiness. *Dis,* from the Latin prefix, means apart or asunder, and *ease* is a state of comfort or rest. The diseased person is a person wanting in ease. An invalid, on the other hand, is someone who is not valid, someone no longer able to bear the burdens of life, or who, for temporary or prolonged periods of time simply cannot function.

As defined by doctors, disease is objective. Causation relates to agents that can be stained, tested for chemical qualities, measured, and described. The laboratory procedures used by medical personnel in hospitals, clinics, and in doctors' offices are objective devices used to determine the degree of seriousness of disability or pathology resulting from disease processes. Determinations are made of organic states such as result from bacteria, viruses, trauma, cellular dysfunction, and various circulatory disturbances.

Broadly speaking, illness—impaired role function—may result from factors not wholly organic, but social, psychological, cultural, and economic. Anything affecting the total well-being of the patient may support the illness and render the patient incapable of normal role performance. It forces dependency and reduces usefulness to the family and other significant people. It cuts off the individual's access to normal enjoyment and satisfaction. The social worker, in addressing him- or herself to other than organic factors, studies and defines illness in its cultural and environmental matrix and assists with the removal of barriers to health from these sources. The increase in chronic disease among Americans has literally changed the meaning of illness for a great many people

In the 1940s infections such as tuberculosis, meningitis, and influenza were still major life threats. Polio was still maiming and killing people into the 1950s. Now, however, chronic diseases—heart disease, diabetes, emphysema, and stroke—are major threats. People have to live with chronic disease, adjust to pain, change habits—diet, quit smoking, exercise, and change employment. With chronic conditions—arthritis, heart disease, some cancers—the patient must be a partner in the care of the disease, in its prevention, and in its deterioration. Social work comes into the picture in helping the patient to adjust, to accept medical regimens, and to relate to the health complex involved in the broadened care aspects of chronic disease. In addition social workers work with dying patients, allowing them to express fears, and help other hospital and medical care specialists deal with their own feelings in working with those who are dying. Illness is always highly individual. For many, illness damages the self-image. Illness forces dependency upon relatives and society, which may be difficult for the ill person to accept. The Essei Japanese man, for instancc, whose rearing emphasizes the interdependence of family members, may develop symptoms, become immobilized, or resort to self-destruction when he can no longer count on a comfortable place of eminence within the family and is forced to accept relief or nursing home care. Illness often minimizes the usefulness of the individual to his or her family and loved ones. When it interferes with the breadwinning function of the wage earner, illness can result in disorganisation of the entire family, and for the wage earner in a loss of self-respect, feelings of helplessness, and despondency.

The enjoyment of the normal functions of the individual is denied to the ill person, whose responses are often distorted and detrimental to normal social relationships. The small child who is ill and who has to be hospitalized for extended periods of time, may lose the feeling of closeness to parents and experience separation trauma.

Some children who are separated even for short periods of time, particularly under unfavourable circumstances for which no preparation is made, carry a scar for many years, if not for a lifetime. Infants and young children who have been hospitalized and separated from their families for long periods of time, who lack the closeness of a vital tie to a parent or other significant person, may suffer irreversible physical and emotional damage, become autistic, distrustful of others, and encounter difficulties in relationships all their lives. The adolescent who suffers from a prolonged illness, who is confined and obliged to curtail activities, may lose peer group support at a time when it is greatly needed in his or her struggle for autonomy and independence.

A wage earner suffering from a "nervous breakdown" clung desperately to symptoms for fear that he would be asked to return to work and a job he could not manage. He recovered only with skilled medical and social work help when he was assured that he would recover and be able to work again and support his family. The aging may use sickness as a method of forcing their children to give them care and attention, A mother, for example, who during her childbearing period was preoccupied with the task of rearing and educating her children, in middle age and retirement found her usefulness often questioned, if not by others by herself. Her children, long since established in their own homes, were independent and did not have the same need for her as when they were younger. She sensed that her role in the family had changed. She chose illness as an escape from the feeling that she was no longer useful, to force her children to live with and care for her. Unconscious regression to earlier states of dependency, helplessness, and illness are common reactions to stress. The ill person may be dependent, helpless, and under the care of others; nevertheless, the sick are also expected to cooperate with the hospital and other individuals who are responsible for assisting in their care and treatment.

Social Work in the Health Care Services: Future Prospects

Since 1965 there has been a continued expansion in the health care field. The bill for Medicare alone was $34.31 billion in 1986; for Medicaid, $24.9 billion. It is estimated that 10.5 per cent of the GNP was spent for health care funding in 1982, which amounts to approximately $1, 365 per person in the United States. The government financed almost half of all the health care related costs. Elderly people, who constitute approximately 11 per cent of the total population, consumed over a third of the health-care dollar. The Gramm-Rudman Deficit Law is forcing re-education in health care costs in 1987. Regardless of the impact of this law, health care services will remain an important concern in the United States.

It is reasonable to predict that social work will continue to have a function in the health services in the decades ahead. Care for the individual already is a widely recognized and accepted function of social work in acute care facilities. Numerous examples have been reported of social work's effectiveness in one-to-one arrangements in general hospitals, medical schools, clinics, and in mental health.

Physicians are not trained to develop social-health solutions. For instance, a recent study reports that elderly patients account for 38 per cent of all days in short-stay hospitals. The elderly are often faced with multiple readmissions, and the elderly person is especially vulnerable to the complex interaction of medical, psychological, and social factors. Social workers can play an important role in helping the elderly and their family members to obtain appropriate medical services by preventing unnecessary hospitalisations, coordinating health planning, and doing discharge planning. Community work is gaining prominence, particularly in the practice of community medicine and in comprehensive mental health centers.

Social workers in medical centers, for example, serve on state medical care advisory committees for Medicaid and Medicare. They also serve on boards on alcoholism and planned parenthood. Increasingly, they are taking leadership on the health team, especially as health care is moving out of the hospital and into the community. Social workers also have been involved in research and evaluation, especially in patient satisfaction measures, which is likely to increase in the years ahead. In various ways social workers are relating themselves increasingly to the community aspects of care. Less is being done at top- or middle-management positions by social workers. But here, too, a few schools of social work are conceptualising theory and offering field instruction for management positions. Schools have done less well in preparing their graduates for roles in planning, policy making, and such administrative functions as budgeting, cost analysis, or in relating to the political processes affecting the health care services.

Social Work and Prevention

The social worker is in a unique and enviable position to contribute to prevention. Social work is health oriented, conceptually and philosophically. It addresses the strengths of the individual or family in a given situation.

As a go-between of services, the social worker is the linkage between the person and a system of support that maintains health, or that may be the means of detecting illness early, or of preventing deterioration of the problem.

Social work organises and develops the community, or mobilizes the resources for doing this. It is often the first to pinpoint needs and to engage in those activities designed to prevent breakdown for the person, the group, or for society. Social work has a resource and service focus and takes the position that no one can be healthy in a sick society.

Social Work in Health Care

Social workers in the health care field work in hospitals, with families, and in public health.

Social Work in Hospitals

Practice in hospitals is a major component of social work in health care. The functions of social work in the hospital include:

1. Assess the patient's psychological and environmental strengths and weaknesses.
2. Collaborate with the team in the delivery of services to assure the maximum utilisation of the skill and knowledge of each team member.
3. Assist the family to cooperate with treatment and to support the patient's utilisation of medical services.
4. Identify with a cadre of other professionals to improve the services of the hospital by an interdisciplinary sharing of knowledge.

5. Serve as a broker of community services, thus providing linkage of patient need with appropriate resources.
6. Participate in the policy-making process.
7. Engage in research to assure a broadening of the knowledge base for successful practice.

Social work is illustrated by the following case of a patient admitted to the hospital for a renal transplant.

> At intake the social worker was responsible for obtaining the history of Paul's illness. She learned that he had an acute renal disorder at age 14. In the years following, he had lived with a fear of death, as well as anxiety over the problems of daily living. During a long period of remission, he married, became the father of a son, was employed in a small family-owned priming business, and lived a "normal" life.
>
> When he was 26 his kidneys failed again and he was hospitalized. After lengthy examinations and consultations, he was scheduled for a renal transplant. The medical team, including the social worker, shared the responsibility for preparing Paul and his family for this operation. The social worker discussed the many ramifications of the operation with Paul's father, who was the donor. It was apparent that although the father was motivated to help, he was also frightened by the prospect of giving up one of his kidneys. He needed the reassurance and support offered by the worker to become comfortable in his lifesaving role, and to dispel his feelings of guilt at his reluctance.
>
> The social worker also was called upon to be the broker for handling the costs of hospitalisation, surgery, and medication. These costs arc often more than a family can handle, and if outside help is not available, can lead to bankruptcy, loss of self-esteem, a lowered standard of living, and serious deprivation. In planning

for money to pay for the transplant, Paul and his family decided to sell the printing business to meet pan of the medical costs. Arrangements also were made with governmental and private agencies to pay the remaining expenses.

In addition to practical problems, Paul and his family had to be prepared for possible rejection of the transplant. The social worker supported and amplified the physician's explanation of rejection.

Two days before the scheduled operation, Paul became ill with a serious respiratory infection, necessitating a postponement. This was dis-appointing and frustrating.

Several weeks after he first entered the hospital the transplant finally was made, but it was not successful. Even though there had been lengthy discussions about the possible rejection, there was much for the social worker to do in helping Paul and his wife handle their extreme disappointment and fear for the future. Paul's father, too, needed reassurance that he had done all he could, that it was not his "fault" that the transplant had not been successful, and that he could live a normal life with just one kidney.

The social work effort concentrated on all members of the family in helping them to sustain each other in this crisis and in introducing them to dialysis, the only means available for cleansing Paul's blood. Since the family lived some distance from a hospital with the necessary equipment for this treatment, it meant a 100-mile trip every other day, plus six hours for the dialysis. In addition, there were the constraints of living imposed by this necessity. All these problems necessitated constant support and help by the social worker.

A breakthrough came when a portable machine weighing 45 pounds became available to Paul. This gave him mobility and greater independence.

As his health improved, and after he had resolved his

hostile feelings about his dependency and had adjusted to his dialysis schedule, he decided to further his education. From the warm association and concrete assistance given by the social worker during his long illness he decided to become a social worker. Encouraged and sustained by his family, the social work school, and the community, he completed his work to become a practicing social worker, feeling that his experience with disease and disability would give him insight into the feelings and problems of others facing death or other medical problems. He stated, "If people can't talk about their disabilities, they'll have a hard time living with them."

Persons who are qualified to help with social factors are important members of the comprehensive treatment team. Their services are related to (1) direct help to the patient, and (2) indirect aid through assistance to the family and/or others. Help to the patient is related to (a) intake, (b) hospitalisation, (c) release, and (d) aftercare. The social worker can be most valuable at the time a patient is admitted to a medical setting. Through use of skills and knowledge, he or she can assist the patient to adjust better to the medical environment and treatment as well as offer help with financial arrangements when necessary. While the patient is in the hospital, the social worker can be of considerable assistance in providing an opportunity for the patient to talk to someone who will listen and who cares. This is usually therapeutically sound and helps in the total treatment plan. If a patient is worried about some problem, he or she is likely to feel better if the anxieties can be verbalized.

The following two case glimpses illustrate other medical-social problems:

A 24-year-old woman was admitted to the emergency ward of a hospital after she attempted suicide for the third time. Because this was a hospital where there was no social service department, the administrator transferred her to another hospital where this service was provided. The main problem for this woman was familial, involving an alcoholic, mentally disturbed husband. It was only after the social worker gave help to the husband and family as a whole that the young woman could live with her situation.

A 15-year-old girl was hospitalized in the psychiatric ward of a general hospital. Part of her problem concerned her relationships with her mother and father. The psychiatrist worked with the girl in the hospital, and the social worker helped the mother and father to understand their daughter better—her needs, their relationships, and what could be done to open the door for communication among them. Through joint guidance of the psychiatrist and social worker, the girl was able 10 leave the hospital and return to an emotional climate at home that was more conducive to satisfactory daily living than it had ever been before.

Social Work and Illness in Family

A family is often controlled by its "sickest" member, with household activities revolving around the unhealthy individual. Small children are asked to curtail their natural exuberance when a parent or an elderly grandparent is ill, and older children are required to perform certain household tasks that previously may have been undertaken by the adults in the family. The family's entire way of life may be reorganised or drastically altered by the sickness of one of its members, and not infrequently, considerable family dysfunctioning results from the illness. Frequently, with the help of services within the community, it is possible for a family to mobilize its resources to care for a sick or handicapped child or adult. Although it is true that illness can foster family disorganisation, it can also result in a constructive use of the family to achieve family unity and goals. Social agencies are available for help. Many handicapped or retarded children can be cared for by their families, either by arranging the family's own resources, by using services within the community, or by a combination of family and community resources. Such resources as community mental health centers, visiting nurses associations, home-maker services, and family service agencies can be called upon to strengthen and support the efforts of families. In his or her role, the social worker performs a function that supports the medical care given to a sick person and in so doing realistically appraises the needs of the family and the "assets and liabilities" within the family and community for meeting these needs.

One purpose of social work is to support and strengthen family life. In doing this the social worker makes use of existing services through referrals or assists in mobilising the untapped potential of the community to prevent illness or to restore the sick and disabled to health and usefulness.

The case of Peter Simpson illustrates the social and psychological components of illness and the function of the social worker in working with a young adolescent and his family. The medical care for Peter in this instance was aided by social services: first, through study and diagnosis, which focused the social and emotional components of his illness; second, by a radical shift in living arrangements for Peter, which his mother was helped to support; third, by referral to and use of child guidance; fourth, by job training and employment for Mrs. Simpson resulting in financial independence and greater personal satisfaction.

Social Work in Public Health

A community is a society of individuals that plans for the welfare of its members for mutual advantage. No community can afford to disregard the needs of people who are ill or who might require medical care even if the family cannot bear the burden without help. Recognising various motives, the community must take steps to protect the health of its members. The sick person, the handicapped one, and the disabled one who cannot get the care he or she needs cannot be a healthy, contributing force within the community. Therefore, in its own self-interest, the community provides hospitals, clinics, and other health services. Public health services have been developed in most communities.

The following case illustrates the role of the social worker in public health services:

> A social worker in the public health department was asked to accompany the public health nurse on a home visit to a young mother whose six-month-old infant was failing to gain weight. Several times in the past month the baby had been brought to the hospital's emergency room in a severely dehydrated condition.
>
> The public health nurse was trying to help the mother, a 19-year-old woman of borderline intelligence, with the tasks of child rearing. The baby's 50-year-old father, formerly a truck driver, was homebound because of a back injury.
>
> On her visit, the social worker noted chat the mother seemed depressed and lethargic and, although fond of her child, seemed uncertain about how to care for him. When the baby cried, she became panicky. Her husband was demanding a great deal of her attention. In addition, the young mother was on bad terms with her own parents, who had disapproved of her marriage, and she did not want to involve them in her problems now.
>
> The social worker found herself working with a family where multiple health problems were interacting. Consequently she referred the father to vocational

rehabilitation for retraining in a skill compatible with his physical limitations, and arranged for a homemaker to help the mother for several weeks so she could observe the details of child care and feeding from a competent model. The social worker also helped the mother reestablish a relationship with her own parents, who proved very interested in the progress of their new grandchild and helpful to their daughter.

Summary

Medical social work is social work in responsible collaboration with medicine. It is practiced in hospitals and clinics and in other settings that commonly are identified with the practice of medicine. The clientele of medical social work are those whose needs are social and psychological and whose functioning has been or is in danger of becoming impaired because of illness, disease, or disability.

The ill person, to the social worker, is one who is not performing adequately in the various social roles appropriate for him or her. There are many factors to illness and, in work with the ill person, the social worker addresses him- or herself to those bearing directly on the person's performance in various roles—employee, employer, husband, wife, or child.

Illness has various and different meanings for the individual, family, and the community. The family's activities often are centered around the sick person, who is in a position to control the activities of the household.

Medical and health agencies within the community are established to assist the family in the performance of its role. The meaning of illness to the community lies largely in the need of the community to promote the health of its citizens. Social workers, particularly those in health care settings, are in strategic positions to give direction to the development of services in communities.

REFERENCES

Bartlett, Harriett M., *Fifty Years of Social Work in a Medical Setting.* New York: National Association of Social Workers, 1957.

Bracht, Neil F., *Social Work in Health Care: A Guide to Professional Practice.* New York: The Haworth Press, 1978.

Davidson, Park O., and Sheena M. davidson, eds., *Behavioural Medicine: Changing Health Lifestyles.* New York: Brunner/Mazel, Publishers, 1980.

Eisenberg, Myron G., La Faye C. Sutkin, and Mary A. Jansen, eds., *Chronic Illness and Disability Through the Life Span: Effects on Self and Family.* New York: Springer Publishing Co., 1984.

Lindenberg, Steven Phillip, *Group Psychotherapy with People Who are Dying.* Springfield, III.: Charles C. Thomas, 1983.

Lonsdale, Gill, Peter Elfer, and rod Ballard, *Children, Grief and Social Work.* Oxford, England: Basil Blackwell, 1979.

Mechanic, David, ed., *Handbook of Health, Health Care, and the Health Professions.* New York: Free Press, 1983.

Prichard, Elizabeth R., Jean collard, Ben A. Orcutt, Austin H. Kutscher, Irene seeland, and Nathan Lefkowitz, *Social Work with the* Dying *Patient and the Family.* New York: Columbia University Press, 1977.

Rehr, Helen, ed., *Medicine and Social Work: An Exploration in Interprofessionalism.* New York:

5

Social Treatment of Mental and Emotional Problems

As much as we may talk about the freedom of the individual to do as he pleases, we are constantly reminded, nevertheless, of the rigorous restrictions which society places on everyone's conduct. Often we do not undertake certain actions because we know that social pressures will preclude our enjoyment of them. When at times we are deviant in our behaviour, it may be at the enormous cost of opposing internal and external restraints. It is not easy for everyone to deviate too much from the accepted social values without receiving some form of punishment. The punishment will in part be from society and in part from conscience.

Today, it is increasingly recognised by both professional and lay people that a large proportion of the population suffers from mental and emotional problems of some kind. These range from disturbances created by current crises to severe illnesses which require the person's hospitalisation.

While many psychiatric social workers deal with hospitalised persons, probably as many or even more work with individuals whose conflicts prevent them from functioning effectively in the community but nevertheless are not serious enough to require hospitalisation.

Treating Methods for Mentally Abnormal

Formerly, interest was focused almost exclusively on the extreme expressions of mental disturbances, known as *psychoses*. People who suffered from these maladies were treated in various ways. The early means of controlling the deviant behaviour of the mentally ill were primarily repressive. They assumed that the mentally sick person was a malicious individual who needed to be coerced into normality.

There are instances in medieval Europe and in early American history where mentally ill persons were actually beaten in order that their "demons" might be punished and cast out. Some of the mentally abnormal even suffered the death penalty. The mentally ill in the early American period were also isolated. Under this form of "treatment" the community segregated an abnormal individual so that he would not present a community problem. The case of Jan Vorelissen, as seen in the Upland Court Records of 1676, illustrates this procedure. Jan, according to the Court, was "bereft of his natural senses and is turned quite mad." Because with his madness he was unable to support himself (there is no family mentioned). It was ordered that a "little block house" be built for him "for to put in the said madman." Another method of supervising the mentally abnormal in the early American period was through a form of the indenture system. At best, however, the indenture means of care was loosely organised and led to many injustices.

The early means of caring for the abnormal were superseded by institutional treatment. In some places the insane were placed in the general community poorhouse along with dependent children, delinquents, prostitutes, and the aged. Elsewhere, special institutions were established for separate categories of need. In such places the care of the mentally sick tended to be more responsible, though it was in actuality simply another means of isolating the individual who was not conforming to community standards of normality. These establishments were a far cry from the modern mental hospitals. The results of these methods of managing the mentally ill proved their inadequacy, and in time new ideas and fresh approaches were formulated to meet the problem.

Attention was given to the possibility of a more scientific understanding of mental abnormality. Leaders in the care of the insane began to be concerned with ways in which the living conditions within mental institutions could be improved. Interest rose in whether or not mental illnesses could be cured or at least made less sever. Thus as early as 1824 the first hospital designed exclusively for the use of mental patients was founded in Lexington, Kentucky. Its establishment showed the advancing interest and knowledge in the problem of the mentally disordered.

Increased Concern for Mentally Ill

Near the middle of the nineteenth century, Dorothea Dix, a remarkable advocate of social reform, appeared on the American scene. Through daring publicity she enabled all to see what horrors existed in the care of the mentally ill. So great at that time were the cruelty and stupidity involved that Miss Dix could write to the Legislature of Massachusetts: "I proceed, Gentlemen, briefly, to call your attention to the state of insane persons confined within the Commonwealth, in cages, closets, cellars, stalls, pens: Chained, naked, beaten with rods, and lashed into obedience," Such indeed were the conditions about a century age in one of the most "advanced" of our states. But, despite these practices, there were some hopeful signs. The formation of the Association of Medical Super-intendents of American Institutions (now known as the American Psychiatric

Association) in Philadelphia in 1844 was a landmark in the development of a sane treatment of mental patients.

Psychiatry, moreover, then and later was searching for the best possible methods. At the turn of the last century it achieved significant insights into the problems of mental illness. While there was a host of contributors, certainly no one was more important than Sigmund Freud. It was he who not only formulated for the first time the dynamics of personality structure and functioning but also developed a psychotherapeutic method for the treatment of emotional conflicts. The psychobiological theory of Dr. Adolf Meyer also helped to usher in the modern psychiatric period of scientific understanding. Concern for the problems of the mentally ill was further stimulated by the efforts of Clifford Beers.

From its early interest in the understanding and treatment of the mental and emotional problems of psychotics, psychiatric social work has broadened its concern to include the understanding of normal behaviour. Much of its practice and its success in the recent decades has been in the services it has developed for normal persons who suffer from temporary emotional upsets.

PSYCHIATRIC SOCIAL WORK

Psychiatric social work as a profession had its origin in the West in the second decade of this century. However, there has been a lot of confusion about the term, psychiatric social work. As far back as 1929 two different definitions of psychiatric social work were formulated in the U.S.A. The first definition emphasises the setting in which social casework is practised. It defines psychiatric social work as "Social casework established within psychiatric agencies as a from of service essential to the medical programme of such agencies." The second definition lays stress on the qualitative aspect of the practice irrespective of setting. It defines psychiatric social work as a practice possessing certain qualities, deriving from knowledge of psychiatric concepts and from the ability to adapt them to the social casework process. According to the second definition, the work of social workers, who find new positions in family welfare agencies or child welfare agencies, has to presume that all activities of psychiatric social workers are *ipso facto* related to psychiatric social work.

A third definition has also been given that psychiatric social workers are those who work with psychiatrists as opposed to those who do not. In the sense a social worker working in a family welfare agency or any agency where the service of a part time consultant psychiatrist is available will say that hers is psychiatric social work.

Since psychiatric social work as a new profession in India was started about a decade ago, it is likely that unless we keep the definition clear, some confusion may arise about the term itself. There are social work agencies where some knowledge of psychiatry could be of help, and could profitably be integrated in the training of social workers practising in those setups. For instance, a superintendent of the Home for Women in Social Distress may benefit by psychiatric orientation but her work in that setup cannot be called psychiatric social work. Again, if a Home engages a consultant psychiatrist whom the superintendent occasionally consults regarding her cases, her work cannot fall within the category of psychiatric social work.

Methods common to all social workers are used in all special fields. In the areas where social work is combined with activities of another field or profession, "differences arise from the special contribution of that field, be it criminology, education, medicine or psychiatry. Upon such differences specialities in social work are based, and from them grows the body of knowledge and experience that is incorporated into the training of workers." We realise then that it is the psychiatric setting which has something special to offer to the practice of psychiatric social work. What then is a psychiatric setting?

The set up is concerned with the practice of psychiatry and mental hygiene; the purpose of the set up is the study, treatment, and rehabilitation of the mentally ill and the mentally defective, prevention of mental disease, nervous disorders and mental defects and promotion of mental health. Psychiatric social work in India should be the practice of social work and not just social casework (as found often in Western literature) in a psychiatric setting, for that is a narrow view of social work.

Casework is after all one method of social work. In the practice of psychiatric social work other methods, such as group work, community organisation and research are also made use of. The emphasis on each method will depend much on the nature of the particular psychiatric setting in which a psychiatric social worker is going to practice.

Some of the psychiatric agencies for adults are as follows: (a) mental hospitals for well-established cases of insanity; (b) psychiatric wards for in-patients of the psychiatry department of a general hospital or other hospitals; (c) psychiatric out-patient clinics, (i) out-patient clinics in general hospitals; (ii) independent out-patient clinics or community mental health clinics; and (iii) psychiatric clinics or mental health clinics or mental health clinics attached to prisons, colleges and industries; (d) day hospitals, which besides being less expensive than mental hospitals or psychiatric beds in general hospitals, give the patient an opportunity to get adjusted to the family and the community while he is under treatment. Patients spend the whole day there and go back home only in the evening; (e) organisations for rehabilitation of mental patients; (f) institutions for adult mental defectives.

For children the following institutions are necessary: (a) child guidance clinics; (b) mental health services at (i) maternity clinics or some child welfare centres; (ii) pre-primary, primary, and secondary schools; (iii) juvenile centres; (iv) certified schools; (v) remand homes; (vi) institutions for dependent children, and (vii) institutions for mentally subnormal children. Psychiatric social work can very well be developed in these setups.

Essential functions of a psychiatric social worker are:

1. To study case situations and complement the examination by the psychiatrist. The psychiatric social worker makes a thorough study of the environment of the patient, covering such aspects as home, work life and social life, and brings out significant facts which have some bearing on his maladjustment. This study enables her to prepare a systematic case history of the patient which throws light on the tension and difficulties in his life and also help her to assess the positive and negative aspects of the environment. The psychiatric social worker is able to throw light on the environmental factors that have contributed to the patient's problems. By interpreting the environment of the patient the psychiatric social worker helps the psychiatrist to understand the patient in his total setting and arrive at a satisfactory diagnosis so as to chalk out a line of treatment.

2. To administer social treatment. This has a very wide range. The psychiatric social worker has very often to explain to the patient or the relatives what the problem is and what is involved in psychiatric treatment, so that

their anxiety is allayed and they can co-operate in the treatment. The social worker has to help the relatives of the mentally defective or the insane, to accept the diagnosis and psychiatric recommendations. The social worker aids the psychiatric treatment by the social treatment, i.e., treatment of environmental problems. She sees that there are no complications in the family, workplace of the patient or in other areas which can serve as obstacles in carrying out the psychiatric treatment. Often the nagging attitude of the members of the family, lack of proper understanding of the problem on the part of the employer or the school teacher (in the case of a child) or the sense of stigma regarding the illness on the part of the patient and his relatives can come in the way of successful treatment. The social worker works with the patient, his relatives and others, directly connected with him in modifying their attitudes. She also tries to bring about a better adjustment between the patient and his family.

In this connection, it is important to remember that the needs of a patient cannot be completely separated from those of his family; he cannot be expected to recover in a hospital if the needs of his dependents are not adequately met. So apart from helping the patient to adjust himself to the requirements of the treatment of his illness, the social worker also helps the family to adapt itself to the new situation. By working with the patient and his family the social worker lessens the patient's anxieties and enables him to complete his treatment without signing out against psychiatric advice.

Social treatment is also geared towards after care. Serious and difficult as are the problems of the person affected with psychosis or neurosis, there are still greater problems of after care. On his return home the patient may find himself a man apart if he continues to live as he lived in an institution. He has to adapt himself to the family. The social worker has to follow up a discharged case very carefully. Though mental illness can be recurrent, every attempt needs to be made in the direction of allaying the anxiety of the discharged patient for whom the danger and the fear of the illness hangs like the sword of Damocles and affects his personality. Besides, his ability to support himself and his family must be restored. Since the illness gives the patient a special position in society, the cure is not complete before the patient is readjusted socially and is enabled either to resume his old position or become reconciled to the new one. Therefore, the social worker very often has to assist a dischargee in securing a job better suited to his mental condition and also in adjusting himself to this new work. She has to pool together community resources like trusts and charities, employment exchanges, housing sections and recreation centres to help the patient.

3. The enlist the co-operation of other social agencies for better discharge of functions of one's own agency and for stimulating interest in dealing with common problems effectively. By working co-operatively with various agencies, the psychiatric social worker is able to interpret her agency and its functions to the community so that the community can seek its aid in time and also give its timely assistance to the agency.

A psychiatric social worker needs to bear in mind that she should not get so deeply involved in intensive treatment of the maladjusted individual that she fails to recognise the importance of general social problems and, therefore, may not take interest in programmes for social change. She needs to study social conditions, develop resources in the community and participate in community planning.

The interdependence of psychiatric social service and

community resources is such that unless all are of high quality, the service itself will be handicapped. If a particular community lacks facilities for various kinds of services to the emotionally disturbed child, the psychiatric social worker is prevented from helping the client adequately. In a community there may not be a play centre for children or special classes for exceptional children. The social worker may recognise these needs of children but will not be able to help them in the real sense of the word unless there are facilities for meeting their needs. Communities vary in the completeness of their welfare services and this fact does affect the adequacy of the service rendered by the social worker. Therefore, a psychiatric social worker has to become indirectly a community builder. She cannot keep her work strictly confined to any setting. She has to interpret the needs of the client to the community and make special efforts to arouse public interest in bringing about certain improvements.

4. To participate in training programmes. Students of psychiatric social work, student nurses, medical students and staff of the agency where the psychiatric social worker is employed as a mental hygiene supervisor or consultant may participate in the training programmes. As contributors to mental hygiene programme in educational institutions or other organisations, psychiatric social workers may or may not have always direct casework function with the clients of the agency, but they have the responsibility of helping the staff of the agency to increase and utilise more effectively knowledge of emotional problems and their implications for physical and mental health, and social relationships.

5. To impart mental health education. In pre-natal and post-natal clinics and nursery schools the psychiatric social worker apart from direct casework service to the

clients, when necessary, imparts mental health education to parents. Sometimes her services are required to promote mental health education in the community. Her work may involve community organisation, publicity, assisting in community surveys, studying mental hygiene needs of communities, development of facilities for more adequate provision for prevention and treatment of mental disease and so on.

6. To participate in the determination and formation of agency policies with a view to socialising the agency setup to meet the needs of clients better.

7. To maintain social work records. This is important for the purpose of social statistics. A full report enables a worker to diagnose the social problems better and check up her social treatment plan. This will also enable her to know whether she is going in the right direction or not. Social care itself is so complex a problem that various factors must be very carefully considered. The social worker must improve her skill constantly. She must be critical of what she does. Recording also helps her in acquiring the habit of observing and writing descriptions carefully.

8. To promote research. The psychiatric social worker can be of immense assistance in the field of research. She enables the patient to accept psychiatric recommendations and encourages her to continue the treatment. Thus psychiatrists are in a position to observe the results of any particular treatment in which they are interested. When a patient does not respond to a certain type of treatment, the social worker can find out for the psychiatrist whether or not the deterrent is a social factor which needs handling before he is expected to respond. Such information would be of help in the verification of his reactions to a particular treatment. The psychiatric social worker can render help

in promoting social research too. She observes the social components of illness, behaviour disorders, etc., and finds out that the community resources are inadequate and can throw much light on the deficiencies. She is able to determine what each case contributes to the knowledge and understanding of human beings and social forces. She observes what a particular case can have in common with other cases which can justify further study to determine the necessity for social measures. Case records of the agency provide ample data for social research. It is needless to add that social research leads to social action for promoting the cause of welfare of patients and their families.

9. To promote therapeutic entertainment measures. The psychiatric social worker attached to hospitals has to entertain patients from time to time to keep them cheerful and help them to overcome their home sickness as well as the boredom of long treatment. She may organise a recreation club with the help of the members of the staff and the patients, and encourage the latter to develop hobbies. Such activities contribute much to the patients' recovery. Through organised recreational programmes the patients learn group participation, take up responsibility for their behaviour, learn discipline in a congenial atmosphere and also overcome their personality defects like shyness, withdrawn behaviour, negativism, etc. In child guidance clinics the therapeutic clubs organised for providing therapy through recreational activities serve a good purpose. When the activities are organised one should keep in view the problems of its young members like shyness, aggressiveness, inability to mix in a group and so on. For instance, through dramatics and puppet shows the members are enabled to give vent to their repressed feelings in a socially acceptable manner. This indirectly helps them to find socially acceptable channels for the outlet of their surplus energy.

In the practice of psychiatric social work it is very essential to have team spirit among the members of the staff of the psychiatric agency. A good teamwork relationship, specially between the social worker and the psychiatrist is absolutely necessary. However, unfortunately both in the West as well as in India there have been occasions when a trained psychiatric social worker's role has not been properly understood. She has been regarded as a person who explains to the families of the patients the psychiatrist's recommendations and finds jobs, boarding homes, schools and recreational centres. Often she has been regarded as an errand girl attached to a psychiatric clinic to carry out specific behests of the psychiatrist. But gone are the days of social manipulation in the field of professional social work. The social treatment that the psychiatric social worker offers has distinct techniques (social work techniques) of its own and her treatment is a part of a plan of total treatment. In the social treatment the psychiatric social worker deals with human attitudes and emotions as well as pools together resources of the community. She has casework techniques at her command for dealing with human emotions. Social casework is a form of psychotherapy as it deals with the treatment of mind. In other words, she handles people's feelings and emotions. It differs from psychotherapy of the psychiatrist in as much as his goal and techniques are different. It is essential that one profession should try to understand the contribution made by another. It does not conduce to teamwork where rigidity exists. It is disconcerting to find in a child guidance clinic that the child should be seen only by the psychiatrist and not by the social worker, and relatives by the social worker. Who should take up the major responsibility for the treatment of the child or his parents? Quite often the parents present a problem which needs the help of a psychiatrist. Sometimes the child would benefit by social work therapy, casework or therapeutic group work. Again, it is amazing to hear why a psychiatric social worker is not allowed to talk to a mental patient; yet she is expected to interpret his problems to the relatives, find him a job or bring about better adjustment on the part of the employer to the patient. The fear that if a social worker talks to the patient, the therapy value of the psychiatric treatment would be lost is unfounded. Quite often the patients bring out so many facts about themselves when they are interviewed in an unhurried atmosphere of goodwill by the social worker that the psychiatrists would benefit by them. There should be an understanding on the part of both the psychiatrist and the social worker about the areas of treatment of the patient. It is not necessary that the psychiatrist should always tell the social worker about her area of work. The psychiatric social worker should also be able to state when a case is being discussed how she would be able to contribute towards the treatment.

An important point needs to be mentioned here that as there is a dearth of psychiatrists, the practising psychiatrist who has a social worker in his team utilises her service more for individualised work with the patient. This expert's intensive work is done from a psychological angle. In other words, the major emphasis is on the patient as an *individual* rather than as a *social being.* She is expected to carry out this work under the supervision of the psychiatrist. Some psychiatric social workers who do this type of work do not realise that they are overlooking the distinct contribution that a trained social worker can make to the field of social work. By training she is a social worker. She is taking up the type of work which a psychiatrist is expected to do. Neither by training is she a psychiatrist nor by her functions does she remain a social worker. There is a dearth of psychiatrists, similarly there is a dearth of trained psychiatric social workers in India. The professional training for each field is different. We do more harm than good to both the professions, for the social worker by doing the job which a psychiatrist with professional training should do remains an assistant to the psychiatrist. She is neither a psychiatrist nor a social worker doing justice to their respective professions. Efforts should be made by the professional organisation of psychiatrists to encourage more people to go in for the training of psychiatrists and develop facilities for imparting such training.

In the treatment of a patient the psychiatrist is there to look at the patient (with major emphasis) as an individual. The social worker has a valuable contribution to make if she concentrates more on the environmental factors that create and affect emotions and attitudes without trying to be a pseudo-psychiatrist or psychoanalyst. Instead of attempting to do psychotherapy of the other type, a psychiatric social worker with due recognition of psychological factors needs to look into the environmental factors intensively. She should study the client as a person in his social content, find out what environmental factors (like culture or religious factors) hamper his happiness, what he and his community can do about these matters and how a social worker can help him. If we accept the fact that what a person is today is the result of all his yesterdays, then it logically follows that today's experience of social living will be a part of his psychic experience of tomorrow. Since a psychiatric social worker can have first hand or direct information of the social situations, she can be well equipped with her unique method of psychotherapy (casework therapy) through deeper understanding of the environmental factors as they affect the personality, and she can also utilise the knowledge of social situations in the social readjustment of the clients. Her therapy needs to be more and more in time socio-psychotherapy and not the psychotherapy of a psychiatrist.

From all that has been said above, it is evident that for psychiatric social work we need the services of well qualified social workers with specialisation in the field of psychiatric social work. Any body just interested in this work will not do. Social work methods have a scientific basis. Methodical skill is essential for scientific social work. It is not simply intuition and common sense. The profession of social work today presupposes a scientific body of knowledge which should be acquired in an accredited school of social work before any individual is entitled to practice it. Very often it is thought that when one concentrates on the educational requirements one is apt to overlook necessary personal attribute of the workers. Our schools of social work do pay attention to personality factors in the selection of students and have been fairly successful in recruiting university graduates of both sexes who possess such qualities as warmth, sympathy and sensitive understanding that are regarded as necessary for the successful practice of the profession of social work. No person should be allowed to engage a psychiatric social worker—unless he or she has specialised in the field, has maturity of judgement and a definite interest in working with people with psychiatric problems. Academic preparation for this type of social work is extremely valuable.

A good combination would be (1) an adequate background of generals education; (2) possession of a B.A. degree, preferably in social science; (3) interest in sick people; (4) ability to overcome fear of and aversion for blood, diseased condition, queer behaviour, including physical violence, etc.; (5) special training in a school of social work, Indian social problems, social legislation, medical information, public welfare and community welfare services, basic social work techniques, namely, casework, group work, community organisation, social research, dynamics of human behaviour, adult and child psychiatry, including psychopathology, treatment of psychoses, various behaviour problems and management of the mentally defective; psychosomatic medicine, social and emotional components of illness, care and rehabilitation, casework in psychiatric settings, child guidance techniques; organisation and administration of psychiatric social service in various settings and so on.

In training psychiatric social workers it is not desirable to limit their training programmes to the psychiatric field only. Some think that a psychiatric social worker under training should have field work experience only with patients. They, however, fail to see that such a procedure will make the worker's vision narrow. She is likely to see a patient in a disturbed state of mind only rather than as a person. Besides, a psychiatric case may have an organic disease, a social problem like unmarried motherhood and poor pecuniary condition. The worker who has no experience of varied human problems may attribute every aspect of the behaviour of the client to his social or emotional.

The field-work programme should give the psychiatric social worker enough ground in working with healthy people as well as people suffering from various organic and mental diseases, and also familiarise herself with various community resources. Therefore, her first field work placement should be in a non-institutional setting, such as a family welfare agency where she can come to grips with personality and family problems. It will be desirable to have a placement in a medical setting too, for many organic conditions lead to psychiatric problems. Besides, the student will learn to resolve the dichotomy of mind and body and try to grasp what happens to the whole man. The student should have supervised field work experience in psychiatric settings both for children and adults. such as in a child guidance clinic, psychiatric out-patient clinic or a mental hospital.

Postgraduate professional training for psychiatric social work in India is imparted for the last 10 years only. It is surprising to learn that many persons object to the postgraduate training of social workers. They feel that a two-year training programme discourages many workers from joining the course when a large number of trained social workers are needed. However, every profession at one point or another in its development has to choose either between emphasis upon quantity or emphasis upon quality, and our country should regret to choose the former.

For erecting a house or building a bridge, we need the services of well qualified and trained engineers. It goes without saying that the training of social engineers who deal with human beings must have adequate training in a postgraduate institute, because they are engaged in promoting the social well-being of individuals, families and groups, and in restoring the victims of diseases and disasters to a useful life. One cannot be satisfied with a three or four months training programme for psychiatric social work. Adequate training cannot be imparted to students in a brief period. It is as absurd as giving a medical degree to a person after a short course of training and allowing him to practice as a physician because we are short of them.

In our country, we need the services of well-qualified male and female psychiatric social workers. Their salary should be in accordance with the training required for the position and the responsibility to be shouldered by them.

At present, the total emoluments of a psychiatric social worker in a mental hospital or an out-patient psychiatric clinic rarely exceed Rs. 250/- a month. Besides, when she is required to visit the patients' homes or contract the employers, she pays the transport charges from her own pocket.

In spite of the fact that there is a great demand for psychiatric social workers, the employment agencies do not pay them handsomely. Consequently, very few candidates prefer to go in for this specialisation in schools of social work. In most of the social work training institutions the largest number of students prefer to specialise in the labour welfare field which in such more paying. It is felt that schools of social work will make arrangements for training of psychiatric social workers, and more candidates will enrol for the training in the field if they feel that there is a demand for them on suitable terms. Adequate salary will attract worker of integrity. They will be imbibed with the spirit of service, and the self-imposed responsibility will induce them to keep in touch with the new developments in this special field.

REFERENCES

Ethel L., Ginsburg, "Psychiatric Social Work," *Orthopsychiatry,* 1923-48 Retrospect and Prospect, New York: American Orthopsychiatric Association, Inc., 1948, 470 - 472.

Lois Meredith, *French Psychiatric Social Work,* London: The Commonwealth Fund, 1940, p. 3.

Porter R. Lee and Marion Kensworthy, *Mental Hygiene and Social Work,* New York: The Commonwealth Fund, 1929, p. 161.

6

Management of Social Welfare

Social welfare is a multifaced concept, welfare of living beings, welfare of mankind and social welfare. Hindu philosophy has repeatedly emphasfised welfare at various levels. The Indian concept *Kalyan* considered equivalent of welfare is in fact much more comprehensive. Even social welfare traditionally was considered in a narrow context referring to the amelioration of the handicapped, the deprived, the poor, the orphan, the destitute, the neglected and the unfortunate victim of unfavourable circumstances. It had its roots in charity, benevolence, humanitarianism and the quest for self-realisation. Even where the State took measures for relief and help it was motivated by charity and benevolence.

In the end of last century century the social costs of industrialisation brought the realisation that the poor, deprived and suffering people were not unfortunate sinners but were victims of an unegalitarian, oppressive, exploitative production system and that they had to be cared for by those benefiting from the system. Marxian thinkers contributed to this conclusion in a major way though other social scientists through their surveys and studies of the working classes and the poor also demonstrated that the poor and the unfortunate were products of the system. Hence, the duty of the system for their well-being.

India during her freedom struggle recognised the need of ameliorating the economic and social conditions of the people in general and the poor, social outcasts and the depressed in particular. Gandhi realised the need of such well being and never accepted that only political freedom was priori to the amelioration of the conditions of the poor, the chronically sick, the socially outcasts and the educationally deprived. Along with his movement for Independence of the country he continued his struggle for social and economic uplift of the people under his constructive programme. The Congress under the leadership of Gandhi and Nehru also recognised the need of national reconstruction and the National Planning Committee was set up under the chairmanship of the latter. When India became free and ventured to draft its Constitution, it had two perspectives in general; a liberal democratic polity represented by the United States and England and a totalitarian socialist state represented by the Soviet Union. Gandhi was a spiritualist-moralist-idealist admiring nature, having more faith in 'good' in the individual and less faith in the 'good' of the state.

Unfortunately, he was taken away from the Indian political scene by the bullets of a fanatic and it was Nehru whose faith in democracy, liberalism, socialism and secularism was well known, guided the destiny of the nation in the early years of its reconstruction. Jawahar Lal was both an idealist and a pragmatist, being a keen student of history, he realised that the goal of socialist order could not be proclaimed immediately but the principles of such a socialistic order could be laid down in the name of the welfare social order. (It was perhaps the influence of Fabian Socialism that he thought of socialistic order through

'Welfare State'). Nehru thus influenced the direction of change and development of Indian polity, and was instrumental for the inclusion of the 'Directive Principles of State Policy' in the Constitution of India. He had repeatedly emphasised that these provisions were not justifiable in courts of law but were 'fundamental to the governance of the state'. Many a times people asked him why these were not made a part of the Fundamental Rights but he always said that it was mandatory for the state to pursue a policy consistent with the principles laid down in this part and any action of the government . . . legislative, executive or otherwise, violating these directive principles was against the spirit of the constitution. Article 38 of the Indian Constitution states: "The State shall strive to promote the welfare of the people by securing and protecting as effectively as it may a social order in which justice, social economic and political, shall inform all the institutions of the national life."

Hence, the corner stone of a welfare social order is social, economic and political justice. In the next Article (Article 39) certain principles of policy to be followed by the state in pursuance of the goal of social, economic and political justice have been specifically laid down. These relate to equal right to men and women to adequate means of livelihood; ownership and control of material community resources for the common good; prevention of concentration of wealth and ownership of means of production detrimental to the common good; parity of wages for men and women for equal work; protection of health of workers and safeguard of women and children against abuse; and above all provision of development facilities to children and youth and protection against abandonment. In the following articles specific areas of social policy and methods of social justice are detailed out. In Article 39A, for example, equal justice and free legal aid are directed; Article 41 refers to Right to Work and public assistance; Art. 45 points to free and compulsory education for children up to fourteen years' age; Art. 45 refers to promotion of educational and economic activities for scheduled castes and tribes; and Articles 42, 43 and 43A direct that humane conditions of work, maternity relief, living wage and decent standard of living to all workers—agricultural, industrial or otherwise—and participation of workers in management be assured. Article 47 requires the State to promote improvement in levels of nutrition, standard of living and health (basic needs) as its primary duties. In the economic field it enjoins on the state to endeavor to organise agriculture and animal husbandry on modern scientific lines, and to promote cottage industries and handicrafts. On the environmental and cultural fronts it directs the State for protection and improvement of environment and safeguarding of forests and wild life (Art. 48A) protection of monuments and places and objects of national importance.

Thus, it will be seen that the state policy of Welfare is wide and is not limited to the handicapped, destitute, delinquent, neglected, poverty stricken and socially unfortunate only. The concept of welfare and a just social order is wide and the approach to welfare is not the "Residual Welfare" but instead the "institutional redistributive" model in the terminology of Richard M. Titmus. Social justice is not only compensatory or ameliorative but is essentially redistributive in character, ensuring equality of opportunities, social status and political rights. This is in keeping with the perspective of the ideals of justice, liberty, equality, fraternity and dignity of the individual, proclaimed in the preamble of the Constitution of India. The Social policy parameters laid down in the constitution are essentially what we profess. The framers of the constitution recognised that India was far from these ideals. The society was ridden with religious, caste and economic strifes, almost over half of the population was living in abject poverty; production was low; country was facing the problem of food; industries were few and production was low; it was dependent on imports and aid; there was hardly any national income which could be distributed; natural resources were untapped and could not be harnessed for productive purposes; basic industries were absent and technical know-how was missing; people's skills were primitive, foreign aid was not easy to get due to poor credibility of the country; and above all the foreign powers were interested to trap the nation in their power games. In the words of Nehru the whole government was welfare and to talk of a welfare ministry or department was irrelevant. This is what he had said in 1953 while talking to a group of youth demanding the setting up of a welfare department in the government. He thought that the residual ameliorative welfare activities could be left to the voluntary sector and the best that the state could do was to encourage and promote their activities. Thus, we find the setting up of the Central Social Welfare Board for encouragement of the voluntary sector.

Present Situation

Even after forty years of freedom India is far from the ideals of the welfare state. The right to work has been incorporated in the Directive Principles of State Policy but is not a fundamental right. The state is not able to fulfill the promises of the Fundamental Rights and the roots of the failure lie in our under-development. In the first four plans the basic strategy was on economic development and it was assumed that increase in GNP and Per Capita Income would enable the State to implement measures for distributive justice. Nehru considered economic production priori to any measures for distribution. However, what ever little economic development has taken place it has only lead to an increase in economic inequalities. The rich have become richer and the poor have become poorer. Development brings with it inflation and this has resulted in the lowering of the real incomes of the people. The purchasing power of the common man has fallen substantially.

The nationalised industries have led to increase in production but who has been the beneficiary? The industrialists, the large trader, and the big zamindar cultivating cash crops. The poor landless laborer, the worker in the unorganised sector, the cottage level producer, the marginal farmer producing mainly for his own consumption, the odd jobber have all fallen below their previous level. Many of them have been thrown out of their traditional abodes and are living at starvation level and in inhuman conditions in our industrial—urban centres. Poverty has shifted from village to city and the relative deprivation has multiplied. There is no social assistance for the unemployed. What ever social security is available is to the organised worker who gets wages much better than the worker in agriculture or unorganised sector or the self-employed artisan.

Social Welfare in a liberal state has to do some social leveling. Our Anti-poverty and Twenty Point Programmes have been focused on these. However, a look at our programmes for the development of the poor clearly show that the effect has been more in the favour of the upper middle and upper classes. Increased economic assistance has helped the officials, the intermediaries, the village elites, the big farmers and manufacturers. Studies are not wanting that demonstrate that over three fourth of the input for the development of the poor in reality benefits the middle and the upper middle classes.

Strategy in the Sixth Plan for removal of poverty was to increase the quantum of social consumption of the poor. This means greater economic and social benefits to the poor. This necessarily means a broad based social assistance programme for the poor. Housing, education, loans for self employment or subsidiary activities, training for new skills, and subsidies for new activities have been major strategies for economic amelioration. There has been reportedly some 'relief' as the proportion of the poor below the poverty line, it is claimed, has decreased. However, the social and economic structure of the classes stands unchanged. In contrast, the conflict between the classes have increased, perhaps the poor have become more conscious of their misery and their exploitation and also because the upper classes/castes are more resentful of the preferential treatment meted out to tne traditionally exploited classes. They argue against positive, enabling discrimination in our constitution and the anti-reservation riots and village feuds between the scheduled castes and the upper castes bear a testimony to this. Similarly, tribals too are rising up at places against the age-old exploiting communities. This awareness of rights amongst the poor and the have-nots is no doubt a healthy sign but the resultant violent conflicts are detrimental to the hearth of the society.

Social Welfare is concerned with the needs of the people and no society can meet all needs of all people at all times. There are hierarchies of needs. Some are basic to existence, some are essential to human development and others are needs of comfortable life. A welfare state has to see that first the needs of existence-food, clothing and shelter must be met, irrespective of the condition of the person, child, woman, adult, sick, unemployed, handicapped, deserted, delinquent, old, infirm, able bodied; in fact whatever his physical, mental or social status. A means of livelihood for the one who can work, and an adequate income for the provider or guardian of the one who is a dependent, or alternatively financial assistance to supplement his income is the *sine qua non* of a humane and just society. People not only should have facilities to live but to grow and develop. The society therefore must provide them opportunities to grow and develop physically, mentally, emotionally, morally and socially. The second level needs are developmental needs. A child born in a society has a right-to grow and develop to his fullest capacities. Education, health, nutrition, recreation and cultural training are his birthrights in the society to which he belongs. Only when the society fulfills its obligation in terms of his developmental needs, it will be able to demand responsibilities from him as its citizen.

The extent to which the society has to discharge these developmental responsibilities depends on the process and duration of development and dependence. In modem societies this period has become longer due to complexity in social, economic and civic life. The fulfillment of these two levels of needs is priori to the consideration of the third level of needs. I have described as 'comfort' needs and some others have described as 'dessert' needs. Unless we had meals, satisfying our hunger and meetings the needs of growth, there can be no claim to a 'dessert'. So long as multitudes of humanity do not get a 'square' meal, dessert cannot be enjoyed. The third level needs no doubt should be fulfilled but not till the time every one's basic and developmental needs have been met.

Social Welfare Policy is not limited only to the issues of distributive justice at the theoretical level. Policy means choices, and issues of social policy imply issues of social choice. Social policy is goal directed and acknowledges that it has to be pursued over a time and in a sequence.

Issues involved are its nature, scope, motives, sponsorship, clientele, personnel, resources, quality and accountability.

The professed and the real policies are to be examined under the various heads. The gap between what we profess and claim and what we really practice or are able to practice always exists. Policy helps us to be watchful that we are not drifting from our path. In the present context in India it is imperative that we examine the policy contents of our practice of social welfare.

Social Welfare is not for the few, or the minority of the under-privileged ones. Welfare of all irrespective of the financial social or physical Status of the persons is the goal of the state. In modern society every one needs opportunities of growth and work; every one is to make his own place in the society. The traditional ascriptive system is being replaced by achievement system. The dividing line between independence and dependence is very thin. The needs are multiple and the cost of meeting these needs from one's private sources is so enormous that without the linkages with the social system one can rarely hope to meet his subsistence and developmental needs. This is an age of inter-dependence. Hence, social welfare is to be univcrsal encompassing all its citizens in its fold. Every one must be eligible to receive and hence every one also must contribute. Eligibility criteria in terms of income or contribution hit at the very root of universal services. Health, education, social security, assistance, personal social services (like guidance, counseling, probation, case work, psychiatric services, old age assistance) all should be available in terms of need.

Traditionally welfare has been helping the unfortunate members of the society unable to cope with the stresses, particularly economic as a human consideration. This helping was on selective basis and charity and relief laws have been based on this criterion. Even charity considered as to who was 'fit' to receive assistance. Either religious mendicants or the destitute, handicapped were given relief. With the development of charity organisation movement and social work eligibility criterion became a principal consideration. This was mostly financial a state of destitution. However, the modem social work does not believe in the priori principle of destitution. Welfare is not a social leveling measure. Instead it is a development benefit available to a person by virtue of his need. Social Welfare aims at the development of the potentialities of all on a differentiated basis depending upon the basic and developmental needs of the individuals. One need not become a destitute to be eligible for assistance. Authors have quoted cases where poor women had to take divorce from their husbands to prove that they were destitutes, or old people had to state that they had no son or daughter who could take care of them or support them. Inability to meet one's needs should be sufficient reason for social assistance. Similarly, old age and lack of resources should be a sufficient claim for old age assistance. Where families or individuals are able to meet basic needs and or development needs, the society should help them for both.

Welfare workers have named the financial and material help rendered by them as benefits enjoyed by the recipients. This clearly indicates something received as profit or aid, to which one has a limited claim and it accrues to him because of someone's charity. It again connotes a 'giver' and 'receiver' relationship and the one indulging in charity is the benefactor and the one receiving it is a beneficiary. Such a relationship between the giver and the receiver is demoralising to the latter and lends an air of superiority to the former.

Social Welfare today rules out such a relationship as

the very object of state is welfare of its people and not merely protection against external attack or internal disorder. Social assistance or social security benefits or personal or correctional benefits are provided as a matter of right to the common people in a welfare state. Similarly, retirement or compensation benefits are essentially rights of the people which they command. In the sphere of education and health, free service facilities, mid-day meals, medical care at public cost, immunisation by public agencies are not benefits given by a 'benefactor' state but is a right of the citizens. In the field of welfare of poor, the aged, the destitute, the delinquent, the scheduled castes, the scheduled tribes, the denotified communities, the children and women, the workers, the victims of calamities, all that help is given for immediate relief or for education, training, or in the form of economic assistance, or counseling and correctional services, are not benefits that some categories of society enjoy. It is what they receive as a matter of right because of the unfavourable circumstance in which they have been thrown and for which it is obligatory for the state to come to their rescue.

Charity organisation societies in their assessment of the help needs were determining the eligibility of the individuals and families which had disabled them from leading independent and self-reliant life and had made them political recipients of public aid.

Taking the clue from medical field as persons who were wanting in their personality make-up and needed to be 'cured' or helped or 'enabled' were labeled as 'cases'. This very process of labeling resulted in a self-image and a relationship set between the relief worker and the individual or family expecting help. This 'case-helper' relationship means that there is some thing wanting in the individual or the family. The Community organisers had a different perspective. They found their cases unable to stand up against the social system and the social workers were just supposed to be advocating on behalf of the weak, the poor, the disabled, the feeble and hence they described their constituency not as cases but as clients whose interests they were trying to serve. This label was a little better than the previous label of a 'Case' as the former means one, who is demanding justice, or his due.

However, the concept of the client also means that he was not able to get his due and needed the assistance of some one who could struggle on his behalf or could stand by him as his agent. This is the typical law-court situation, where one can get justice only through an intermediary not by himself. This is an elitist approach to justice not a people's approach. The individual is the master and the state is subservient to his interests. He is claimant of his rights. He may or may not have an 'advocate'. The state is to ensure the delivery of his 'due' to him. No wonder, in the Indian Constitution the Directive Principles of State Policy directs the provision of free legal aid. In the field of social welfare the help must come even if the claimants are unaware of their needs.

Social welfare has its roots in voluntary action and in India too traditions of voluntary action are age-old. No doubt instances of state intervention for welfare are quite numerous. Even the British followed the policy of neutrality in social welfare but health and education were the areas of state action. The British health services were in response to the needs of the employees of the company but their educational activities were definitely to spread modern science and the British philosophy and literature in this colony. In 1950, though the Constitution had declared welfare of the people as the goal of the state but in the first plan social welfare was largely left to the voluntary sector. Voluntary work is good, but it does not become universal, a civic right of the people and accountable in the sense a public programme can be. It can be innovative but its patterns vary. For a Universal national system of welfare, the state has to own and run it. In some countries where the goals are socialistic but the private sector is large in the industrial sector, the tendency is to be awed by the economic success and material productivity of the private sector. Education and health are being left out in the private sector. Firstly, privatisation results in the differential nature of these institutions. The rich who pay get better quality of services and the poor get substandard facilities. However, many a times the so-called paid services are substantially at state cost and to the detriment of the interests of the common man. The paying wards in the public hospitals and medical colleges and differential payments in schools aided by the government are an example of the point.

Recently there is another example of privatisation of services. Even big hospitals are being built by private companies. Contribution made to them are free from Income Tax, their profits are free from tax, their equipments are free from import duty and then they rceive grants sometimes as block grant and sometimes prorata for keeping some beds free for state government cases. Who are these cases? Are they really the common men and women who pay the substantial part of the tax or they are influential 'Very Important Persons', or the government bureaucrats, their family members and friends who get these quality services indirectly paid by the tax payer? There are some issues which the social workers must ponder upon. India's experience of government aid to the voluntary agencies needs close analysis.

After the beginning of the first plan the Central Social Welfare Board and State and Central governments have been giving grants in aid for various programmes. After over forty years we can see that dependence on state money has increased and most of the agencies have been dependent upon government grants. The quantum of voluntary mobilisation of resources in proportion to the grant is on the decline. Besides, their services are staffed by poorly trained personnel and the staff turn over has been very high. Continuity of services has been lacking. The innovative work done earlier is hardly discernible now. Though the record of government programmes is also not very encouraging but it is for different reasons. Besides, tax money cannot be allowed to be spent at the sole discretion of private individuals and as a measure of political patronage, as they are not accountable to the people.

Voluntary agencies had mostly lay persons in rendering services, either volunteers or paid. The later were less educated and had no training in helping methods. Today when welfare services aim at enabling by assessing needs of individual, group or community and rendering professional help by developing the potentialities of the people through a cooperative effort, or rendering a professional service like medication, or surgery or specialised education, welfare services cannot be left to untrained personnel. Nor can it be left to civil servants who have a different orientation to manage the affairs of the state.

Our institutional and personal services need to be manned by professionally trained social workers just as hospitals need doctors, schools need trained teachers and machines need skilled technicians and engineers. Professional worker does not mean only a paid worker as many people are prone to think. The hall mark of a profession are its value system, its distinct body of knowledge, specialised skills ana a code of conduct or discipline. A profession is a self-regulatory system with a commitment to its constituency. A civil servant is committed to the interests of the bureaucratic system. The value orientations of the two are different.

In India there is no dearth of professionally trained social workers. Besides, all jobs in the welfare field need not be manned by professionally trained persons. Semi-professional or para-professional workers can perform a variety of roles. In fact, a job analysis of placements and positions in the welfare field needs to be made, to identify the knowledge and skills required at different levels. The levels of job performance should be identified and training at various levels should be organised. However, with experience and further training they should have opportunities of upward mobility in professional and organisational hierarchy. This will maintain professional interest and motivate them to improve upon their knowledge and skills. This will also result in greater professional identification and higher worker morale. The organisations too will benefit with continuous improvement of skills and involvement in the work.

Civil servants have a disadvantage as their primary identification is with the organisation and they are interested in the perpetuation of the bureaucratic system. They generally identify the institutional goals of the organisation and consider the objectives of the constituency only secondary. Besides, they are apt to conform to procedures and letters of law and rules and inflexible in their approach. In a welfare department controlled by the civil servants at the top, and following a bureaucratic style and values of work, there is a tendency of even the professional workers ultimately becoming professional bureaucrats as is well evident in the departments of health, education and more so in social welfare, where the proportion of the professional workers is small and many a professional positions are manned, unfortunately, and irrationally by civil servants or lay men. In fact a clear personnel policy in the welfare sector needs to be formulated.

ROLES OF SOCIAL WELFARE AND CHANGING CONCEPTIONS

The historical evolution of social welfare, presented in the previous chapters pointed out the changing emphasis on social welfare at different periods of history. In India, the earliest conception of what has now come to be known as 'social welfare,' was *Dana,* and the philosophy underlying it was known as *Dana Dharma* or *Dhamma. Dana* literally meant sharing, and *Dharma* had a variety of meanings, ranging from duty or obligation to charity or equity. During the medieval period when Muslim kings ruled the country, charity was known as *Khairat.* The goal of social welfare has been described at different times in Indian history as *Lokasangraha, Loka Sreya* and *Sarvodaya.*

In the west, it was known as charity or philanthropy before the industrial revolution and even after, until about the second decade of the nineteenth century. After the middle of the last century, during the Charity Organisation Movement in England, the term 'scientific charity' gradually gained currency. As late as 1897 in the U.S.A., Mary Richmond was saying that the new profession had no name and for want of a better name she called it the profession of applied philanthropy. The term 'social work' was introduced in the U.K. by about the 1920s.' We do not know when the term 'social welfare' came to be used.

Recently there have been several attempts in the west to identify the different conceptions of social welfare and sometimes these are also referred to as models of social welfare.

Somewhat similar to the institutional view of social welfare is the development concept of social welfare which was defined as: 'Welfare activities as a frontline function of modern industrial society, in a positive collaborative role with other major social institutions working toward a better society.' Later, Richard Titmuss formulated the well-known three models of social policy which incorporated the two previously mentioned concepts of social welfare.

'The Industrial Achievement Performance Model incorporates a significant role for social welfare institutions as adjuncts of economy. It holds that social needs should be met on the basis of merit, work performance and productivity....'

'The Residual Welfare Model is based on the premise that there are two 'natural' (or socially given) channels through which an individual's needs are properly met; the private market and the family. Only when these break down should social welfare institutions come into play and then only temporarily....'

'The Institutional Redistributive Model sees social welfare as a major integrated institution in society, providing universalist services outside the market on the principle of need. It is based on theories about the multiple effects of social change and the economic system, and in part on the principle of social equality....'

Romanyshyn believes that in the U.S.A. they are increasingly moving toward an institutional (or developmental) concept of social welfare. He contrasts the institutional concept with the residual concept and then identifies certain characteristics of the former. The developmental concept is a frontline, normal provision of resources meant for all people and given as a matter of right of citizenship. It views social problems as structural in origin, and not as a matter of individual, moral or personal defects, and social welfare as a public responsibility. The goal is the welfare of society through maximising development of all individuals. We may discern many common elements between this conception of social welfare, Rammohun Roy's conception of *Loka Sreya* and Gandhi's conception of *Sarvodaya*.

As the concept of social development became popular due to the efforts of the U.N.O. and organisations associated with or affiliated to it and also as a result of an attempt to link social welfare to the emerging trend in planned national developmental programmes, a new term 'developmental social welfare' was coined to refer to this broadened conception of social welfare. At first, a long phrase such as 'social welfare geared to social development' or 'social welfare in a developmental context' was used to describe this vague new idea. Gradually, the shorter, more convenient term 'developmental social welfare' became popular, especially in international gatherings on social welfare. However, it was very soon discovered that while the christening ceremony was over, no one had seen the baby. What did this new baby look like? Thus it was that Kulkarni was invited to describe the characteristics of developmental social welfare in Nairobi in 1974. Kulkarni attempted to describe what developmental social welfare is. According to him, social welfare becomes developmental when it attempts institutional change as different from maintaining or strengthening the existing structure.

The developmental social welfare is a macro-level conception which aims at meeting, in progressive phases, a total national need or deals with the entire social problem in its national magnitude, with a view to eventually liquidating it. This macro-level conception implies a broader orientation than the traditional residual welfare model which is usually concerned with the handicapped and the vulnerable sections of the population. Functional efficiency is another characteristic of developmental social welfare. This implies that it is not enough that the motive for social welfare is based on good intentions.

The resources provided for social welfare have to be very efficiently utilised, borrowing some of the methods and techniques of modern management both for the economy of resources as well as for a better impact on the recipients. Lastly, Kulkarni mentions that a significant new function of social welfare in a developmental context is preparing for change. In these days, most countries are attempting a planned change of their societies and this leads to unplanned social consequences. According to him, there is no instrumentality other than social welfare to foresee the unplanned consequences of planned change and forestall them by providing adequate services. What Kulkarni has done is to paint a picture of developmental social welfare in a broad outline, by singling out some of its major characteristics as he sees them. The task of designing a pattern from these characteristics on the basis of some key concept(s) is left to the reader. The description of developmental social welfare as provided by Kulkarni is by and large acceptable, except on some points. One of these points of difference is the reference to functional efficiency as an essential characteristic of developmental social welfare. It is difficult to accept the implication that inefficiency in the implementation of programmes and services is an inherent characteristic of the traditional residual social welfare. It is not inconceivable to consider an efficient planning and implementation of a traditional social welfare programme for groups like the physically or mentally handicapped. Nor are examples wanting of organisations functioning very efficiently.

Similarly, functional efficiency may not be an inseparable part of developmental social welfare which may be implemented efficiently or inefficiently. In other words, functional efficiency is independent of the residual or developmental model of social welfare. It may be, though this needs to be proved, that by and large the traditional model of social welfare in the past exhibited functional inefficiency. However, it is not certain that developmental social welfare always has a characteristic of functional efficiency. On the contrary, there is reason to believe that there may be considerable inefficiency as a result of the huge growth of the bureaucracy, when comprehensive welfare programmes covering the entire population are implemented by the state machinery. Kulkarni has not defined clearly what he means by functional efficiency. If reference to modern management methods and cost-benefit techniques are any indications, then he seems to be referring to the economic concept of efficiency in the planning and use of resources. This concept is under attack in the field of welfare economics on very valid grounds. First of all, it is based on the Pareto principle that it is possible to plan for the welfare of a whole society, without getting bogged down into the problems of individual conceptions of welfare. Following the Pareto principle, there is the further argument by the Paretians that such an approach can be made objective and value-free. That the Pareto principle is not as neutral as it is made out to be and that it has an implicit ideology has been brought out very effectively by Rowley and Peacock. It is rather strange that critics of economic planning, who in the past have pointed out the narrow economic concern of planning and its preoccupation with growth-based concepts of national aggregate indicators, and who have argued for a broader concept of social planning, should now plead for the economic concept of efficiency.

In another context, a similar disagreement has been expressed by Sen and Naqvi who have stated that allocation of resources for education should not be argued on the basis of investment in human capital. Our criticism may be countered with an argument that what is implied is not the narrow economic concept of efficiency, but an expansion of it into a broader concept of social efficiency. Assuming that such is the implied argument, though it has not been so stated, it may be mentioned that such a concept has not been developed so far. Kingsley Davis has remarked that there is no adequate and precise concept of social efficiency even at a theoretical level, not to speak of the development of operational tools and techniques of social efficiency. In the light of these observations, we cannot accept that functional efficiency is a necessary or inherent characteristic of developmental social welfare. Another characteristic of developmental social welfare, according to Kulkarni is to foresee and forestall the need to deal with unplanned consequences of social change. This is rather a narrow view of preparing for social change. The concept itself permits a fuller and a richer development. If many countries are committed to institutional changes through national plans for development, it becomes essential that the population of these countries who are mostly traditional and conservative in their outlook have to be prepared for accepting planned social changes.

An excellent example is the programme for family planning. In most traditional societies, due to a variety of historical and social factors, the size of the families tend to be larger, and generally people are not either aware of the possibility of planning the size of the family, or convinced of the desirability of it. In such a situation, it becomes the task of social welfare which claims to be developmental, to prepare people to accept the value of a small family norm and then persuade them to implement it. In our view, such a programme is an essential part of preparing the people of a society for social change, if the intended change is to be relatively smooth and free from tensions and conflicts. We may restate this characteristic of developmental welfare as the preparation of people to adopt social change, adapt to it and absorb the consequences of change, whether intended or unintended. One of the prominent characteristics of developmental social welfare is that it is concerned with the prevention of social problems.

As Kulkarni has rightly noted, developmental welfare is essentially preventive in nature. The concept of prevention is open to a variety of interpretations, ranging from the very narrow micro-level prevention in a curative context, to a very broad conception of prevention which implies the general improvement in the living conditions of the people as a whole. Frequently, in discussing the concept of prevention, there is an implicit, if not an explicit borrowing of this idea from the field of medicine. In medicine prevention is classified into three categories: primary, secondary and tertiary preventions. This classification evolved at a time when concern was centred on the control and cure of disease in a clinical model. The tertiary prevention refers to the prevention of further deterioration and consequent severe damage in the physical condition of a patient who may be suffering from a disease. The secondary prevention refers to protecting other people who may be in close contact with the patient from the possible infection of disease.

For example, if a family has an infective case of pulmonary tuberculosis, then the entire family is exposed to the risk of infection. When this has been detected, the secondary preventive measures would include the radiological and laboratory investigations of other family members for finding out if any of them has the infection already. In case any member of the family is found; to be infected, the early detection will help to control the disease from spreading. The primary prevention refers to specific immunological measures taken to prevent a population from the danger of infections from a disease organism. A familiar example is the inoculations routinely carried out these days against small pox, diphtheria and polio among the children. From time to time, there have been attempts to borrow and adapt this medical conception of prevention to social welfare.

One of the earliest attempts was by Rapoport. A recent attempt is by Kendall. (It appears that social work, especially professional social work is unable to free itself from borrowing concepts from medicine and compares itself continually with the medical model.) This medical classification of prevention is inapplicable to social welfare, because of the inadequate scientific progress in the areas of development of knowledge, discovery of specific instruments of prevention and development of a clear-cut typology of social problems, despite the aspirations and explorations by social workers. For example, if we wish to speak of primary prevention in social welfare, we do not have a product comparable to a vaccine which could safeguard people against poverty or illiteracy. So it serves no purpose to borrow ideas indiscriminately from the field of medicine.

As the Seebohm Committee Report has rightly pointed out that it is more appropriate to speak of general prevention and specific prevention. The term general prevention refers to all those measures which may improve the living conditions of the people such as provision of employment, removal or minimisation of inequality of incomes, better conditions of work at factories, mines and plantations, adequate housing facilities, strengthening of the vital nutritional elements in the food intake of the people, especially the vulnerable sections, etc. The specific prevention refers to those measures which are aimed at controlling or preventing a particular social problem about which we have reasonably dependable knowledge of causation and prevention. For example, efforts to reduce the incidence of the physically handicapped by improvement of roads, effective traffic regulations, proper use of safety measures in the factories, improved nutrition and comprehensive immunisation of vulnerable population against crippling diseases.

It may be noted that the concept of general and specific prevention as outlined here is essentially a macro-level conception. It does not refer to general and specific preventions with reference to a single person and a family or a small group of population which have been the focus of attention in the traditional conceptions of social welfare. It is in this quantitative as well as qualitative sense that prevention appears as an essential characteristic of developmental social welfare. At the same time, it is not incompatible with the micro-level approach to prevention. In fact, they are complementary to each other. In the light of the above descriptions of developmental social welfare, we may proceed to discuss the roles and tasks to be performed by social workers. A review of the recent literature on social welfare and social work reveals that a variety of roles and tasks have been identified, by different authors. David Drucker, on the basis of his analysis of the voluminous literature on social welfare and social development, identified five roles for social welfare: *social policies and planning in development; ensuring social justice* with particular reference to more equitable distribution of the national wealth; the essential need for *participation by the people* in policy formulation, planning and implementation; improving the social and cultural infrastructure by *institution building;* and social work helping methods. Drucker makes reference to the role of the social worker as an institution builder. While he has not elaborated this idea, it is full of potentialities for further development.

In the developing countries, the main problem for the government in providing welfare measures is the relatively backward state of economy and the extreme scarcity of resources. Despite the professed goal of the welfare state by the politicians in power in these countries, it will be a long time before they could approximately reach the situation which obtains at present in welfare states like the U.K. and Scandinavian countries. When resources are not available to be distributed among the people, it is not very relevant to speak of the role of the mediator between resource systems and the people in need. To say this is not to completely exclude this role. Whatever resources that are provided in education, health and welfare could be made available to the people in need by a variety of actions by the social workers. However, it is our contention that more often in the developing countries the major problem is the lack of resources which are needed by the people. This requires that the social workers in the developing countries work towards the goal of creating organisations and institutions which will provide the services which are urgently needed by the community.

In order to do this, it will be necessary to mobilise the material and non-material resources from within the community and outside. What is more, some of these communities which are likely to be mostly the disadvantaged and the weaker segments of the society, may even need the active assistance of the social worker in helping them to establish a proper infrastructure for developing and delivering the services. A good example is the work of Ela Bhatt of Ahmedabad who was recently awarded the Magsaysay Award. The practice of methods that facilitate social work, which is identified as a separate role by Drucker, do not seem to fit in with the new conception of social welfare.

Gore has stated the following as the developmental tasks of social welfare: to promote broader social values which are necessary for development such as equality, social justice, secularism, universalistic norms, rationality and also commitment to national unity; to represent, argue, and press for the interests of the disadvantaged; to identify the dysfunctional consequences of change and to institute services which will smoothen the change; to develop new services to maximise the utilisation of available social services.

In other words, anticipating changing needs during social developmental process, creating service structures to meet these needs, and for this purpose participating in the formulation of social policy and social planning are the developmental functions of social workers.

Pinkus and Minahan have formulated seven tasks for social work which they define as planned change effort. Their many references to planned change and social policy and planning in their model of social work practice, indicate that their conception of social work is definitely not the traditional residual model of social work. It is perhaps very similar to the broader concept of social welfare as described by Kulkarni and Drucker. The seven tasks stated by Pinkus and Minahan can broadly be grouped into four functions: to enable the people to cope with their problems by making use of their own capacities and resources; to act as mediator between people with needs and the resources provided by the society. This includes also the task of facilitating people's access to the resource system and influencing them to be more responsive to the needs of the people; the provision of concrete material goods and services which is termed by the authors as the task of dispenser of material goods and services; contributing to the formulation and modification of social policies. We may ignore for our purpose, the performance of the traditional role of the agent of social control which is also mentioned by them.

It is interesting to note that despite their emphasis on planned change efforts, in their statement of tasks there is none that directly and obviously deals with the role of an agent of social change. When we consider that they have mentioned as one of the tasks, the functioning as an agent of social control, this omission of a change agent function or task is glaring and significant. It may be argued that this is implicit in the description of other tasks. The task that can be considered for such an implicit idea is that of contributing to the development and modification of social policy. It is also implicit to a minor extent in the task of facilitating interactions and modifying and building new relationships between people and social resource systems.

In a very recent *Report of the Working Party on Social Work Task* by the British Association of Social Workers, there is an attempt to distinguish between social service and social work functions. It is recognised, however, that 'the boundaries between social work and social service are necessarily blurred'. The Report includes a list of twenty social work roles, of which five roles can certainly be considered as appropriate roles in developmental social welfare as described by Kulkarni and Drucker. These roles are: Mobiliser of Resources, Agent of Social Change, Public Educator, Researcher, and Advocate. There is a specific mention of the change agent role which was missing in the Pinkus and Minahan list. In addition to these, another five roles like Mediator, Manager, Director and Consultant may be considered as social worker roles in both the traditional and developmental conceptions of social welfare.

Some social work educators in India strongly object to the social worker role of provision of material goods and concrete services, which they associate with the lady-bountiful do-gooder role of the charity era and thus find it inconsistent with the non-sentimental, objective, professional social worker role of enabler. This issue has been brought into sharp focus, as a result of experimenting with 'open' community placements for fieldwork in slum communities and especially in the relocated settlements of the urban slum population, where the emphasis has been on the developmental preventive conception of social welfare. When there is no adequate organised public or voluntary provision of basic minimum survival needs of the population, what enabling role can a social worker perform? Is it not like singing songs of Kabir (in this case the professional chorus of enabling) to the hungry millions as mentioned by Gandhi?

It may be relevant to emphasise the enabler and mediator roles in the U.K., U.S.A., Canada and many economically developed European countries, that do not face the problems of acute mass poverty, and where the state spends 12 to 16 per cent of its GNP on social security, including provision of income maintenance programmes, so that no one is deprived of the basic necessities of life. It is significant that even in these countries, dispensing of material goods is stated as one of the function's of social work.

This critical survey of the literature on the conceptions and roles of social welfare, especially with reference to the developmental social welfare, may be concluded with a brief statement of the nature of developmental social welfare and its roles. The goal of developmental social welfare is *primarily* to meet the basic needs of the large majority of the people who live and work in dehumanising conditions, and progressively to work towards the improvement in the quality of their lives. This implies that social welfare is an integral and essential part of national plan for social development. The concept of social development will vary to some extent according to the present social situation of the country, its national consensus on the goal, values, nature and elements of a new society that is aimed at, and the plans and strategy for development. Whatever may be the concrete expression of the constituent elements of such a society and the means to achieve it, it will necessitate significant changes at the organisational, institutional and social structural levels.

Social welfare is an active participant in the developmental process and may be referred to as developmental social welfare. It is a macro-level conception with a major emphasis on prevention of social problems, without however neglecting the urgent necessity of caring for those sections of the population, which are at present handicapped, destitute or in other forms of social distress. While it aims to be universal in its approach to prevention or alleviation of human distress, based on the citizen's right to organised social provisions, it may begin by concentrating on those sections of the population whose needs must receive priority over others. This conception of developmental social welfare broadly corresponds to Titmuss's institutional-redistributive model. But there are certain differences between these two conceptions which should not be overlooked.

The term role may be defined as analytically identifiable units of behaviour or activities which are expected of or associated with the implementation of welfare. It is impractical to work out a long and detailed statement of such roles, because increasingly we face the problem of artificially separating certain behaviour or activities, which seem to be very much a part of several roles. On the other hand, too broad and inclusive a statement of roles may be very vague and lack discreteness. The task of describing these roles, is thus a formidable one. But a modest attempt, which draws upon the work of others is made in that direction.

Social Critic

This is a role familiar through social welfare history by the work of social reformers who have felt strongly about certain aspects of society—whether social customs, or social conditions which needed change. The criticism is aimed not at an individual condition but at a structural defect. It is ideological and frequently involves polemical exchanges. It may be buttressed by reasoned, logical, and scholarly arguments put forth in the form of articles in popular journals, publication of books, and lectures at public meetings or on the radio and T.V. Some of these activities may be done with emotionally charged, subjective, and somewhat exaggerated accounts of individual or group suffering through the same media as described above. Rammohun Roy, Iswar Chandra, Vivekananda, Dayananda, Agarkar, Ranade, Chandawarkar and Gandhi typify a long tradition of the first category and B.M. Malbari and Jotirao Phule exemplify the second.

This also includes the work by modern social policy analysts and researchers who contribute to scholarly journals, or address academic gatherings or bring out serious academic publications like research monographs, books, etc. There may be also publication of pamphlets and use of mass media to build up public opinion on an issue. Sometimes they link up with the political processes in the society, whether directly as contributors to the formulation of policies, programmes and election manifestos of a political party or tangentially by irregular, but formal associations as experts or sympathetic intellectuals. Richard Titmuss in the U.K., and K.N. Raj, Dandekar and Rath in India belong to this distinguished academic category of influential social critics. This description of the role of a social critic incorporates the BASW classification of roles of consultant, public educator and researcher.

Institution Builder

At a different level from the role of an organiser, though including many elements of it, is the role of the institution builder which was discussed earlier. The organisational element is also here, but it is not always linked to a social movement. It is a creative, resource-mobilising and infrastructure-building activity which results in the birth of a new institution or an organisation to meet a hitherto-neglected group of needy population, usually at a local level (at least to begin with). Illustrious examples of this would be Fatma Ismail and Jai Vakil in Bombay, and Mira Mahadevan in Delhi, who pioneered services by creating new institutions to serve the physically handicapped, mentally retarded children and organising mobile creches for children of women construction workers, respectively. The work of earlier social reformers like Sasipada Banerjee and D.K. Karve who established homes for the widows also belong to this category.

Organiser

The work of social critics sometimes leads to the creation

of an organisation which is essential for propagating the new ideology by recruiting more converts to it, and for mobilising popular or official support in favour of advocated changes and carrying out a series of actions to achieve the goal. Rammohun Roy organised the Brahmo Sabha, Vivekananda established the Ramakrishna Mission, M.G. Ranade founded the Indian Social Conference and Gandhi started a number of organisations like Harijan Sangh, Hindustani Talimi Sangh, etc. In recent years, Vinoba Bhave brought into existence the Sarva Seva Sangh through the federation of seven existing organisations. In all these efforts, the central common element is a new social-political or religious movement which is being launched (or has been launched already). It needs to be sustained, strengthened and extended through organised efforts of committed cadre of workers.

Mediator

This is a familiar role discussed in the context of the traditional model of social welfare. It is based on what Richard Crossman has called as the availability theory. It presupposes the availability of an adequate organised provision of a variety of goods and services, whether through state machinery or through volunteer organisations. This role of a mediator assumed prominence with the advent of the welfare state which undertook to provide for the population minimum necessary services against certain risks, that were beyond the ability of the people concerned and for which they could not be blamed. The limitations to the practice of this role in the context of the economic conditions of the developing countries has already been commented upon. This role is relevant to the extent certain social services have been made available by the society and some of these may be meant exclusively for the benefit of a designated group in need such as social assistance for the aged and the handicapped; and the client group may be either ignorant of the provision or unable to secure it without assistance, because of the procedures involved. An intervention by the social worker may sometimes influence the 'available resource' system to be sympathetic and responsive to the request by the client or client group. It may be practised with the outside organisations whose services are needed by the client or inside a multi-professional service organisation like hospitals, courts, and the schools.

Enabler

This is one of the oldest and most familiar roles which evolved during the period of social workers' intense quest for a professional status in the U.S.A. It was emphasised, especially as part of the practice of case work and counselling in relation to the persons' emotional problem(s) in the area of interpersonal relationship such as material problem, parent-child problem, employer-employee problem, etc. It was also based on the unstated assumption that basic survival needs of the client have been met in some way or at least they are not the primary problems for which the client needs assistance. In developing countries like India, sometimes there is an inappropriate overemphasis on this role, due to the failure to recognise the situational differences between them and the developed welfare societies like the U.K. and U.S.A. It may also be a clever way of hiding the social workers' helplessness to help (or rationalisation, to use the Freudian term).

Provider of Concrete Goods and Services

This is perhaps, the oldest of all the roles of social workers dating back to the charity era. It includes the direct face-to-face actions between the clients and the social workers whereby their material need is inquired into, assessed and then a decision taken on the request. This may be followed by the actual provision of benefits in cash or kind like food, shelter and clothing. It is estimated that in the U.S.A. 50 per cent of the federal outlays in 1973 benefiting the poor was in-kind benefits. The situation is similar in the case of social workers' clients in the U.K. According to one estimate almost half of the tasks performed by the social workers in the U.K. are of such in-kind benefits. How much more prominent and relevant would this role be for social workers in countries like India where mass poverty prevails?

It has been stated earlier that the conception of developmental social welfare is inclusive of traditional social welfare. Accordingly, we may view traditional social welfare and developmental social welfare as a continuum, each occupying one end of the line of continuum. The latter conception may cover however, a greater portion of the line. Out of the eight social welfare roles discussed here, the first four roles may be distributed at the developmental social welfare end of the continuum and the last two (Provider of Concrete Resources and Enabler) roles, at the traditional social welfare end. The remaining two roles (Institution Builder and Mediator), may straddle the blurred centre where one conception merges with the other.

WELFARE PROJECTS IN URBAN AREAS

Slums and congested localities are the product of urbanisation and industrialisation. The Advisory Committee appointed under the chairmanship of Sri Ashok K. Sen in 1958 estimated the number of slum houses totally unfit for human habitation at about 11.5 lakhs. On this conservative estimate, the total population living in sub-human standards would be about 60 lakhs. Poverty, ignorance, disease, over-crowding, malnutrition, neglect of children, prostitution, juvenile delinquency, crime, gambling, gangsterism are some of the problems of slums and congested localities. Increasing, lethargy, manual inefficiency and anti-social outlook, are the consequences of slums which sociologists have summed up as 'slum mentality'. Another feature of the slums is that they take a few months to find roots but decades to be cleared. Slum is a common feature in all the industrially advanced countries, what is necessary is to improve the conditions of slum dwellers by slum clearance or improvement. Again in the words of Sen Committee, "the problem is not just one merely of clearing the site and putting up structures afresh to a well-thought out plan and design. The problem in the last analysis is really one of a development which will do away with the disease and ignorance, unemployment and poverty". There are three aspects of working with the slum communities:- *(i)* Slum clearance, *(ii)* Slum improvement and *(iii)* Slum prevention.

Whereas the slum clearance and slum preventing fall within the purview of housing departments and municipalities, certain aspects of slum improvement fall within the purview of social welfare programmes: Slum improvement may again consist of two aspects: (1) providing basic civic amenities, and (2) basic welfare services for all sections of the community taking family as a unit. Welfare aspects have to go hand in hand with slum clearance, lest the newly built colonies deteriorate into slums again.

In the two plans, we have been concentrating on the rural development schemes and very little attention was paid to the urban development. The Central Social Welfare Board has undertaken a scheme of Urban Projects for providing welfare services in slums and congested localities of big towns. Some of the municipalities and corporations are also undertaking this work. In fact, the work of slum improvement has to be done in co-operation with the voluntary social welfare and development agencies, municipalities and other departments like Health, Education, Housing etc. As has been said above, while providing welfare services in a slum community, we have to take into consideration the mental and social level, the need and resources of the community. A voluntary agency could undertake the work of slum improvement in co-operation with the municipality of the town. The municipality could be persuaded to improve the sanitation and water supply of that area by providing drainage, latrines, conservation services etc., and the housewives in the area could be persuaded to ensure personal cleanliness and cleanliness of the surroundings. Similarly, the municipality could provide street-lightening, public baths, some materials for paving streets in the locality, a school and the social worker could help the community to make use of the school, keep the streets clean, maintain the baths properly. If a child has to perforce earn in order to supplement the income of the family some facilities for free schools should be provided in the evening or at night without undue fatigue. This will *prima facie* look child labour but we cannot shut our eyes to reality. Thousands of children in slums and poor localities are supplementing their family income. For some time, we have to accept this and help children in pursuing: studies while they cam for the family. The mothers will have more time for work, if the babies could be footed after in creches or in *Balwadies*. Cleaning and bathing of the children, milk feeding, recreational and educational programmes could be organised in the evening when the women are free from household duties. Adult education, cultural gatherings and craft training could be organised. The organisation could also help the mothers in undertaking an economic project, to supplement their family income. In the field of housing, the organisation could help the members of community to take advantage of the scheme of low-cost housing etc., or in building damp-proof walls, latrines, soak-pits and providing ventilators. The families could be helped to make use of existing medical facilities or if they do not exist, services like maternity and child welfare and general medical aid could be provided with a referral service to other institutions. In regard to the coverage of welfare activities, the welfare centres could provide services to 500 families, consisting of 5,000 individuals—men, women and children.

Activities and Services

For Women Welfare

Women's clubs, arts and crafts classes, referral and placement services for the destitutes, lone and unattached women, family planning and other welfare services.

For Youth Welfare

Scouting, hobby clubs, camping and excursions, use of scout camps and youth hostels, vocational guidance, employment information bureau, youth counselling.

For Child Welfare

Ante-natal and post-natal advisory services, infant health centres, creches, pre-primary schools, school health service, children's play centres, recreational and cultural activities for children, school social work service— making use of school facilities in the area, milk distribution.

Common Activities

Cultural and recreational programmes, social education programmes, placement and referral services for the aged and the infirm, the destitute and the delinquents etc., helping in building homes, paving of streets, making soak-pits, etc.

Work Stages

Survey

The first step in organising community services is to carry out a simple and quick survey. The survey schedule for the community should include information on the following points:

1. Area and the locality, 2. Number of families, 3. Total number of men, women, and children, 4. Economic stratification of families of the area, 5. Nature and extent of the existing services, like schools, dispensaries, recreational centres, craft centres, etc., 6. Availability of accommodation, volunteers and good leaders in the community, and 7. Felt-needs of the community.

Meeting Leaders

After the necessary information regarding the locality has been collected, it may be necessary to have a meeting of the local leaders in order to discuss the various needs and resources of the community so that a worthwhile programme for organising welfare activities is chalked out. Even if all the members of the community are not literate, still there may be some leaders who are respected by that community. They should always be associated with the development work. Care should be taken to see that as far as possible help of the minimum number of people should be taken from outside. The co-operation of the local municipal councillor, representing that area, local volunteers, local teachers and any other important persons could be enlisted.

Budget

The receipt side of the budget should show grants from various sources, subscriptions, fees, donations in cash and kind and voluntary services from various local agencies. Services of the volunteers should also be enlisted for providing various services like medical aid, training in arts and crafts, building houses, social education etc.

Policy and Evaluation. The policy for running all programmes should be laid by a committee consisting of local people and social workers. Any programme for community development will not yield desired results if the programms is not periodically evaluated both by the workers and an outside agency, in order to judge community's participation, the methods used in meeting its needs and the results achieved.

Fund-Raising. Next step will be fund-raising. The resources of the community in terms of cash, kind and voluntary services likely to be available for this purpose should be assessed for the purpose of promoting welfare services. Various methods of fund-raising including community chest have been described in subsequent pages.

Organiser. There is a need, to have a full-time community organiser who could be accepted as the leader of the community. He will be the chief person responsible for the organisation of the centre and he is to be a multipurpose worker. He should be able to maintain accounts, carry on necessary correspondence, initiate the programme, ensure community participation, maintain liaison with other agencies and supervise the work of other paid staff. He should be a person trained in community organisation work, and mature enough to be able to win the confidence and participation of the community.

Principles. The main purpose of a welfare centre is not only to provide services either to a group or all members of the community but to make the welfare centre as nucleus of work for mobilising cooperation of all agencies and members of the community. The community and the various agencies—governmental and non-governmental—could help the community organiser directly or indirectly.

In a community there may exist number of agencies running services for women, children, physically handicapped, providing medical aid, maternity and allied services etc. A community centre should, therefore, make use of these services in its work. There is also a need for neighbourhood and coordinating councils to plan new social welfare services and coordinate the work of existing agencies—voluntary and governmental. This aspect of community organisation has been dealt with in another book 'Introduction to Social Work' by the author.

The philosophy behind community organisation work is that any service or an agency in community should be organised by the local people and should not be an end in itself but should be a means of organising the community to be aware of its problems and needs. They should be able to develop an attitude of self-help and readiness to meet its needs with its resources. Any outside help unless it is intended to serve as a stimulus to use local resources to meet needs will create dependence of the community on outside help which is not healthy. Urban community development scheme of Delhi Corporation was based on this philosophy. It aimed at developing and using local leadership for solving community's problems. The scheme does not envisage any direct services. Workers connected with urban community development have watched with interest the results of the scheme of Delhi Corporation.

NIGHT SHELTER AND DORMITORY

With the growth of large cities, there is a greater influx of rural population to the cities in search of employ meat in the industrial establishments. The low salaries and, inadequate housing provided by the industry compel a wage earner to find out cheap accommodation. Sometimes low-paid workers sleep on the footpaths. These unfortunate people are not only subject to the rigours and vagaries of weather but are also exposed to social and moral dangers. Therefore, a scheme of providing shelter to the homeless has to be worked out in order to protect them from exploitation and prevent the spread of anti-social activities. Night shelters are very necessary in big urban areas and industrial cities with slums etc. We have also to consider the case of pavement dwellers. There are four categories of people which are usually found on pavements:—

- Couples with children leading normal life.
- Children and orphans between 3 and 10 years of age in whom no one is interested.
- The aged and the infirm, the diseased.
- Unmarried adults.

A visit to the pavement dwellers in the morning has an unpleasant effect on the mind. Some people are still sleeping long after the sun has risen. Some are busy burning fire for the morning meals. The children are helping the mothers in the meals and some people are whiling away their time in gossip. While arranging for shelters, we have to bear in mind this typc of the pavement-dwellers and their needs.

Location

The welfare services in a community are incomplete without providing shelter to the shelterless. Therefore, a shelter should be located in a congested and busy area of the town which is approachable by all kinds of poor people who need shelter. The shelter could provide accommodation to 50 to 100 persons depending upon the accommodation available in the locality. The kind of people who will use this accommodation are Riksha pullers, shoe shine boys, petty hawkers, cart pullers and persons doing other small jobs in the town. These shelters are not meant for beggars. Separate night shelters should be provided for (a) boys upto 16 years (b) adults and (c) women.

Resources

It may not be possible to depend upon the limited resources of the organisation for running a shelter. Therefore, an organisation intending to ran a shelter has to tap, all public and private resources in the community. It may be possible to get accommodation from the municipality or a philanthropist on nominal rent. Grants are now available from the Central Social Welfare Board and other governmental agencies for this purpose. Part of the resources could be raised by donations and by charging fees varying from 25 to 50 P. per person per night from the inmates depending upon the local conditions *e.g.*, rent paid for the building and average earning of the inmates.

Other Requisites

In addition to a building, a Night Shelter requires the following:—

- Necessary equipment, beddings, carpets, floor mats, blankets, pillows etc.
- A radio or a television set and other indoor play material.
- Arrangement for vocational training for the unemployed inmates.
- A Care-taker with an Attendant.

A Care-taker should be a trained person capable of giving general guidance and counselling to the inmates. His duties are more or less like a hostel warden. Whare facilities are limited, it could work as night shelter only and not a dormitory. Efforts should be made to provide facilities for sleeping, bathing and cultural activities and first-aid, developing the shelter into a kind of residential dormitory, where the inmates could keep their belongings, have after-noon rest, and be looked after during illness. Later, efforts could also be made to organise a cooperative of the inmates and the warden could also help in employment and placement facilities.

Centres for Social Welfare

Social welfare has come to embody a distinct concept which refers to welfare of those sections of community which are in need of special care, *e.g.* women, children, physically handicapped, etc. Social welfare services have become all the more necessary because the community has to take over some of the functions of the family because of modem living, working conditions, disintegration of caste system and joint family system, as the modem family is unable to fulfil the needs of women and children.

Thus, social welfare is not a negative concept, but it aims at maintenance of sound family conditions and their promotion to more positive state of welfare. The rural community has so far not been provided with the basic and elementary services for health and education *e.g.*, a balwadi, a social education centre, medical aid etc.

Principles. In organising welfare services for women and children, we have to bear in mind the same principles as mentioned in urban community development and rural development schemes. We should not impose any service on a community which does not want it. There may be resistance to send the children to schools or to make use of the services of a trained midwife instead of an indigenous *Dai.* In such matters, the Extension Agency should work slowly in order to get these new services accepted by the community. This resistance to the new services, which, though useful to the community, may be due to lack of confidence of the rural community in the agency. But, if these services have relation to the felt-needs of the community, they are sure to succeed. There are instances to show that sometimes, in spite of good deal of time, money and energy spent on welfare programmes, the community did not participate, co-operate, or even respond favourably to them.

The ultimate aim is, therefore, to help the community to help itself. The test of the success of such a programme will be the extent to which these programmes can be run, even after the agency withdraws from the area. For this purpose a quick survey of needs and sources of the area will be very useful basis to begin the work.

It is important to create an urgency of the need and a psychology of success by choosing objectives which are not difficult to fulfil. It is also advisable to take up programmes, which can show within a reasonable time, tangible and demonstrable results, the value of which can be readily appreciated by the community. It is also advisable to take up programmes for which local co-operation is readily available. As has been said in the previous pages, there should be one agency for different development programmes for a particular area.

Therefore, any agency, working in a rural community should organise multi-purpose activities and assistance from other agencies should also be secured in order to enrich the programmes and to aim at necessary coordination. The activities should run on defined lines with certain amount of regularity in the work. The frequency of the different activities should vary from activity to activity, depending upon the need and the resources. The following are some of the programmes which could be included in the programmes of a welfare centre in the community:—

Special Programmes

Registration and reference of individuals needing special care.

Staff: The staff of a multipurpose welfare centre will consist of the following:

- Gramsevika (Women Village Worker) trained in various aspects of welfare, e.g., balwadi, craft classes for women, social education work, general medical aid, etc.
- Craft Instructor, trained in at least two local crafts, which are useful in the area.
- A midwife or a trained *Dai* for taking up anti-natal and post-natal work.
- The cooperation of the local women leaders including teachers could be secured for organising weekly and periodical activities as mentioned above.

Building. It may not be necessary to have an elaborate building for running a welfare centre. The buildings constructed under local development works or by the Central Social Welfare Board could be obtained. Otherwise a small hut could be obtained rent-free from the community. The construction of the building should not be different from the type of the cottages in the community. A welfare centre be located inside a village. It should be in the most central place in the village, which is accessible to women, and children.

Equipment. A centre needs balwadi equipment which pre-ferably should be prepared locally by the *Gramsevika,*

Balsevika, if she had proper training and understanding of the concept of a balwadi. Equipment for maternity services could be obtained from International Organisations like the W.H.O., U.N.I.C.E.F. and C.A.R.E., through the Government.

The Kasturba Gandhi National Memorial Trust has been running multi-purpose welfare activities, centres, throughout the country, with the help of local leaders. These centres have also been collecting money for running of services. The Central Social Welfare Board started about 500 projects with five centres each to provide the services mentioned above, but they have now transferred this work to Manila Mandals, and other suitable organisations, since the Board is now working only in the community development areas. Therefore, voluntary agencies can take up this work at least in the areas not covered by the community development work. In doing so, they could, if possible, obtain the assets already created by those centres, which have also prepared the community for acceptance of such a programme. It will not be difficult for any organisation to work in this area. Even the areas covered by Community Development will need extension services for women and children and voluntary agencies could always start welfare centres in co-operation with the Community Development Authorities. Financial assistance is also available from the Central Social Welfare Board for running centres in the rural areas, not covered by Community Development and Welfare Extension Projects.

The Rural Development Department has worked out a scheme of promotion of voluntary action in rural areas. This includes promotion and strengthening of rural Mahila Mandals (women's clubs) which are capable of undertaking activities for women and children with assistance from concerned departments.

Welfare of the SCs & STs

Since social welfare aims at providing services for the weaker sections, we shall now discuss problems of the scheduled castes and the methods of organising this community to help itself. The scheduled castes are also known as untouchables, *Harijans,* depressed classes etc. The castes in India were mainly based on one's occupation. A person born in a particular occupation or community was supposed to pursue the occupation of his family and no other. This was done purely with a view to having an occupational division in the society. Casteism was not only prevalent among Hindus but among the Muslims and the Christians. This is an indication of the fact that the basis of the caste was occupation. This is borne out by the trade names prevalent in India. If one's work was of a clean and pure nature, he was considered as 'high', while if it was dirty and unclean, it was looked upon as 'low'. The origin of untouchability as an institutionalised practice, however, cannot be traced with any certainty. Another version of the origin of the caste was the need for purity of blood. Some say that the basis of caste was *Varnas.* Whatever may be the origin of untouchability, it is, quite clear that members of scheduled caste community have suffered from economic and social disabilities.

Many individual reformers like Raja Ram Mohan Roy, Pandit Madan Mohan Malviya, Thakkar Bapa, Keshab Chander Sen, Shri K.R. Rao, Mahatma Gandhi, Dr. Ambedkar etc. and social organisations like the Brahmo Samaj, Christian Missionaries, Arya Samaj, Harijan Sevak Sangh, Ramakrishna Mission, etc. have done quite useful work for the welfare of this community but because of difficulties under the foreign rule and a large population of the Scheduled Castes consisting of over seven crores, their work could not achieve any material and substantial results.

However, an atmosphere under which any organisation could organise worthwhile programmes was created.

Gandhiji's Role. The word *'Harijan'* was coined by Gandhiji, which means 'God's people'. He fought this evil not only from the social reform point of view but also on political basis. He said, "Unless and until, we befriend the *Harijans* and treat them as our brothers, we do not treat humanity as one brotherhood. The whole movement for the removal of untouchability is a movement for the establishment of universal brotherhood, and nothing else." Gandhiji fought against the British decision to give separate political entity to the *Harijans* as distinct from the Caste Hindus. On the social side he fought against those who did not allow *Harijans* to enter temples, public places, like restaurants or to have access to wells, village *chopals* and even localities in which caste Hindus live.

With the dawn of independence, a new chapter has been opened for the Harijans. Under Article 17 of the Constitution untouchability has Been abolished and its practice in any form is forbidden. Other provisions of the Constitution provide for special care for their education and economic interests, reservation of seats in the legislature and civic services. The constitutional safeguards and financial provisions for welfare services cannot achieve the desired results, unless the community itself organises to help its member,.

It is not necessary here to repeat the methods and principles of community organisation, as these are basic to any community development programme. Here we shall discuss only the various areas of work which can be taken up by voluntary agencies interested in working with communities for community development programmes. One of the most important areas in which an agency with network of branches could work is removal of untouchability and creation of an atmosphere in which the Harijans could have a definite social status. The programmes designed for the removal of untouchability consist of:

- Publicity and propaganda by use of simple audio-visual aids.
- Throwing open of wells, temples, eating places, etc. to the members of the community.
- Observance of national, religious and social functions,
- Arranging and encouraging of inter-caste marriages and giving them due publicity.
- Helping the administration to punish those who practise untouchability.
- Adoption of children by *Harijan* and other castes.
- Providing welfare services to the poor members of so-called higher castes along with members of scheduled caste?.

Educational programmes of the scheduled castes include schools for Harijan children particularly girls, encouraging parents to send their children to the schools seeking scholarships for poor Harijans, admitting children in schools with children from all communities. Residential industrial schools for the Harijan children can be run with success by the voluntary agencies with necessary state assistance. Other areas of work for voluntary agencies are providing drinking water facilities, housing, health and medical services, social education programmes to discourage drinking and preparation of illicit liquor. In addition to these programmes a welfare agency can with advantage organise a community centre with programmes for all sections of population in a locality inhabited by members of scheduled castes whether they are in urban, slum, congested or poor localities or in the rural areas. These services, as mentioned in the earlier pages, are in the nature of balwadies creches, nursery schools, maternity services, medical aid, cultural and recreational activities for all age groups, youth clubs, dormitories and shelters for the unattached and the shelterless, activities necessary to promote and improve their economic life, legal aid and social reforms. The set up, contents and principles of running welfare services for the scheduled castes are not different from those of the services for the other urban or rural communities. Only additional requisite is the understanding of the social disabilities under which this community has suffered.

The requirement for the programme is a small building with two or three rooms, necessary equipment for *balwadi*, creche etc. play material, library books, minimum furniture, a trained educated and experienced worker to work as an organiser, helped by part-time workers one each for creche *Balawdi*, crafts, medical aid, maternity services, youth recreation, their number depending on the type and number of activities undertaken by the agency on the basis of local needs and/or resources.The Central Social Welfare Board is assisting welfare agencies providing these services in the urban areas to members of all castes and creeds. In case an organisation is working exclusively for the welfare of scheduled caster, it can get assistance for developing such programmes from the Department of Social Welfare. Grants are also available from the State Departments, for running schools, residential and non-residential, hospitals and dispensaries, housing etc., organising and improving industies for the scheduled castes. So far, we have discussed welfare programmes for the urban communities in the slums, congested and poor localities, rural community and the scheduled castes.

Among the backward communities, we shall now deal with services for the tribal community. There are at present in India 20 million backward and scheduled tribes. Some of these are Gonds and Baigas in Madhya Pradesh, Santhals in Bengal and Bihar, Nagas in Assam and Nagaland, Bhils in Bombay and Rajasthan, Warlies in Maharashtra, Todas in Madras, Khonda in Orissa, Gadies in Rajasthan and Punjab, Oraons and Mintas in Bihar. Broadly, these backward classes go under different names such as Aboriginals, *Adivasies,* Tribals. This is historical. It is said when Aryans invaded India, they came in contact with aboriginals who did not try to mix with them and tried to main-tail: their separate culture. Even to-day the tribal population lives near jungles, rivers, mountains but away from the so-called civilised population in order to maintain their separate existence.

The anthropologists have tried to divide these tribes in the following three main groups according to physical features:

- The proto-australoids, who are similar to Waddid group.
- The Mongoloids, who are found among the Naga tribes of Assam.
- The Negriot, with frizzly hair, who are found in Andamans. They seem to be the oldest.

The tribals have since started coming in contact with outside world. The contacts of various tribes with the civilised world varies from tribe to tribe. Therefore, the degree of civilisation of the tribes, if that can be determined, varies. A committee constituted-by the Indian Council of Social Welfare recommended that the Indian tribal can be divided into four main divisions:

Tribal. Those who still live away from the civilised world in the forests and still maintain their pattern of life.

Semi-Tribal. Those who have more or less settled in rural areas and taken to agriculture and allied occupations.

Accultrated. Those who have migrated to urban and semi-urban areas and are engaged in ordinary occupations and have adopted some of the traits of culture of the civilised population, at the same time continuing contacts with their tribal culture.

Totally assimilated. Those who have been totally assimilated in the normal urban way of life.

The way of life of tribals in different regions is different, but there are some characteristics which are common to all these tribes, since basically all live a primitive life. The common characteristics are:

- Primitive and simple way of life in the state of nature,
- Shy of strangers and distrust in a non-tribal,
- Love for drink and dance,
- Nomadic life,
- Murders and crimes common,
- Habitation in the less easily accessible and remote areas,
- Hunting considered as a ritual,
- Religion akin to Hindus, idol worship (Hill Gods),
- No script, illiteracy, ignorance,
- Prevalence of polyandry and late marriages, the youth sleep in the dormitory. (Not among all tribes).
- Existence of democratic institutions akin to Panchayats.
- Common occupation,—agriculture, fishing, hunting,

poultry, dairy, farming, coal-making, honey collecting, pottery, painting, carving and other handicrafts. Weaving (among Nagas).

During the pre-independence period, the Government tried to solve their problem by declaring, areas called secluded areas, which were placed under the -Governor-General. This was done purely on political grounds and reasons of security. In spite of the advice of the anthropologists, nothing was done for these people. The foreign missionaries which worked under the patronage of the British Government also exploited the tribal population. They were only busy with conversion to Christianity. This was done after giving them some material benefits and social services. This approach of the missionaries, however, helped in bringing the tribals in contact with the outside world and these contacts did change their way of life to some extent. The forest contractors are also responsible for the plight of the tribals. The tribals did not get their due share in the forest wealth. Not only outsiders were appointed on these jobs but even where the tribals were appointed, their ignorance was exploited and they were not paid adequately for the jobs dons by them. They were deprived of the property due to indebtedness. Apart from exploitation from the outsiders, the very way of life of the tribals, their ignorance, traditional medicine, superstitions etc., are also responsible for their decay. The efforts so far made to ameliorate the conditions of the tribals include the following steps taken by the Government:

- Constitutional safeguards,
- Financial provisions in the Five Year Plans for their welfare,
- Appointment of a Commissioner for welfare programmes,

- Creation of welfare departments and ministries in the State?,
- Appointment of Backward Classes Commission,
- Reservation of seats in the Union and State legislatures,
- Reservation of positions under the Government for the tribals, and
- Tribal Commission.

Among the individuals the names of late Thakkar Bapa, late Mr. Varrier Elvin, Dr. B.H. Mehta and Mr. L.M. Srikant, and among the voluntary agencies, the names of Indian Council of Social Welfare, Bhil Sewa Mandal, Vanvasi Sewa Mandal, Bhartiya Adimjati Sewak Sangha, Ramakrishna Mission. Servants of India Society and Christian Missions may be mentioned. They devoted their energies and efforts for the uplift of the tribal people.

Approach to the Tribal Problems

We have discussed the approach of the British Government and the missionaries to the tribal problems. Even today people have different ideas about the method of handling tribal community. One school of thought believes that we should not at all interfere in the tribal affairs and leave them wherever they are, without thinking of any changes in their way of life. The other school which terms this approach as museum-piece approach feels that we should help the tribal people in changing their traditional and primitive way of living and that after a course of time, they should lead the same life as other communities in India are leading and they should also be benefited by the progress civilised society is making through the development of science. In this connection, it is worthwhile to mention here the stand taken by the Government of India as indicated in the speech of late Pandit Jawahar Lal Nehru, late Prime Minister of India at the Tribal Conference held in 1952.

> "The Government of India has no intention of forcing anything on these people by way of religion, language or mode of living. We want to win confidence of the tribal people. Let them maintain their separate social existence. We have to preserve their simple civilisation. While doing so, stress should be laid on providing facilities on basic education, improvement of economic life, preservation of forests and creation of employment."

Programmes

The programmes which can be taken up for the welfare of the tribals by the voluntary agencies are: protection of forests through co-operatives, grain golas, associating tribals with exploiting forests, improving methods of cultivation, educational programmes including running of residential schools with training local tribal crafts, public health and medical services including maternity and child welfare and other programmes of economic upliftment. The type of services to be run in a tribal area will depend largely on the local needs. The services to be run in different areas have to be different, based on the felt-needs of each community. What is important is the understanding of the needs of the tribal population in which an agency is working and the basic approach to the problems. A person working with a welfare agency has, therefore, to understand the principles of working with a tribal community, which though are derived from the basic philosophy of community organisations will be different from the principles underlying work with other communities.

Principles

Keeping this basic policy in mind we now proceed to analyse some of the principles governing work with the tribal community, based on the principles of community organisation. These principles are:

1. No community can remain stagnant and isolated from the rest of the world in this atomic and space age.
2. We should not impose any thing on a tribal community by way of religion or culture. We should create conditions under which they can maintain and enrich their culture.
3. We should react the level of the tribal community in working with them. The changes must be gradual and in a degree desired by them. All the welfare schemes should, therefore, relate to their life pattern. Nothing should be taken from them unless we have some substitute ready.
4. The workers should have sufficient knowledge of anthropology. They should also have understanding of the tribe with which they are working, as each tribe has its own peculiar way of life and separate problems. Scientific surveys should also be undertaken to understand the problems of the tribals.
5. In devising welfare schemes for the tribals, the sole consideration should be their acceptance and easy identification. What we think good for them may neither be good nor acceptable.
6. We should start our work on the basis of social and cultural values of the tribe and not only educate them in their own script but should also try to develop their own script through their local people. The tribal community should, therefore, develop on the lines of its own genius. Efforts should also be made so that tribal culture also influences the life of the other population.

7. A welfare programme in a tribal community should be all comprehensive, administered through one administrative unit. We should also avoid over-administering these areas. The tribal institutions and tribal people should be associated with administration of welfare programmes. The plans should be simple to operate, understandable and capable of yielding spectacular and tangible results which are important to the tribal community. It should also be seen that the various schemes operate simultaneously, so that there is no delay in one, which might affect the progress of the other.

Therefore, the principle of isolation is not good to follow, nor should the agency decide what is good for them, but the programme should be integrated with their values, and should be in consonance with their pattern of life.

7

Humanistic Psychology

Humanistic psychology is only a single recent expression of an old intellectual tradition, a tradition with roots in ancient Greek, Hebrew, and Asian philosophy. There really is no one set of humanistic beliefs; humanism has taken different forms in different historical eras. It has emerged whenever people have felt that some system or authority—political, moral, or intellectual—was undermining human dignity or human unity (Fromm, 1967; Hawton, 1961). Much early humanistic writing was directed against religious dogma. For example, sixteenth-century writers such as Desiderius Erasmus and Sir Thomas More protested that the Church often asked people to blindly adhere to religious doctrines, thus undermining their dignity by robbing them of the freedom to think for themselves. Furthermore, the Church often pitted Christians against non-Christians, when it should have been promoting tolerance and brotherhood (de Santiallana, 1956, pp. 27-30, 92-95).

Humanistic philosophy flourished most widely during the eighteenth-century Enlightenment, when the writings of Locke struck such a responsive chord. Before Locke, political and religious authorities often argued that people were innately wicked and therefore required repression. But if Locke were right—if people were solely the products of their environments—then one had only to change the environments to perfect them and make repression unnecessary. Furthermore, if inequalities were not innate but the products of circumstances, one could erase these too.

The Enlightenment spirit, then, was quite optimistic; unlimited human progress seemed possible. To achieve the greatest progress. Locke, Voltaire, and others turned to science. They believed that the scientific method—the open-minded, cautious verification of hypotheses through empirical evidence—would produce the knowledge that would better the condition of all (Berlin. 1956, pp. 11-29).

The Enlightenment beliefs in science and environmentalism have continued to play a role in some humanistic thinking. However, no single set of beliefs has ever claimed the complete loyalty of all humanists. In fact, in modern psychology, the combination of science and environmentalism took on a form which began to strike some as too rigid and narrow, leading to a new humanistic revolt.

Modern Scientific Psychology

Modern scientific psychology grew out of a deep admiration for the achievements of physics, chemistry, and the other natural sciences. Many psychologists felt that if psychology could only follow the example of these sciences, it too could accomplish great things. They proposed that psychology, like physics, strive for the objective, quantitative measurement of isolated variables and the formulation of abstract laws. At first, in the latter part of the nineteenth century, scientific psychology was led by Wundt and his colleagues, who tried to analyse consciousness into basic elements, as physicists and chemists had done. This effort, however, seemed to lead to a dead end, and by the second decade of the twentieth century the scientific banner had been taken over by another group, the behaviourists. The behaviourists, as we have seen, argued that we should confine ourselves to the measurement of overt behaviour and the way it is controlled by observable stimuli in the external environment. The inner world of thoughts, feelings, and fantasies, they argued, has little place in scientific psychology. Many behaviourists have seen themselves within the humanistic tradition; they have been trying to develop scientific techniques that will better the human lot.

As we have seen, experimenters have used behaviour modification techniques to alleviate fears, temper tantrums, and other problems. They also have devised new instructional methods. Behaviourists, like their Enlightenment predecessors, have held that their environmental, scientific approach will produce the greatest human progress. The Humanistic Revolt in Psychology Early on, however, some psychologists had misgivings about the behaviouristic brand of science.

During the first half of this century. Gordon Allport, Carl Rogers, Abraham Maslow, and others argued that behaviourism, whatever its merits, was producing a very one-sided picture of human nature. Humans, they argued, do not consist only of overt responses, nor are they completely controlled by the external environment. People also grow, think, feel, dream, create, and do many other things which make up the human experience. The behaviourists and others, in their emulation of the physical Sciences, were ignoring most aspects of life which make humans unique and give them dignity. These humanists were not at all opposed to scientific investigation, but they argued that psychology should address itself to the full range of human experience, not just the aspects that are most readily measurable and under environmental control. For some time, these writers were calling out in the wilderness; their views were far removed from the mainstream in American psychology. But in the 1950s their writings began to attract increasing attention, and a humanistic movement in psychology was born (Misiak and Sexton, 1973, pp. 108-9). The humanistic psychologists' call for renewed attention to inner experience has aligned them with the existential and phenomenological movements. With the existentialists, the humanists have held that the living person must take priority over any abstract, scientific system. With the phenomenologists, the humanists have pointed to the need to suspend our ordinary ways of classifying people from the outside; instead we should try to understand how the world feels to people from the inside. Modern humanistic psychology, then, developed primarily in reaction to behaviouristically oriented approaches.

Humanistic psychology's relationship to the second main branch of psychology, psychoanalysis, has been more ambivalent. Many humanists have appreciated the psychoanalytic attempt to explore the inner world at its deepest levels. However, humanists have also felt that the psychoanalysts have been too pessimistic about human capacities for growth and free choice. Whereas the behaviourists have seen people as exclusively controlled by the external environment, psychoanalysts have viewed people as dominated by irrational forces in the unconscious. Perhaps, humanists have suggested, psychoanalytic theory has been too colored by the study of patients with crippling emotional disorders, humanists have proposed that people, to a much greater extent than has been realised, are free and creative beings, capable of growth and self-actualisation (Maslow, 1962, pp. 189-97). The modern humanistic movement in psychology, then, sees itself diverging from the two dominant forces in psychology, scientific behaviourism and psychoanalysis. For this reason, humanists sometimes call their movement the third force." To get a more concrete picture of the kind of work humanistic psychologists have been doing, we will now review some of the ideas of the man who is considered the father of modern humanistic psychology, Abraham Maslow.

Maslow

Biographical introduction. Maslow (1908-1970) was born in Brooklyn, New York, the son of poor, Russian immigrant parents. He was a shy, unhappy boy. Although he liked high school, he had trouble adjusting to college. He attended the City College of New York, Cornell University, and finally the University of Wisconsin, where he earned his B.A. degree and stayed on for graduate work in psychology. Maslow began his career squarely within the scientific mainstream. He received rigorous experimental training under E.L. Thorndike and Harry Harlow and wrote a standard textbook on abnormal psychology (Wilson, 1972. pp. 115-34). In fact, Maslow said that early in his career he was sold on behaviourism (Misiak and Sexton, 1973, p. 113), and in a sense he never repudiated it; he always realised that people are subject to conditioning from the external environment. What increasingly annoyed him was behaviourism's one-sidedness; people also have an inner life and potentials for growth, creativity, and free choice.

Maslow's ideas. Maslow's first step in the direction of a humanistic psychology was the formulation of a new theory of motivation (1943). According to this theory, there are six kinds of needs: physiological needs, safety needs, belongingness needs, love needs, self-esteem needs, and, at the highest level, self-actualisation needs. These needs are arranged in a hierarchical order such that the fulfillment of lower needs propels the organism on to the next highest level. For example, a man who has a strong physiological need, such as hunger, will be motivated by little else, but when this need is fulfilled, he will move on the next level, that of safety needs, and when these are satisfied, he will move on to the third level, and so on.

In his major works, Maslow was most interested in the highest need, the need for self-actualisation.. Self-actualisation, a concept borrowed from Goldstein (1939), refers to the actualisation of one's potentials, capacities, and talents. To study it, Maslow examined the lives and experiences of the most healthy, creative people he could find. His sample included contemporaries and acquaintances, such as the anthropologist Ruth Benedict, as well as public and historical figures, such as Thomas Jefferson and Eleanor Roosevelt (1954. pp. 202-3). Maslow's key finding was that the self-actualisers, compared to most people, have maintained a certain independence from their society. Most people are so strongly motivated by needs such as belongingness, love, and respect that they are afraid to entertain any thought that others might disapprove of. They try to fit into their society and do whatever brings prestige within it.

Self-actualisers, in contrast, are less conforming. They seem less molded and flattened by the social environment and are more spontaneous, free, and natural. Although they rarely behave in unconventional ways, they typically regard conventions with a good-natured shrug of the shoulders. Instead, they are primarily motivated by their own inner growth, the development of their potentials, and their personal mission in life (1954, pp. 223-28). Because self-actualisers have attained a certain independence from their culture, they are not confined to conventional, abstract, or stereotyped modes of perception. When, for example, most people go to a museum, they read the name of he artist below the painting and then judge the work according to the conventional estimate. Self-actualisers, in contrast, perceive things more freshly, naively, and as they really are. They can look at any painting—or any tree, bird, or baby—as if seeing it for the first time; they can find miraculous beauty where others see nothing but the common object (Maslow, 1966, p. 88). In fact, they seem to have retained he creative, open approach which is characteristic of the young child. Like the child, their attitude is frequently absorbed, spellbound, popeyed, enchanted" 1966, p. 100). Unfortunately, most children lose this approach to life as they become socialised.

In a sense, then, self-actualisers are good phenomenologists. They can suspend or go beyond conventional ways of ordering experience, Maslow also likened their approach to a "Taoistic letting be" to an appreciation of objects without interfering with them or attempting to control them (1962, p. 86). He suggested that psychologists can learn much from self-actualisers' phenomenological and Taoistic approaches. Instead of fitting people into theoretical categories and performing experiments on them, psychologists should first simply watch and listen to people with a naive openness. If they did this, they would be open to new discoveries. Maslow reworked his ideas over the years and was not always systematic in the process. But by and large, his overall position was as follows:

1. Humans possess an essential, biological, inner nature, which includes all the basic needs and the impulses toward growth and self-actualisation (1962, p. 190; 1971, p. 25).
2. This inner core is partly species-wide and partly idiosyncratic, for we all have special bents, temperaments, and abilities (1962. p. 191).

3. Our inner core is a positive force which presses toward the realisation of full humanness, just as an acorn may be said to press toward becoming an oak tree. It is important to recognise that it is our inner nature, not the environment, that plays the guiding role. The environment is like sun, food, and water, it nourishes growth, but it is not the seed. Social and educational practice should be evaluated not in terms of how efficiently they control the child or get the child to adjust, but according to how well they support and nourish inner growth potentials (1962. pp. 160-61. 211-12).
4. Our inner nature is not strong, like instincts in animals. Rather, it is subtle, delicate, and in many ways weak. It is easily drowned out by learning, by cultural expectations, by fear, by disapproval, etc." (1962. p. 191).
5. The suppression of our inner nature usually takes place during childhood. At the start, babies have an inner wisdom with respect to most matters, including food intake, amount of sleep, readiness for toilet-training, and the urges to stand up and to walk; Babies will also avidly explore the environment, focusing on the particular things in which they take delight. Their own feelings and inner promptings guide them toward healthy growth. However, socialising agents frequently lack respect for children's choices. Instead, they try to direct children, to teach them things. They criticise them, correct their errors, and try to get them to give the "right" answers. Consequently, children quit trusting themselves and their senses and begin to rely on the opinions of others (pp. 49-55, 150,198-99).
6. Even though our inner core, with its urge toward

self-actualisation is weak, it rarely disappears altogether—even in adulthood. It persists underground, in the unconscious, and speaks to us as an inner voice waiting to be heard. Inner signals can lead even the neurotic adult back to buried capacities and unfulfilled potentials. Our inner core is a pressure we call the "will to health," and it is this urge on which all successful psychotherapy is based (pp. 192-93).

7. There area few people—"self-actualisers"—who have remained deeply responsive to their inner natures and urges toward growth. These people are less molded and flattened by cultural pressures, and have preserved the capacity to look at the world in a spontaneous, fresh, childlike manner (pp. 207-8).

Humanistic thought has taken various forms through the decades. During the Enlightenment, humanism became linked to an environmental outlook and the scientific enterprise. The hope was that the creation of improved environments, aided by scientific knowledge, would lead to better living conditions for us all. In contemporary psychology, the behaviourists continue to pursue the goals of the Enlightenment.

In recent years, however, the behaviouristic approach has struck many humanistic psychologists as too one-sided. Maslow and others have objected that behaviourism leaves out too much that gives human life its richness and dignity. By focusing on how external behaviour comes under environmental control, it has ignored our inner world and our spontaneous urges toward health and independence. If we are to create better environments, they must not simply be those that control behaviour but those that foster and support the intrinsic creative forces.

REFERENCES

Ainsworth, M.D. S. (1962). The effects of maternal deprivation: A review of findings and controversy in the context of research and strategy. *Public Health Papers. 14.* Geneva: World Health Organisation.

Almy, M., Chittenden, E., and Miller, P. (1966). *Young Children's Thinking.* New York: Columbia Teachers' College Press.

Ames, L.B. (1971). Don't push your preschooler. *Family Circle Magazine, 79, 60.*

Appleton, T., Clifton, R., and Goldberg, S. (1975). The development of behavioural competence in infancy. In F. D. Horowitz (Ed.). *Review of Child Development Research* (Vol. IV). Chicago: University of Chicago Press.

Aries, P. (1960). *Centuries of Childhood: A Social History of Family Life* (R. Baldick. trans.). New York: Knopf. 1962.

8

Developmental Theory

DEVELOPMENTALISTS AS HUMANISTS

If Maslow's ideas sound familiar, they are, Maslow and the modern humanistic psychologists have, without making much note of it, drawn heavily upon the developmental tradition. Since Rousseau, developmentalists have been preoccupied with the same basic problem as Maslow: Children, as they become socialised, quit relying on their own experience and judgments; they become too dependent on conventions and the opinions of others. Thus, the developmentalists, like the humanists, have been searching for an inner force that will guide the individual toward a healthier, more independent development.

Intrinsic Growth Forces

Where Maslow speaks of a biological core which directs healthy growth, developmentalists refer to maturation. Maturation is an internal mechanism which prompts children to seek out certain experiences at certain times. Under maturational urging, children regulate their cycles of sleep and eating, learn to sit up, walk, and run, develop an urgent need for autonomy, master language, explore the widening environment, and so on. According to Gesell and others, children, following their own inner schedule and timing, are eminently wise regarding what they need and can do. So, instead of trying to make children conform to our own set schedules and directions, we can let them guide us and make their own choices—as Maslow proposed.

Nevertheless, as Maslow observed, it is often difficult for us to trust children and the growth process. We seem to have particular difficulty believing that children can really learn on their own, without our direction and supervision. But developmentalists have tried to show that they can. Montessori, in particular, tried to show that if we will open-mindedly observe children's spontaneous interests, they will direct us to the tasks on which they will work independently and with the greatest concentration and sense of fulfillment. They will become absorbed in such tasks because the tasks meet inner needs to perfect certain capacities at certain points in development. Thus, we are not forced to take charge of children's learning, to choose tasks for them, to motivate them by our praise, or to criticise their mistakes—practices which force them to turn to external authorities for guidance and evaluation. Instead, we can trust their maturationally based urges to perfect their own capacities in their own ways. Maslow might have pointed to Montessori as an educator who was thoroughly humanistic in her faith in children's intrinsic creative powers.

Not all developmentalists, of course, are as nativistic as Gesell or Montessori. As we have seen, Piaget. Kohlberg, and the cognitive-developmentalists doubt that biological maturation directly governs the stages of cognitive development. Nevertheless these theorists also look to children's independent activities, rather than to external teachings, as the source of development. Children, in their view, are intrinsically curious about the world and reach out for new experiences that lead them to reorganise their cognitive structures. Thus, the cognitive-developmentalists also share the humanists' faith in intrinsic capacities for self-directed learning.

Interestingly. Maslow's thoughts on adulthood also were foreshadowed by earlier developmental theorists—especially by Jung. Maslow pointed out how the well-socialised adult, whose inner potentials for self-actualisation lie dormant, will ill hear inner voices calling for attention. Jung used nearly identical language to describe the crisis of middle life. Prior to middle age, the individual typically concentrates on adjusting to the external, social world, trying to do things that bring social success and prestige and developing those parts of the personality that are suited for this goal. In middle life, however, social success loses its importance, and inner voices from the unconscious direct one to attend to the previously neglected and unrealised parts of the self. The individual increasingly turns inward and considers the discovery and rounding out of the personality more important than social conformity.

Thus, developmental theorists, like the modern humanistic psychologists, have tried to uncover intrinsic growth factors that stand apart from pressures toward social conformity. At the same time, however, some developmental theorists have been more pessimistic than the humanists about the chances for any substantial improvement based on intrinsic forces. In particular, the Freudians have felt that because maturation brings with it unruly sexual and aggressive impulses, a good measure of social repression will always be necessary. Erikson has viewed maturational growth somewhat more positively than Freud, calling attention to the maturation of autonomy, initiative, industry, and so on, but he too has felt that the other sides of these strengths—shame, doubt, guilt, inferiority, and so on—are inevitable. No child, for example, can become completely autonomous, for societies will always need to regulate the child to some extent. Still, Erikson hopes that we can raise children so that they can gain as much autonomy, initiative, and as many other virtues as possible.

Furthermore, Freudian therapy relies heavily on inner growth forces. Recall how Freud once asked a psychiatrist if he could really cure. When the psychiatrist responded that he could not—that he could only remove some impediments to growth as a gardener removes some stones or weeds—Freud said that they would then understand each other. The psychoanalyst's reliance on intrinsic growth processes is quite evident in Bettelheim's school. Bettelheim does not try to make disturbed children behave in normal ways, but he tries to provide certain conditions—love, acceptance, empathy—which will enable children to feel it is safe to take steps toward growth on their own. The physician treats patients in essentially the same way. The doctor does not actually heal a cut but only cleans and stitches the wound. The rest is up to Nature. Any cure, in psychotherapy or in medicine, partly relies on forces toward health that are out of the doctor's control. The doctor puts his or her faith in innate forces toward health.

Thus, developmental theorists, like the humanists, have tried to discover the nature of intrinsic growth forces and to devise educational and therapeutic methods based upon them. And, to a considerable extent, developmental writers had been working on these tasks long before the modern humanistic movement in psychology even began.

Romanticism

Theories that extol the virtues of Nature and biological forces, as opposed to society, are often called Romantic. In this sense, Maslow, as well as Rousseau and the maturationists, are strongly Romantic. Rousseau, in fact, is often credited with the origin of Romantic thought.

Another aspect of Romanticism is a fondness for the past. This attraction is quite evident in Maslow; he looked upon infancy and childhood as times when we were more closely in touch with our natural urges and possessed a more spontaneous and creative outlook. As children, he said, we perceived the world more freshly, directly, and imaginatively than we typically do as well-socialised adults. Maslow recognised the value of mature, adult thought, but he also felt that we need to learn to regress temporarily to more childlike modes of experience.

Rousseau, too, "romanticised the past." He suggested that we were happier and more independent as savages, and he saw childhood as a potentially happy and innocent time in which we live in close harmony with Nature. In modern developmental theory, perhaps the most thoroughgoing Romantic was Schachtel, who contrasted the richly sensuous experiences of infancy and the open curiosity of childhood with the stereotyped, conventional thought of most adults.

Neither Rousseau nor Schachtel, however, clearly specified ways in which we, as adults, might recapture childlike modes of experience. For such a conceptualisation, we are particularly indebted to Werner. Werner suggested that we continually engage in a process called microgenesis, beginning each new thought or perception at primitive levels before moving on to more advanced forms of cognition. Thus, the primitive modes of experience are continually available to us. Ordinarily, Werner observed, we do not engage in primitive imagery in a very full way, but we do so when we are most creative, when we truly begin anew. At these moments our impressions become particularly rich and sensuous; for primitive images are fused with emotion, sensation, and imaginative qualities. Creative thinking, of course, does not stop with such images; it goes on to articulate and structure them. Nevertheless, Werner emphasised, creativity begins with a responsiveness to early forms of experience—a view shared by the psychoanalysts who speak of "regressions in the service of the ego."

Not all developmentalists, we should note, have been very Romantic. The cognitive-developmentalists, in particular, have generally been unimpressed by the distinctive virtues of childlike thinking. Piaget observed that we continue to use early sensori-motor schemes and cognitive operations, but he saw nothing special in the imaginative, fanciful thinking of the preoperational child, and he never suggested that creative people regress to it. Similarly, Kohlberg has never seemed impressed by the concept of regression. In his view, stages of moral reasoning simply reflect increasing levels of cognitive adequacy, so there is no point to regressing to earlier stages.

Not all developmentalists, then, have placed a special premium on childlike modes of thought. All developmentalists, to be sure, have argued that childhood thinking has unique qualities, but not all developmentalists have been so enamored with these qualities that they have urged us to recapture them. Still, a Romantic attraction to childhood is one theme that runs through a good deal of humanistic psychology and developmental theory.

Phenomenology

Another central component of modern humanistic psychology is a phenomenological orientation. This orientation or method includes what may be called a "phenomenological suspension." One tries to suspend one's theoretical preconceptions and customary categories and tries to see people and things as recently and freshly as possible—to see them as they really are. This approach, as we nave seen, was the starting point of Rousseau's developmental philosophy. Rousseau argued that children have their own ways of seeing, thinking, and feeling, and that we know nothing about these; we therefore must refrain from investing children with our own thoughts and take the time to simply observe them, listen to them, and let them reveal their unique characteristics to us.

Later, Piaget and Montessori emphasised the same point. The ethologists, too, may be said to employ a phenomenological suspension. Before an ethologist forms any hypothesis or builds any theory, he or she first simply tries to learn about and describe as much about a particular species as possible. To do this, ethologists believe, we must observe animals in their natural habitats, not in the laboratory. In psychology, phenomenology usually implies a second step. Phenomenological psychologists usually suspend preconceptions in order to enter into the *inner* world of the other. They try to open themselves to the other's direct experience, to see things through the other's eyes. Developmental theorists have been less consistent in taking this second step. Those who have worked the hardest to learn about children's inner worlds are Schachtel and the psychoanalysts. Schachtel tried to gain insight into the infant s unique modes of perception, and the psychoanalyst Bettelheim, for example, constantly asks himself, "How does the world look and feel to this child?"

Other writers, however, have been less interested in perceiving the world through the child's eyes. Gesell wanted us to be open to children's own needs and interests, but he primarily observed their external motor behaviour. Werner gave us insights into how the world might look to the child—how, for instance, it might appear full of life and feeling—but he mostly discussed the child's mental life from the *outside,* analysing it in terms of concepts such as differentiation and integration. Similarly, Piaget provided valuable insights into the young child's unique experiences—how objects change with momentary perceptions, how dreams seem real, how morals seem imposed by authorities, and so forth—but Piaget, too, primarily examined the young child's thought from the outside, analysing it in terms of logical structures. The ethologists also primarily look at behaviour from an external point of view. A knowledge of how the world looks to children (and adults) at different stages will not be easy to come by. Young children are not sufficiently verbal to tell us how the world appears to them, and infants cannot tell us anything at all.

One approach may be the study of spontaneous interests. For example. Montessori showed how young children attend to minute details and are concerned about anything out of place. These observations give us two clues concerning the young child's perceptual world. Young children also seem to perceive life where we do not, and they may be particularly interested in objects, such as cars, balls, or balloons, which, with a little imagination, take on human qualities. It would seem important to record every aspect of the environment which children find uniquely interesting. To structure such studies, we might follow the lead of Martha Muchow, who observed how children of different ages responded to typical settings in their everyday environments, including a landing dock and a department, store. By noting the things that children find particularly interesting, as well as those that they ignore, we can begin to form a picture of how the world appears to the child at different phases of life.

Universals

Readers who have already learned something about

developmental psychology will notice that this book neglects or skims over certain topics. We have not discussed, for example, differences among children or adults on I.Q. tests. Other topics that have received only minor coverage include cultural differences in personality development and sex differences. The various differences among people, which are partly the product of environmental factors, are tremendously important. If we are ever to redress artificial social inequalities, we need to know how they are formed.

However, the differences among people have not been the developmentalists' primary concern. Instead, they have searched for developmental forces and sequences common to all peoples. This search, as Chomsky suggests (1975. pp. 130-33) probably reflects, as much as anything, an ethical orientation. Developmentalists, like humanists, are trying to show how, at the deepest levels, we are all the same. Developmentalists shy away from topics concerning how one person is better than another and focus, instead, on what Maslow calls our "biological brotherhood" (1962, p. 185). They want to show that, at bottom, we all have the same yearnings, hopes, and fears, as well as the same creative urges toward health and personal integration. Hopefully, an appreciation of the positive strivings that we all share can help in the building of a universal human community.

In formulating a new version of humanism, Maslow and others have, without making much note of it, drawn heavily upon the developmental tradition in psychology. First and foremost, they have joined the developmentalists in their search for intrinsic growth forces that can lead to healthy development. Second, the humanists have joined those Romantic developmentalists who have looked fondly upon earlier periods as times when we were more in tune with Nature and had a more spontaneous-outlook. Third, the humanists' call for a more phenomenological science has been, to an extent, anticipated by developmentalists, for many developmentalists have suggested that we cannot appreciate the growing child's unique ways of thinking and learning unless we approach them with something of a naive openness. Finally, both humanists and developmentalists have been primarily concerned with the universal aspects of human development, with the urges toward growth and health that we all share.

REFERENCES

Ainsworth, M.D. S. (1967). *hifanct in Uganda: Infant Care and the Growth of Love.* Baltimore; Johns Hopkins University Press.

_____ (1973). The development of infant and mother attachment. In B. M. Caldwell and H. M. Ricciuti (Eds.). *Review of Child Development Research* (Vol. 111). Chicago: University of Chicago Press.

Aitchison, J. (1976). *The Articulate Mammal: An Introduction to Psycholinguistics.* New York: University Books.

Als, H. (1978). Assessing an assessment: Conceptual considerations, methodological issues, and a perspective on the future of the Neonatal Behavioural Assessment Scale.

Appleton, T., Clifton, R., and Goldberg, S. (1975). The development of behavioural competence in infancy. In F. D. Horowitz (Ed.). *Review of Child Development Research* (Vol. IV). Chicago: University of Chicago Press.

Aries, P. (1960). *Centuries of Childhood: A Social History of Family Life* (R. Baldick. trans.). New York: Knopf. 1962.

9

Effects of the Physical Structure of the School Environment

Most psychological theories of child development under the influence of Freud stress the early experiences of the child in the family as the main determinants of future social, emotional, and even intellectual development. As we have seen, a second major force in the socialisation process is the peer group. A third and often neglected agent is the school. Although most discussions of the school concentrate on teachers, tactics, and texts, the structural features of the school environment merit consideration. Does the size of the school that a child attends make any difference? Similarly, do such factors as seating arrangements, class size, wall color, and ventilation affect the child's scholastic achievement, his attitudes toward school, or the degree to which he actively participates in class and extracurricular functions? Although it is impossible to answer all these questions, recent research has given us answers to at least some of them.

Big School, Small School: The Effect of School Size

The large school has authority: its grand exterior dimensions, its long halls and myriad rooms and its tides of students all carry an implication of power and rightness.

The small school lacks such certainty: its modest building, its short halls and few rooms and its students, who move more in trickles than in tides, give an impression of a casual or not quite decisive educational environment. (Barker and Gump, 1964, p. 195) But that is only an outside view. And appearances are often deceiving. To find out how schools of different sizes look from the inside was the aim of a research project conducted by Roger Barker and Paul Gump of the University of Kansas. These investigators were concerned with the extent of student participation in extracurricular functions in small and large schools.

They wanted to learn whether or not large schools offer more, and more varied, activities for their students than smaller schools and whether this meant that the student in the large school has a richer experience. High schools ranging in size from 35 to 2,287 students participated in the study; all were located in an economically, culturally, and politically homogeneous region of eastern Kansas, and all were controlled by the same state authority. The results were surprising.

Although the largest school had twenty times as many students as a small school in a near- by county, there were only five times as many extracurricular activities. More importantly, the large and small school do not differ greatly in terms of the variety of activities that they offer. The small school is small in enrollment but not necessarily limited in opportunities for activity and participation. Barker and Gump compare it to a small engine in that "it possesses the essential parts of a large entity but has fewer replications and differentiations of some of the parts" (Barker and Gump, 1964, p. 195) With fewer students but nearly as many participation opportunities, one would expect that more students would be more involved in more activities in more important ways in the smaller setting.

This is precisely what the researchers found. The proportion of students who participated in district music festivals and dramatic, journalistic, and student government competitions was three to twenty times as great in the small, as contrasted with the large, institution. Students at a small school would participate in twice as many activities over their high school career. Moreover, there would be greater variety in their activities if they attended a small school. The kinds of positions occupied by students at large and small schools differed as well. Small-school adolescents were more likely to hold positions of importance and responsibility than their peers at a large school. In light of these findings, it was not surprising to learn that the rewards and satisfactions derived from participation differed for students in these two types of environments. Students from the small schools reported: . . .more satisfaction relating to the development of competence, to being challenged, to engaging in important actions, to being involved in group activities and to achieving moral and cultural values [while large school students reported) more satisfaction dealing with vicarious enjoyment, with large entity affiliation, with learning about their school's persons and affairs and with gaining "points" via participation. (Barker and Gump. 1964, p. 197).

Further analysis revealed that these differences were largely due to the fact that a greater number of pupils held responsible positions in small schools. There is one other way in which the two types of institutions differed. In the small-school setting there were many more pressures to participate; students themselves felt more obligation and responsibility to play an active role in their school functions, and they felt that their peers expected them to participate more. One outcome is that there were fewer "outsiders," that is, students who were left out of most extracurricular activities, in the smaller schools. Comparisions of marginal students, or potential dropouts, with regular students indicated that the marginal students felt few pressures to participate in large schools. On the other hand, in small settings the two types of students felt similar pressures to participate in extracurricular affairs. This greater sense of identification and involvement of the marginal students in the smaller school may be part of the reason that dropout rates are lower in small schools. The question of whether or not school size affects academic progress is, unfortunately, left unanswered. Class size rather than institution size probably would be a better predictor in this realm.

However, if we view the school as a socialisation agency, it is clear that much of the school's influence in transmitting social and cultural values comes through these extracurricular functions. Not only does the research of Barker and Gump provide important information about the impact of school size on student behaviours, but it also serves as a remainder that much of the learning taking place in school is not in the classroom. The main implication of this study lies in the answer to the question that guided their research: "What size should a school be?. . . sufficiently small that all of its students are needed for its enterprises. A school should be small enough that students are not redundant" (Barker and Gump, 1964, p. 202).

The Spatial Arrangement of the Classroom

One of the most obvious features of the learning environment is the *rectangular* classroom. Why not a round class or a square one? Or does it matter anyway? According to one design expert—The present rectangular room with its straight row of chairs and wide windows was intended to provide for ventilation, light, quick departure, ease of surveillance and a host of other legitimate needs as they existed in the early 1900's.... The typical long narrow shape resulted from a desire to get light across the room. The front of each room was determined by window location, since pupils had to be seated so that window light came over the left shoulder. Despite new developments in lighting, acoustics and structures, most schools are still boxes filled with cubes each containing a specified number of chairs in straight rows. There have been attempts to break away from this rigid pattern, but experimental schools are the exception rather than the rule. (Sommer, 1969, pp. 98-99).

Maria Montessori once described the children who have to exist in these traditional classrooms as "butterflies mounted on pins, fastened each to a desk, spreading the useless wings of barren and meaningless knowledge they have acquired" (Montessori, 1964, p. 81). Does a pupil's location within the classroom make a difference? Are individuals in front more active than those in the rear? Are those in the center more active than those at the aisles, regardless of the type of room? Consider the seminar room first.

Sommer (1969) compared the participation of college students at the side tables with those sitting directly opposite the instructor. Students sitting opposite the teacher participated most, while those at the side tables talked very little. Finally, while students tended to avoid chairs adjacent to the teacher, when they were "stuck" in these positions they pretended that they weren't there by being silent. Participation in straight-row arrangements seems to be determined by location as well. Sommer found that first-row students participate more than students near the rear and centrally located students participate more than the fringe dwellers.

This location-participation relationship is a very common

one and by no means restricted to college students. In a study of elementary and high school classes, it was reported that the center-front pattern emerged regardless of grade level (first, sixth, and eleventh), sex or age of teacher, or subject matter (mathematics or social studies) (Adams and Biddle. 1970). The effect was so consistent that this spatial location was termed the action *zone* of the classroom. Seat choices may have psychological implications. Levinger and Gunner (1967) found that students who typically sat at the rear of a classroom placed greater psychological distance between themselves and the teacher; these investigators had used a projective test in which students arranged geometric forms and silhouettes on a felt background to index psychological distance in their study. How such "distance" develops is not clear.

Children may sit near the back of the class because of some fear of or alienation from the teacher; on the other hand, the psychological barrier may develop out of the spatial arrangements themselves. Finally, what about class size? In spite of the frequency of discussion and debate concerning the "optimal" class size, there is a surprising paucity of relevant investigations. An exception is an early study by Dawe (1934), in which she examined the effects of kindergarten size on pupil participation. In classes ranging in size from fifteen to forty-six children, the number of comments made by each child during a controlled discussion period was recorded. As class size increased, not only did the total amount of discussion decrease, but a smaller per cent of the children participated; when they did talk, their average amount of participation was likely to be less. Nearly forty years later, Tuana (1969) found a similar inverse relationship between participation and class size at the college level. It will come as no surprise to college students to learn that a mere 2.3 questions per class was typical in the large lecture class. As in the earlier classroom studies, those students in the two front rows of the center section of a lecture hall asked almost half of the questions. Another third of the questions came from students sitting along the side aisles. The "faceless mass" in the middle, to use Sommer's description, participated very little. This suggests that the location-participation link may be even stronger as class size increases. The result of course, is an increasingly large proportion of children being excluded systematically from an active role in their education. If children do learn more by participating more, then the data are clear: smaller classes are preferable.

The findings concerning participation, size, and seating are consistent with a more general proposition governing social interaction, namely, that verbal communication is more likely when the potential conversationalists have eye-to-eye contact. In general, if you sit closer, you will participate more.

Size alone is not the only important factor; density, or the amount of space per pupil, makes a difference. In one recent study, preschoolers listened to a story or watched a teacher demonstration under crowded or uncrowded conditions. Visual attention to the teacher and to the educational materials was less when the children were spatially crowded than when the children listened in an uncrowded setting (Krantz and Risley, 1977).

In light of these findings, it is encouraging to see trends toward greater flexibility in arranging classroom space. Movable furniture is becoming increasingly popular, as in the "school without walls," an open-plan architecture designed for team teaching in which several grades share a large open space (Gump and Ross, 1977). However, merely providing flexible space and movable furniture does not guarantee that innovative teaching will necessarily follow. In one Texas experiment involving fully portable furniture, Sanders (1958) found that the equipment rarely moved in actual practice. This failure to take advantage of the flexible facilities is even more surprising in light of the fact that only 1.4 minutes were required to make a major rearrangement of the furniture. Other investigators have found similar results. For example, in one comparison of traditional and modem classrooms the teachers were "quick to emphasise that the large classroom had not changed their teaching methods" (Rolfe, 1961, p. 192, cited by Sommer, 1969). Clearly, teachers must learn to use space and facilities; without direct instruction concerning the possibilities offered by new classroom arrangements, it is unlikely that few substantial changes in individual class activities or teaching techniques will actually take place. As Sommer wryly commented; "if the school traditions make straight row arrangements immutable, even though the chairs are portable, portable chairs serve only to increase the workload of the janitors who have to straighten the rows every evening" (Sommer, 1969, p. 104).

Structure of the Classroom

The teacher can organise her classroom in a multitude of ways. For example, she can arrange to have students participate in the decision making; she can organise her class into small groups; she can arrange for students to help each other; or she can organise classroom activities in the traditional manner. In this section we will focus on the consequences of different types of classroom organisation.

The classic study of differing leadership styles on classroom climate was that of Kurt Lewin and his colleagues (Lewin, Lippitt, and White, 1939) Groups of five 10-year-old boys, organised into clubs for recreational purposes, were assigned leaders who had been instructed to be either "authoritarian," "democratic," or "laissez-faire" (permissive) in their orientation. The democratic leadership style was superior to the other two leadership approaches in a variety of ways. The boys in the democratic groups were more productive (even in the leader's absence), happier with both their leader and their group, and less hostile toward each other. The laissez-faire leadership produced disorganisation, boredom, inefficiency, and quarrels, while the boys in the authoritarian groups were either passive or rebellious, were aggressive in their peer interaction, and showed little capacity to work efficiently in the leader's absence.

Open *Versus* Traditional Classroom

Many of these differences in teacher style that Lewin originally investigated have reappeared in more recent investigations of the effects of the open classroom versus the traditional classroom. Originally developed in Great Britain, the open-classroom philosophy is based on the assumption that children learn best by actively participating and becoming involved in their own learning rather than being passive recipients of knowledge. Here is a description of the open classroom. In the open classroom, it is rare for all the children to be engaged in the same activity at the same time. They do not sit at rows of desks, dutifully listening (or pretending to listen) as their teacher lectures in front of the room. Instead, they tend to be scattered around the room—at tables, on couches, or on the floor-working individually or in small groups. A typical view of an open classroom might show us two youngsters stretched out on a rug reading books they have chosen from the classroom library. The teacher is at the math table, showing a small group of children how to use a set of scales to learn about relative weights. Two children in the writing comer are playing a word game. And one child is taking notes on the nursing behaviour of the class guinea pig. Other children are working individually or in small groups at desks or tables. A sense of purpose pervades the room attesting to the children's interest in their various learning activities. (Papalia and Olds, 1975. p. 463)

But do children learn more and dislike it less in open classrooms? Problems plague attempts to evaluate the effects of open classrooms since the back- grounds of children in these two types of schools or classrooms tend to differ. However, some tentative conclusions can be suggested. Open-classroom children do not appear to learn more in terms of conventional achievement areas (Featherstone, 1971), but they do like school and their teachers more than children in formal or traditional schools (Groobman, Forward, and Peterson, 1976). Moreover, children in low-structure classes engage in more prosocial behaviour and more imaginative play but are more aggressive than children in a more highly structured environment (Huston-Stein, Freidrich-Cofer, and Susman, 1977). There are other positive benefits as well. Harvey and his associates (Harvey. Prather, White. and Hoffmeister. 1968) found that children in open classrooms exhibited freer expression of feelings, more voluntary participation higher independence, and a larger voice in classroom activities. Activity level as reflected in both the amount and diversity of goal-relevant activity, was higher in these classes. Novelty of their answers was higher, and there was less emphasis on rote answers and solutions. On the other hand, not all kinds of children fare well in open classrooms. Some children may perform better under a more structured type of classroom regime.

It should come as no surprise that the open classroom so far seems to fall far short of being a panacea. Other widely acclaimed innovations in education such as

Summerhill (Neill, 1960) have been similarly disappointing when you look carefully at their overall record of success (Bernstein, 1968). Even if most experiments in education do not survive intact, however, valuable aspects of their programme may persist and eventually that American public schools will convert to the open classroom model, many schools already offer both tvpes of classrooms, the traditional and the open, attempting to assign become absorbed by mainstream educational institutions. Thus, while it is unlikely students and teachers to the one which seems best suited to their own needs, predispositions, and abilities. (Hetherington and Morris. 1978, p. 321)

TEXTBOOKS

What's Wrong with Primary Readers?

In the past decade there has been a reawakening of interest and concern with children's readers. Educators have recognised that children are influenced not only by their teachers and peers but also by the reading material to which they are exposed. Primers serve an important socialising function. Many of the attitudes and cultural values that are slowly emerging during the early school years are directly shaped by the content and themes of these textbooks. In addition, these readers play an important role in determining the child's attitudes toward the task of reading itself. Particularly for children Who have had little encouragement to read before entering school and, therefore, have little appreciation of the value of books and the rewards of reading, primers with lively, interesting, and relevant content would seem to be necessary to interest them in books and reading.

However, most evaluators of available readers give these texts a failing grade. Here is one such evaluation of the current status of the American reader:

> The reading textbooks used in the first grade were inappropriate in terms of interest value. They concealed the results of life in America, hiding not only its difficulties and problems, but also much of its excitement and joy. They featured Dick and Jane in the clean, Caucasian, correct suburbs, in houses surrounded by white fences, playing happily with happy peers and happy parents. They contained a dearth of moral content which could have high interest values. They presented a monstrous repetition of pollyanish family activities They offered no new knowledge. They contradicted the everyday experiences of children in general since most American children seldom, if ever, experience the affect-less situations depicted in the books... the stories were so predictable in outcomes that little, if any, of a child's incentive to continue reading was derived from the story content. (Blom, Waite. and Zimet. 1970, p. 433)

Other surveys have unearthed further deficiencies. For example. Klineberg (1963) has pointed out that in addition to distorting the picture of current American society, these texts pay little attention to foreign nationalities. Maybe it is just as well, for when other national groups are depicted it is -often in stereotyped terms or in an unfavourable light. It is not surprising that American children are markedly ethnocentric.

Moreover, textbooks carry hidden agendas to the young about sex-role mythologies in our society (Busby 1975). A recent analysis of first-, second-, and third-grade readers revealed evidence of a stereotypic portrayal of male and female roles (Saario, Jacklin, and Tittle, 1973). Boys were portrayed as demon- strafing significantly higher amounts of aggression, physical exertion, and problem solving, while girls were often cast as characters engaged in fantasy, carrying out directions, and making statements about themselves. Nor were these rigid sex-role pictures restricted to child story characters. Adult males were portrayed more often as engaging in constructive- and productive behaviours, physical activity, and more problem-solving behaviour. On the other hand, adult females were presented as conforming and were usually found in home or school settings. Males were found more frequently outdoors or in business. Finally, young male characters significantly more often receive positive outcomes as a result of their *own* actions; girl characters receive positive outcomes, but they are more often because of circumstance. This kind of sex-role stereotyping, in fact, starts very early in children's literature: other studies of picture books for preschoolers reveal a very similar pattern (Weitzman, Eifler, Hokada, and Ross, 1972).

Direct evidence that the children themselves are dissatisfied with their classroom readers comes from a recent comparison of the content of first-grade primers and the library selections made by first graders when they had a free choice (Wiberg and Trost, 1970). The marked discrepancies between the two sets of books underlined the differences between children's reading interests and primer content. Unlike the play and Pollyannaish themes of the primers, the children's library choices emphasised folk tales, lessons from life, nature, and real-life events that had both sad and happy endings. Activities involving boys and older children were more frequent in the library books, as were stories about foreign countries. Moreover, although boys and girls read the same books in the classroom, clear sex differences in book preferences were evident when the children were given a choice. Boys preferred books with boy activity stories and prank and information themes. Girls, on the other hand, showed no preference in terms of the sex appropriateness of the activity, but did choose pet books frequently. These data suggest that if children's interest in reading is to be stimulated, some radical redesigning of primers is necessary. The children themselves can, in fact, point the way to more realistic and relevant texts. Not only do young children know what they want; what they want is probably better for them!

Some Implications of Traditional Readers

What are the implications of these elementary school readers for children's academic progress and for their emotional, social, and cultural development? One would expect that children would be much more involved and motivated if the content of the reading material were relevant to their own background, interests, and experience. It is likely that many children simply "tune out" at a very early age due to the perceived irrelevance of school as reflected in these primers If this is the case, one would expect differences between reading ability of children exposed to the "Dick and Jane" stories and those taught to read with more sophisticated, realistic, and relevant materials. In fact, children do comprehend more when reading high- than low-interest material (Asher, Hymel, and Wigfield, 1976).

In related work, Asher and Markell (1974) have demonstrated that the reading scores of boys, even more than girls, are affected by the interest value of stories. Fifth graders were given passages to read that were of either high or low interest. When boys had the, chance to read stories about astronauts and airplanes, they read much better than when they read low-interest stories. Moreover, the typical difference in reading level between boys and girls was not present when the material was interesting. Girls, on the other hand, tended to be less affected by the interest level of the stories. Although there is no simple solution to the problem of lower reading achievement of boys in elementary school, this study suggests that more attention should be paid to motivational factors. Boys can read better if the material turns them on!

Settings may make a difference as well. When popular paperbacks were introduced into an elementary school library, the student use of the library did not change until the atmosphere also changed. To remove the drab classroom look of the library, one enterprising librarian added a large, shaggy. red carpet to the middle of the library, scattered colorful pillows around and removed most of the tables and chairs. "So many kids flocked in to sprawl on the carpet and read that she eventually had to ration the space" (Mehrabian. 1976, p. 155).

Nontraditional Readers

Do ethnic readers, that more realistically characterise ethnic and racial groups, make any difference to children's reading? Although the issue is far from settled, one early investigator (Whipple. 1963) did find differences in measures of word recognition and oral reading accuracy between children taught with traditional primers and those introduced to reading through a multiethnic reading text. The children using the new text, one which portrayed the diverse ethnic and racial groups in American society, had higher scores on both measures. Probably these effects would be particularly marked for non-Caucasian, non-middle-class children. Is it at all surprising that these children feel alienated from the school system when the system presents such a uniformly consistent but irrelevant and foreign set of values? Even for white middle-class children the misrepresentation of our society promoted in the typical primer has detrimental effects. Readers provide an excellent device for exposing these socially naive children to some of the other racial and ethnic groups that compose American society-a needed lesson in cultural learning.

Possibly many of the stereotypes that often underlie current white middle-class prejudices would be eliminated by a more realistic presentation of the current American scene. In one study, the use of multiethnic readers increased the positive attitudes of white children to their black classmates (Litcher and Johnson. 1969).

Fortunately readers are changing, and a number of publishing firms are producing primers that include children of more than one ethnic background as story characters, and that represent boys and girls in less stereotyped fashion. In spite of these trends, many critics (Oliver, 1974) still contend that texts "have not kept pace with a changing society,' (Graebner, 1972, p. 52).

A Closing Comment on Texts

Perhaps the most appropriate way to close this section is to offer the following plea that texts not only need to recognise differences in sex and race, but should be generally more aware that:

> The real world is more varied than the one depicted in elementary readers. Boys and girls, and men and women, are fat and skinny, short and tall. Boys and men are sometimes gentle, sometimes dreamers. Artists, doctors, lawyers, and college professors are sometimes mothers as well. Rather than limiting possibilities, elementary texts should seek to maximise individual development and self-esteem by displaying a wide range of models and activities, lithe average is the only model presented to a child and therefore assumed to be the child's goal, most children—and most adult—would probably be unable to match the model. (Saario. et al., 1973. p. 399)

SPECIAL CHILDREN, SPECIAL NEEDS?

Mainstreaming

Not all children learn at the same pace or in the same

way. Some are Slower to learn; others learn faster than their classmates; some are blind or deaf or in a wheelchair. A major issue of the 1970s has been the question of whether or not these "special" children should be placed in separate classes or whether they should be integrated into regular classrooms. In the world of special education, this shift toward including children of all abilities in regular classrooms is known as "mainstreaming" and in the mid-70s this became a law. Supporters of this new legislation cite some powerful arguments but few hard facts. They argue that mainstreaming will result in higher levels of achievement, both academically and socially. Second, they suggest that this move away from special isolated classes to regular school setting "does a better job than a segregated setting of helping children adjust to and cope with the real world when they grow up. " (Brenton, 1974, p. 23). Third, they assume that exposure to a wide range of "children will help normal children understand individual differences in people and it will also help to diminish stereotyping of children with various types of handicaps or disabilities (Brenton. 1974). In spite of the legal fact of mainstreaming there are skeptics.

The physical needs of severely and profoundly retarded children necessitate the employment of additional personnel and the use of specialised architectural arrangements, equipment and facilities which cannot be established in every overcrowded regular classroom. The centralisation of these children in regional special classes allows a focus and concentration of therapeutic time and effort. In contrast, the distribution of these children across scattered regular classes would lead to a tremendous waste of therapy time lost in traveling to various schools, The regular classroom teacher serving 20 to 40 children cannot be expected to meet the educational, physical, social and emotional needs of children with severe. . . . A token gesture of integration cannot replace an intensive, carefully planned developmental education Programme. (Smith and Akrans, 1974 p. 501)

Nor is it just academic progress that may sometimes suffer from mainstreaming. Integration of retarded children may lead to increased social rejection (Gottlieb 1978) by their nonretarded peers. Elementary school children express liking for retarded children than nonretarded children, and increased contact through integrated classrooms leads to increased rejection of the retarded (Goodman, Gottlieb, and Harrison, 1972). Other evidence indicates that in a school with no interior walls. retarded children, were more rejected than in a school with walls and segregated children (Gottlieb and Budoff. 1973).

As long as people judge others by their abilities, increased contact with those who are relatively less expert may lead to less rather than more acceptance. (Asher, Oden, and Gottman. 1977. p. 42)

Perhaps the most reasonable view is one that encourages flexibility in response to the individual needs of the children in the schools. Hobbs summarises this view:

In schools that are most responsive to individual) differences in abilities, interests, and learning styles of children, the mainstream is actually many streams, sometimes as many streams as there are individual children, sometimes several streams as groups are formed for special purpose, sometimes one stream only as concerns of all converge. We see no advantage in dumping exceptional children into an undifferentiated mainstream; but we see great advantage to all children, exceptional children included, in an educational programme modulated to the needs of individual children, singly, in small groups, or all together. Such a flexible arrangement may well result in functional separations of exceptional children from time to time, but the

> governing principle would apply to all children: school programmes should be responsive to the learning requirements of individual children, and groupings should serve this end. (1975, p. 197)

The Gifted

"What number is that which, being divided by the product of its digits, the quotient is 3, and if. 18 be added, the digits will be inverted? He flew out of his chair, whirled around rolled up his eyes and said in about a minute, 24. Multiply in your head 365, 365, 365, 365, 365, 365 by 365, 365, 365, 365, 365, 365.. . . in not more than one minute said he, 133, 491, 850, 208, 566, 925.016, 658, 299, 583, 255!" (mid-19th century child prodigy, Barlow, 1952, p. 43).

"I was standing at the front of the room explaining how the earth revolves and how, because of its huge size it is difficult for us to realise that it is actually round. All of a sudden, Spencer blurted out, 'The earth isn't round.' I curtly replied, 'Ha, do you think it's flat?' He matter-of-factly said, 'No, it's a truncated sphere.' I quickly changed the subject. Spencer said the darndest things" (Payne, Kauffman, Brown, and DeMoff, 1974, p. 94).

Just as there are special problems in organising the best type of education for retarded and handicapped children, similar problems exist for the exceptionally talented children. Should these extremely bright children be accelerated and be permitted to begin school early, skip grades, and graduate ahead of their age-mates? These are controversial issues. Some argue that acceleration is necessary to maintain interest and motivation. Critics retort that the accelerated child's intellectual needs may be met at the expense of the child's social and emotional development Since the accelerated child is with older peers, he or she may be socially isolated. However, this is probably another "myth," since very bright children often seek out the company of older children and of adults. As Terman (1954), one of the earliest leaders in the study of the gifted child, noted, bright children are usually far ahead of their age-mates not just intellectually, but socially and physically as well.

Support for acceleration comes from a new programme at Johns Hopkins University, called "Study of Mathematically Precocious Youth." In the programme seventh and eighth graders with exceptional talent for mathematics are identified. These children are helped through a variety of special programmes to move ahead at an accelerated pace in mathematics. Other educational alternatives for gifted children include enrichment programmes, which avoid accelerating the child's grade level: These include extra work on the same level of difficulty, but more of it. One critic termed this form of enrichment "busywork" (Stanley, 1976).

A second type involves "irrelevant academic enrichment," which consists of setting up a special subject or activity meant to enrich the educational lives of some group of intellectually talented students. For example, a special class in science or social studies might be arranged as a supplement and diversion for the bored high-IQ students. Another form of enrichment is "cultural", which involves supplying aspects of the performing arts such as music, art, drama, dance, and creative writing or offering instruction in foreign language. Critics argue that these opportunities are often unrelated to the area of the child's talent and do not provide full opportunity for the development of these areas of unique talent. Although still controversial, the case for acceleration *versus* enrichment is gaining support.

THE TEACHER

By far the most important figures in the school are the teachers. In this section we will examine who they are, what they do, and what effects they have on their pupils' academic progress and social and emotional adjustment. As we will see in our later discussion of sex roles, teachers are usually female and tend to treat boys and girls differently in their classroom interactions. In this section, we focus on other aspects of the teacher's behaviour. Do teachers' early impressions of how smart a child is make a difference? The teacher plays variety of roles in the classroom as evaluator, disciplinarian, and social model. The way that she manages each of these roles can affect her pupils in a variety of ways. Even before teachers are acquainted with their pupils, teachers may have expectations that will affect the children's future academic performance.

Teacher Expectation and Academic Success

Although many teachers would probably deny it most of them form impressions early in the school year concerning the probable performance of the incoming group of students. These expectations come from a variety of sources, such as the pupil's past academic record, achievement test scores, family background, appearance, and classroom conduct history. Do these prejudgments of the child's performance have an impact on the child's actual scholastic success or failure? It is possible to investigate the impact of these naturally developed expectations on the child's performance by soliciting predictions from teachers early in the year and then determining how closely the child's output conforms to the teacher's prediction. A more powerful technique involves experimentally planting an expectation concerning certain children in a classroom and then assessing to what degree the expectations will be fulfilled. Rosenthal and Jacobsen of Harvard University (1966, 1968) have carried out such an experiment. In a number of elementary school classes, teachers were informed, that 20 per cent of their students were "intellectual bloomers who would show unusual intellectual gains during the academic year" (Rosenthal and Jacobsen, 1968, p. 66). The critical 20 per cent was, of course, randomly chosen. In order to assess the impact of teacher expectations, the children were administered an IQ test before the experiment commenced and again after eight months of additional classroom experience with the "expectant" teacher. Would the children labeled as academic bloomers show a larger improvement than nonlabeled control children in the same classroom? For the school as a whole, those children for whom the teachers had been led to expect greater intellectual gain showed a significantly greater increase in IQ scores than did the remaining students. However, the effect was most marked in the lower grade levels. In fact, the lower the grade level, the greater the effect.

But is the gain reflected in academic performance as well? To find out, the children's report cards were examined, and in one area, reading, there were marked effects. Children who were expected to do well were judged by their teachers to show greater advances in their reading ability. Again, the gains were most marked at the lower levels. Finally, classroom behaviour was affected, as indicated by the fact that the "experimental" pupils were rated as higher in "intellectual curiosity" than the control children.

To determine whether these advantages would persist when contact with the expectant teacher was terminated, Rosenthal and Jacobsen retested the children after two full academic years. Before this final retest the children had spent a year with a teacher who had not been given favourable expecations. Although the younger children had been easier to influence initially, they had lost their advantage by the final follow-up evaluation. However, after the delay the older children, that is, those in the third to sixth grades, who had shown smaller gains in the early stages still showed the effect of the original expectancy manipulation. As the authors suggest, continued contact with the expectant teacher seems to be necessary for maintaining the effect in younger children, while older pupils are better able to maintain their advantage autonomously.

However, Rosenthal and his self-fulfilling prophecy in the classroom has met with severe methodological criticism (Elashoff and Snow, 1971; Jensen, 1969; Thorndike. 1968). In spite of some failures to find a Pygmalion effect, there has been corroboration of the central finding by other investigators for Head Start children, retardates, and institutionalised adolescent female offenders. Nor is the expectancy effect restricted to academic learning situations; Burham and Hartsough (1968) have demonstrated the expectancy effect with swimming ability in a group of children at a summer camp.

How can we explain the Pygmalion effect? Rosenthal (1973) has proposed four factors that may account for the effect. First, people who are led to expect good performance from a pupil may create a warmer social-emotional *climate* for their special students; research has indicated that when teachers think they are dealing with a bright student, they are more friendly and supportive than when they view their students as less capable.

Another factor is *feedback* for the student's performance; how often does the teacher respond to the child by rewarding her right answer or correcting her errors. A study by Brophy and Good (1970) illustrates that this may be a factor in the expectancy effect. After teachers named their high and low achievers, these investigators recorded the amount of feedback provided these two types of pupils. The teachers ignored only 3 per cent of the high achiever's answers, but they ignored 15 per cent of the low achiever's responses. Students that teachers view as high achievers may do better, in part, because they get more feedback from their teachers.

A third factor is *input,* or the amount of teaching that children may receive. Beez (1968) led some teachers in a Head Start programme to expect poor performance from their "below-average" children while other teachers expected good performance from their "bright" children. Teachers taught the bright children more. For example, 87 per cent of the teachers of the bright children taught eight or more words, while only 13 per cent of the teachers of the below-average children tried to teach that number of words. As a result, the teacher expectations were confirmed: over 75 per cent of the bright children learned five or more words, while only 13 per cent of the dull children learned five words.

Expectancies of good performance may not only translate into more teacher input but may also lead teachers to demand more *output* from students as well (Rubovitz and Maehr; 1973). As Rosenthal notes, teachers "call on such students more often, ask them harder questions, give them more time to answer and prompt them toward the correct answer" (1973, p. 62). In summary, at least four factors may aid in explaining the Pygmalion effect: the climate of the classroom; differences in teacher feedback; teacher input; and opportunities for student output. The case is not closed, but these studies do raise an important question: "How much of the improvement in intellectual performance attributed to the contemporary educational programmes is due to the content and methods of the programmes and how much is due to the favourable expectancies of the teachers and administrators involved?" (Rosenthal and Jacobsen, 1966. p. 118).

Teacher as an Evaluator

The dominant impression of students is that schools are first and foremost places of evaluation, not of learning. Nowhere else in society is the individual scrutinised for so long a time or as intensely as he is in school. This scrutiny usually takes the form of constant testing and examination. (Covington and Berry, 1976) The way that teachers organise evaluation procedures makes an important difference to children's attitudes, motivation, and performance.

Some children are typically anxious in test-taking situations, while other children are relaxed in these evaluation settings. Every teacher has heard students say, "I really knew the material, but I was so uptight in the exam my mind went blank" or "I just can't take exams; I get so tense." Are these just glib student rationalisations or can test-taking anxiety seriously affect academic performance? High-anxious children do perform especially poorly on measures of academic skills, classroom learning, and verbal problem-solving ability, areas critical to a child's progress in school (Hill, 1972). However, these types of children are not less capable than their low-anxious peers, and it is the type of evaluation or test-taking setting that accounts, in part, for the poor performance of high-anxious children. To demonstrate the role of different types of evaluation procedures on children's performance, Hill and Eaton (1977) tested children's arithmetic performance under two conditions. In one case, time limits were imposed so that children could complete two-thirds of the problems they attempted, but failed to complete the remaining third. In an optimising condition, the time limit was removed, which minimised the failure experience and permitted the children to complete all the problems they attempted.

Under the time-pressure condition, the high-anxious fifth and sixth graders showed three times the errors, took twice as long on each problem, and cheated twice as often as low-anxious children. In contrast, in the optimising condition in which the time pressure was removed high-anxious children caught up, going just as fast and performing just as accurately as their low-anxious peers. Nor is this general pattern restricted to "time pressure"; a number of other optimising conditions have been identified that focus on the child's expectations for adult approval or disapproval based on performance.

In a study by Williams and Hill (1976), children performed under one of four conditions: (1) a standard condition involving typical test instructions, (2) a diagnostic condition in which the examiner indicated that the information gained from the test would be used to help teach the children, (3) an expectancy-reassurance condition in which the examiner indicated that the problems are difficult, most children miss quite a few of them, and the children shouldn't worry if they miss some of them, and (4) a normative condition in which the examiner indicated he was interested in knowing how children go about doing problems and so the children shouldn't even put their names on the test booklets. Together these studies suggest that the performance deficits of the high-anxious children ... were due to motivational and test-taking factors and not to learning deficits, since the deficits were removed by simply modifying the testing conditions" (Hill, 1978, p. 6). Evaluation is not going to disappear from the school scene, but it is clear that closer attention to the way in which evaluation is provided can help rather than hinder children's progress.

Teacher as a Disciplinarian

Teachers not only are evaluators, but spend a good deal of their time as disciplinarians. How effective are different teacher-control techniques for achieving and maintaining classroom order, and what effect do teacher tactics have on children's motivation? Although it might be predicted intuitively that praise more effective than disapproval, a systematic analysis of the use of praise is necessary before any conclusions concerning its effectiveness can be drawn legitimately. Other questions require consideration as well. How important are classmates in achieving classroom control? Can the power of the peer group be effectively harnessed by the teacher to achieve more effective discipline?

Operant Reinforcement in the Classroom

Recent attempts to apply operant reinforcement principles to classroom control have been very successful (O'Leary and O'Leary, 1977). In some cases, social reinforcement in the form of verbal approval is used whereby teachers are taught to praise appropriate behaviour and ignore disruptive behaviour. However, in some cases ignoring disruptive behaviour and praising appropriate responses is not - powerful enough to establish control. This may be particularly likely in a classroom where a few individual children continue to be disruptive under a praise-and-ignore regime. When other children observe their peers behaving disruptively without any negative consequence, they may become disruptive themselves.

Under the modern version of these programmes children accumulate points or tokens for good behaviour, which they can then exchange for material rewards such as candy. peanuts, comics, or toys. Numerous studies have demonstrated the effectiveness of this approach for controlling children in classrooms (O'Leary and O'Leary. 1977). But token economies may not always be necessary, and, in fact, may undermine children's interest in their school activity—under some circumstances.

As the study in Box 14-2 illustrates, activities that are intrinsically interesting may lose their appeal if rewards are provided. While this study implies that token economies should be introduced in classrooms only when necessary and not as a routine practice, there are many classroom activities, such as learning multiplication tables, that may be unappealing. In such cases, tokens or extrinsic rewards can often increase children's interest in these classroom activities (Feingold and Mahoney, 1975). Token economies have a place in the classroom, but care needs to be exercised in choosing the target activities. Teachers are not the only control agents; peers can often achieve classroom control as well (McGee, Kauffman and Nussen, 1977). Two experimental studies will illustrate this point.

In one study (Barrish, Sanders, and Wolf,- 1969) a fourth-grade class was divided into two teams and any misbehaviour (for example, talking in class or leaving your seat without permission) by any team member resulted in a loss of privileges for the whole team. The privileges were events which are available in almost every classroom, such as extra recess, first to line up for lunch, time for special projects, stars, and of course the fun of winning the contest. These investigators found that individual contingencies resulting in group consequences were very effective in reducing disruptive classrooms. However, the effect was present only in the class period (math) where the peer game was in effect; there was little generalisation to other periods (for example, reading). Only when the game was introduced in the reading class did a, drop in disruptive behaviour occur. This suggests that 'generalisation' is no magical process, but rather a behavioural change which must be engineered like any other change [O'Leary et al., 1969, p. 13]. A related study by Schmidt and Ulrich (1969) indicated that team competition may not be necessary. These investigators were able to lower the level of classroom noise by making any individual violation of a previously specified noise ceiling result in loss of prlvileges (extra time in gym period) not just for the individual but for the whole class.

This procedure seemed to work just as well as the competition procedure used by Barrish and his colleagues and avoided some of the undesirable consequences that between-group competition may produce, such as increased intergroup hostility (Sherif and Sherif, 1953). As Bronfenbrenner notes in his recent *Two Worlds of Childhood: US.* and *U.S.S.R.* (1970), the technique of peer control is used regularly in Russian school classrooms.

Turning the Tables: Student, Control of Teacher Behaviour

Student control is not limited to their classmates; students can control their teachers as well. By applying the same operant principles that teachers have successfully used to control their pupils, children have been taught to modify their teachers' behaviour. In one California classroom, a group of 12- to 1 5-year-olds were taught to reward positive teacher behaviour by smiling, making eye contact, and sitting up straight (Gray, Craubard, and Rosenberg. 1974). At the same time they were taught to discourage negative teacher behaviour with statements like "It's hard for me to do good work when you're cross with me." The results were striking: Over a five-week intervention period, there was a fourfold increase in the rate of positive teacher behaviour, while negative teacher behaviour was completely eliminated by the end of the intervention period. When these student behaviour engineers were instructed to discontinue reinforcing their teachers, the rate of positive teacher behaviour dropped.

Other studies (Bates, 1975; Berberich, 1971) confirm these findings and underline the influential role that students can play in modifying teacher behaviour. The same bidirectional principle that characterises parent-child interaction clearly applies to teacher-student interchanges as well.

Self-monitoring: Power to the Pupil

Teachers and peers are not the only source of pupil control; children can exercise self-control. One of the most promising techniques for improving children's classroom conduct, concentration, and achievement is *self-monitoring.* Self-monitoring is a system by which students are taught to keep track of their own classroom behaviour on a daily basis. Here is how it worked in one fifth—and sixth-grade classroom with an individualised mathematics instruction programme (Sagotsky, Patterson, and Lepper, 1977). Children could proceed at their own speed in this programme. Some of the students received self-monitoring instructions.

Peer-Teacher Approach

Not only can peers aid in controlling their classmates, but they can function as peer-teachers as well. Older children are cast in the role of assistant teachers and given responsibility for teaching younger children. Although the details of different programmes vary most involve some kind of instruction session for the "helpers" in which they learn the techniques of relating to and teaching younger children. In addition, to coordinate the tutoring programme with the younger child's regular classroom experience, assistants often meet with the teacher of the child that they are aiding. The results are encouraging and indicate that both tutor and pupil benefit in a variety of ways (Allen, 1976; Sheehan, Feldman, and Allen, 1976).

First, both partidpants showed greater academic progress in the tutorial subject. Cloward (1967) found significant changes in reading achievement over a five-month period: not only did the tutored pupils show a gain of 6.2 months in reading level in contrast to a gain of only 3.5 months for nontutored control children, but the tutors gained as well. In fact, over a seven-month period the tutors improved an average of nineteen months in reading level.

More recently, Allen and Feldman (1973) found that the experience of being a tutor can benefit low-achieving children. Children who are low achievers often have a record of failure and tend to be passive participants in any learning exchange. Motivation and involvement will increase in the tutoring situation, and so these investigators argued that low achievers would learn better when placed in the role of peer-teacher than when studying alone. Ten low-achieving fifth graders whose reading scores were at least one year below average grade level served as tutors; ten third graders were the tutees or learners. Subjects participated for ten consecutive weekdays for a two-week period: for every alternate day the fifth-grade tutor either taught a third grader for twenty minutes or studied the material alone. By the end of the two-week period, tutoring resulted in significantly better performance than studying alone for the low- achieving fifth-grade children. These gains were made in spite of the fact that the third graders learned equally with the tutor or studying alone. The tutoring effect in this case had more impact on the tutors than the tutees. While follow-up studies are necessary to determine the stability of these gains, these results point clearly to the effectiveness of the peer-teacher programme.

Moreover, other benefits have been reported. Lippitt and Lippitt, for example, summarised some of these additional effects, teachers of younger children who receive help say that their youngsters show increased self-respect, self-confidence, and pride in their progress. They are less tense, can express themselves more clearly, are better groomed, and have improved attendance records.

As for the older students, working with their juniors provides valuable learning experiences in addition to giving them a chance to be appreciated by teachers and younger students. They learn how to help someone else learn. They learn to relate to a younger child. They get a chance to work through, at a safe emotional distance, some of the problems they have in relation to their own peers or younger siblings. Ordinarily, older children might not be interested in the social skills involved in getting along with people, but they are highly motivated to learn them when learning those skills enables them to do a better job of helping the younger children. Academically, too, older students benefit from being crossage helpers. Children who might have had no interest in reviewing subject matter which they did not understand when they were in the lower grades make a tremendous effort to fill the gaps when they are responsible for helping someone else understand. (1968, p. 4)

Although other investigators have reported similar effects (Allen, 1976; Deering, 1968; Kuppel, 1964), systematic research is required to determine the critical factors that account for the effectiveness of these programmes. Children can clearly serve as effective helpers for their classmates and for younger pupils and may, in the process, help themselves.

Teacher as a Social Model

Just as parents and peers serve as models for the developing child, recent evidence suggests that young children imitate their teachers as well. However, not all teachers are likely to be imitated, nor are all children equally likely to copy their teacher's actions. In a recent study Portuges and Feshbach (1971) have isolated some of the teacher and observer characteristics that affect the degree of teacher imitation. Groups of 8- to 10-year-old boys and girls were shown movies of a female teacher presenting a geography lesson, using either a rewarding or critical teaching style. The "positive" teacher responded approvingly to correct answers, while the negative model rebuked the pupils in the film for their errors. In addition, the models exhibited different distinctive incidental movements, such as cupping the ear or clasping the hands. To assess the extent to which the children would imitate the teacher-model's distinctive mannerisms, the children were required to "teach a geography lesson" to two life-sized dolls. The rewarding teacher was imitated more than the negative instructor. The use of a positive approach, then, apparently enhances teacher influence by making it more likely that the pupils will imitate the teacher's behaviour. However, the strength of the effect varied with the sex and social class of the observing child. Girls imitated the female teacher-model more than the boys did; girls probably view the role of teacher as more sex-appropriate than do boys. Moreover, middle-class children imitated more of the teacher's gestures than did lower- class observers. It was the middle-class girls who imitated the model to the greatest degree, while lower-class boys were the least influenced by the teacher-model. The implications of this social class difference will be explored in detail in a later section. Other studies suggest that the children may imitate their teacher's typical problem-solving style. As we saw earlier in our discussion of cognitive style, impulsive children exposed to reflective teachers become more reflective in their problem-solving strategies (Yando and Kagan, 1968). Teachers as well as parents and peers serve as influential models for children. We have examined teachers and tactics; now we turn to an evaluation of texts.

SOCIAL CLASS, RACE, AND THE SCHOOL

It has been estimated that the school has a cumulative effect on the lower-class child such that "by the third grade he is approximately one year behind academically, by the sixth grade two years behind, by grade eight two and one half to three years retarded academically and by the ninth grade a top candidate for dropping out" (Rioux. 1968, p. 92). For the middle-class child the picture is very different: rather than dropping out, he is much more likely to go to college than his lower-class peer (DeLury, 1974).

Why the social-class difference? Many answers have been offered, Recall our earlier discussions of the cognitive and linguistic differences between lower- and middle-class children. At that time, it was noted that those differences are present and detectable before the child ever reaches the schoolroom. So it may not be entirely the school's fault; children of lower-class backgrounds are simply not as well prepared to fit Into the middle-class culture of the classroom. But it is the aim of education presumably to teach children regardless of their background.

Children of lower-class backgrounds are not the only ones who have special difficulty with the school system. Children of different racial and ethnic backgrounds often fail to achieve their full potential in our schools. In this section, we examine the roles that parent and teacher attitudes and expectations play in the academic performance of children of different racial and ethnic backgrounds.

Finally, we will critically evaluate one solution to the problem of poor progress in school among minority group children—desegregation.

Middle-Class Bias of the School

First of all, the fact that the school is a middle-class institution, espousing middle-class values and staffed by middle-class teachers, puts the child from a lower-class background at a disadvantage from the outset.

> The lower class child experiences the middle class oriented school as discontinuous with his home environment and further, comes to it unprepared in the basic skills on which the curriculum is founded. The school becomes a place which makes puzzling demands and where failure is frequent and feelings of competence are subsequently not generated. Motivation decreases and the school loses its effectiveness.. . . (Deutsch, 1964, p. 255)

In contrast, for the middle-class child,

> The school is very central and is contiguous with the totality of his life experiences. As a result there are few incongrituties between his school experiences and any others he is likely to have had and there are intrinsic motivating and molding properties in the school situation to which he has been sensitised. . . . faculty orientation with his family orientation. (Deutsch, 1964, p. 255)

> Simply by virtue of their class membership, middle-class children have an advantage over their lower-class peers.

Parent Attitudes Toward the School

Part of the reason for this feeling of discontinuity stems from the different orientation to the school system that middle- and lower-class parents provide their children. There are clear social class differences in the manner that children are introduced to the school. Hess and Shipman (1967) studied this problem by asking black middle- and lower-class mothers to indicate "what she would tell her child on the first day of school before he left the house" (p. 69). It was assumed that the answer to this inquiry would tap the parental attitude toward the school. The lower-class mothers tended to give their children unqualified commands concerning how to behave in school. Little or no rationale for their directives were provided: "sit down," "don't holler," and "mind the teacher" were typical of the answers. On the other hand, the middle-class mothers tended to use a more cognitive, rational orientation which provided the child with some explanation for the rules that the school would impose on the children's behaviour. For example, a middle-class mother might instruct her child: "You shouldn't talk in school because the teacher can't teach so well and you won't learn your lessons properly." Consider the implications of these different orientations for the child in the classroom. The child who is given the imperative orientation is likely to view the school as a rigid authoritarian institution governed by inflexible and unexplained rules and regulations. This attitude may lead to overzealous acceptance of absolute answers and less likelihood of inquiry, curiosity, and debate. The child's interest and involvement would probably be low. In contrast, the child given the rational, cognitive orientation will be more likely to expect that answers should have reasons underlying them. A spirit of inquiry is kindled in the middle-class child which probably delights the teacher and, in turn, aids the child's progress. In fact, if these motivational and attitudinal consequences are true, one would expect performance differences between the two groups. Hess and Shipman found a clear relationship between the mother's orientation and the child's mental performance; the use of an imperative approach was associated with low performance in several areas, including lower IQ scores among children of imperative mothers.

Moreover, the differences are not simply in the initial orientations but also in the amount and quality of home support for academic achievement. A number of studies have indicated that the child's perception of parental support and interest in his or her academic progress is significantly related to the child's actual school performance and the child's attitude toward school (Crandall, 1972). Class differences are clear: there is more likely to be support from middle-class: parents than from lower-class parents for scholastic achievement and success (Katz, 1967).

Many lower-class parents are involved and interested in their children's school work. It has been found that when lower-class parents are more knowledgeable about the school system and have higher levels of aspiration for their children, it is associated with the achievement of good grades for their children (Greenberg and Davidson, 1972). Parental involvement can make a difference.

Lower-class parents not only are less likely to provide encouragement, but are often less able to help the child in school tasks. Often their own education is limited, and as the child moves to higher grades, the parents are increasingly unable to assist their children or even appreciate the usefulness and relevance of the school's demands. Incidentally, the frustration experienced by many middle-class parents in trying to comprehend the "new math," for example, suggests that this problem is not restricted to lower-class parents. With increasing specialisation and curriculum innovation it may be necessary to teach the parents as well.

Problem of Appropriate Models

There are other problems encountered by lower-class

children which tend to lessen their chances for scholastic success While the middle-class children can adopt their parents as models of scholastic achievement, the lower-class children must look elsewhere. Their parents are simply inappropriate models from which to learn the attitudes and values necessary for school success. The teacher, of course, provides an alternative model and if the child could identify with and emulate the actions and attitudes of the middle-class teacher, chances of succeeding in the school system would increase. However, as Portuges and Feshbach (1972) found in their study of social class differences in teacher imitation, middle-class white children imitated the teacher more than did the lower-class black children. This is consistent with other evidence that middle-class children are more likely to aspire to the teaching profession than are lower-class children Whether or not these black students were rejecting the teaching role or merely the *white* teacher is left unanswered. One might expect that more black teachers with whom the disadvantaged black pupils could more readily identify would result in a more positive attitude toward school among black students. If the child does adopt the teacher as the primary model, this may emphasise further the discontinuity between the child's home life and the school.

Social Class and Racial Differences in Teacher Attitudes

How much of the blame should the teacher assume for the failures of the lower-class child? The teacher, of course, has been a favourite target; a number of investigators have blamed the white middle-class teacher's lack of appreciation of the problems of the disadvantaged as a primary cause of the lower class child's scholastic plight. An angry and outspoken advocate of this view is Clark The clash of cultures in the classroom is essentially a class war, a socioeconomic and racial warfare being waged on the battleground of our schools with middle-class and middle-class aspiring teachers provided with a powerful arsenal of half-truths, prejudices and rationalisations arrayed against hopelessly outclassed working class youngsters. (Clark, 1965, p. 129) Support for the claim that teachers fail to understand and appreciate the differences in background, experience, and values of lower-class children comes from a study by Groff (1963). In his search for the reasons for dissatisfactions in teaching the culturally disadvantaged child, he found that 40 per cent of the 294 teachers interviewed cited the "peculiarities" in the personalities of the children as the major cause of dissatisfaction.

There is little doubt that this is due to the middle-class outlook of the teachers. In an investigation by Gottlieb (1964), the attitudes of white middle-class teachers and black teachers with lower-class origins were compared. When asked to indicate the factors that contributed to job dissatisfaction, the white teachers cited "clientele" factors, such as lack of parental interest and student behaviour or discipline problems. In contrast, the black teachers tended to see such factors as lack of proper equipment and overcrowded conditions—rather than the students—as their major sources of discontent. Teacher race and background were related to their perceptions of their students as well. When asked to check those adjectives which came closest to describing the outstanding characteristics of their children, white teachers most frequently selected "talkative," "lazy," "fun-loving," "high-strung," and "rebellious" to describe their lower-class pupils. Black teachers, however, saw their pupils in a much more positive light and checked such adjectives as "happy," "cooperative," "fun- loving," "energetic," and "ambitious." It would appear that the

Negro teachers are less critical and less pessimistic in their evaluations of these students than the white teachers, probably because many of them have themselves come from backgrounds similar to that of their students and yet have managed to overcome social barriers and status. (Gottlieb, 1964, p. 353)

It is not just the failure to appreciate differences in customs, values, and background that leads to the lower-class or black child's lack of success. It has been proposed that biases of teachers may lead to these children being assigned lower grades than their middle-class or white peers. The correlation, however, between teachers' grades and a child's scores on standardised achievement tests, over which the teacher had no control, does not differ for black and white children (McCandless, Roberts, and Starnes, 1972). There is little evidence of bias in grading against black students. In fact, if anything, the reverse situation occurs. That is, while achievement scores of white children are higher than black children, their grades are not. Of course this study is not definitive in ruling out bias; it simply shows that it is not evident in grading practices. But discrimination comes in many forms. The finding that the black and white children's grades are similar in spite of achievement differences may suggest another kind of bias, unrealistic feedback. Do black children receive dear and realistic information about their performance, or do teachers give the black children good grades in spite of their performance? If so, this could seriously interfere with the children's progress toward mastering school tasks.

A recent large study in urban high schools by Massey, Scott, and Dornbusch (1975) is relevant. Black and Spanish-surname students, in comparison with Asian and "other white" groups, received lower grades and scored lower on math and verbal achievement tests, but these low-achieving black and Spanish students maintained generally *positive* conceptions of their skills in these academic subjects. What accounts for this discrepancy between academic self-concept and their actual performance? Half of these low-achieving black and Chicano students believed that they would not usually receive poor grades for inadequate work or low effort. Moreover, the low achievers, even more than their higher-achieving white or Asian classmates, viewed their teachers as warm, friendly, and dispensing more frequent praise. The authors summarise the implications of their findings as follows—The academic Standards and evaluation system found in the schools did affect the students' assessment of their effort and achievement. Low achievers, especially black students, were allowed to delude themselves into thinking they were doing well.... (Massey Scott, and Dornbusch, 1975)

This is a pattern of institutional racism that Perpetuates inequality. The aim of evaluation is to provide children, regardless of their social class or race, with accurate feedback, so that they can, in turn, set realistic goals. All children can achieve, but only by providing guides concerning their strengths and weaknesses can they reach their full potential.

Implications for the Lower-Class Child

What are the implications of middle class teachers' frequent failure to understand the lower-class child? Often resentment, dissatisfaction, aid a sense of bewilderment characterise the middle-class teacher in ghetto schools. Attempts to teach are often abandoned in favour of primitive control tactics. In fact, Deutsch (1960) has estimated that lower-class children receive one-third less actual teaching than their middle-class peers. The teacher spends almost 80 per cent of the school day disciplining students or engaging in non-educational duties, such as collecting milk money. The teacher then becomes redefined as a disciplinarian, and since the teacher spends less time in educating students, they learn less, become increasingly bored, and become even more disruptive. The result is a vicious circle: a tougher control policy and even less teaching.

The upshot is that many teachers tend to regard being assigned to teach in lower-class schools not as a challenge but simply as a less desirable, less prestigious placement. For many it is merely a necessary first step to a "better" job; the aim is not to learn to adjust to the situation but to apply for transfers as soon as the system's regulations permit. This may contribute to the fact that one out of every two children from the bottom rung in society will drop out before completing high school (Cervantes, 1965).

Clearly any programme aimed at improving the academic progress of lower- class children should not be restricted to content and curriculum innovations. Drastic alterations in teacher preparation and teacher attitudes are necessary. This education should include an extensive exposure to lower-class life and lower-class values. Once teachers decide that lower-class pupils can learn, maybe they will learn. One lesson that Head Start has taught us is that children of all backgrounds can learn. Next we turn to the final topic: desegregation, and examine whether this is a route to achievement of educational equality.

SCHOOL DESEGREGATION

Few topics have generated as much public concern in the last two decades as the desegregation of American schools. In 1954, the United States Supreme Court mandated an end to segregated education in a classic case entitled *Brown V. Board of Education.* Desegregation was expected to correct these ills, and recently there has been an evaluation of how successful desegregation efforts have been in achieving these goals. Here are the main expectations that emerged from the 1954 decision:

1. For whites, desegregation will lead to more positive attitudes toward blacks.
2. For blacks, desegregation will lead to more positive attitudes toward whites.
3. For blacks, desegregation will lead to increases in self-esteem.
4. For blacks, desegregation will lead to increases in achievement. (Stephan. 1978, p. 221)

How accurate were these early predictions?

First, are whites and blacks less prejudiced toward each other after going to school together? The evidence is mixed. Some studies (Singer. 1967) find that black and white children in *naturally* integrated schools are more accepting of each other than in segregated schools. Other investigations indicate that blacks and whites had more negative attitudes toward the other group in integrated schools—particularly if integration is forced rather than voluntary (St. John, 1975). The manner in which integration is reached makes a difference as well. Linney (1978) compared black children who were bused to achieve desegregation with those black children who remained in the same school and achieved integration by the addition of white students to their school. After desegregation, the black children who were bused were rated as more aggressive and less prosocial by both their new peers and teachers, while the nonbused black children were not viewed differently following integration.

Modifying racial attitudes is complex, and merely placing

black and white children in the same school does not mean that they will necessarily interact with each other. In their extensive four-year longitudinal study of the effects of desegregation in River- side, California, Gerard and Miller (1975) conclude that the "data we have examined point unmistakably to the conclusion that with the exception of playground interaction, little or no real integration occurred during the relatively long-term contact situation represented by Riverside's desegregation programme. If anything we found some evidence that ethnic cleavages became somewhat more pronounced over time" (p. 243). In recent years the rise of ethnic pride has meant that spontaneous cross-race mixing is less likely, and integration may foster this type of in-group orientation. To illustrate, black children in one city who were bused to achieve integration increased in black separatist ideology more than did nontransferred siblings (Armor, 1972). How is self-esteem affected? Again, the findings are mixed and inconclusive. Some report increased self-esteem among black students, while others report either no effect or decreases in self-esteem, especially in academic self-concept (St. John, 1975). One difficulty with this area is the underlying assumption that the black child has low self-esteem and that desegregation will improve the black child's self-image.

However, the assumption of the black child's low self-image has been challenged by several studies (Rosenberg and Simons, 1972. Soares and Soares, 1969), which have shown that black children's self-image is at least as positive as that of white students. Even when a gain in self-esteem is clear, the factors which account for this change are uncertain. Possibly such changes are "a by-product of improved achievement, increased attention by faculty to black educational needs, a greater sense of black unity, or still other factors" (Evans and McCandless, 1978, p. 485). There is more support for the final prediction concerning increases in the achievement of black students in integrated schools. In only 3 per cent of the studies does desegregation lead to a decrease in achievement, while in 29 per cent of the studies, an increase occurs (Stephan, 1978). This means that in 68 per cent of the studies, the achievement of black children was unaffected by integration.

Moreover, even when there are changes, not all academic areas are equally affected: Increases in mathematical skills are reported more often than gains in verbal or reading skills (St. John, 1975; Weinberg. 1975). The most consistent effects concern the age of the child at the time of integration. In general the earlier the desegregation occurs, the more beneficial it is for students in terms of achievement-test performance. In one careful study, groups of black city children in kindergarten through the fifth grade were randomly chosen to be bused to suburban white schools (Mahan and Mahan, 1970). After two years the children transferred in kindergarten through the third grade gained significantly more than the nontransferred students on both intelligence and achievement measures. For those transferred in the fourth and fifth grades the gains favour the nontransferred control group on both measures. In spite of modest gains, the achievement gap between black and white children remains after integration (Gerard and Miller, 1975; Linney, 1978; St. John, 1975).

Finally, black children may sometimes pay a hidden price for shifting to integrated schools. These children may suffer a loss of academic status as a result of losing their place at the top of the class, in terms of performance, by being shifted to a class where white children more often occupy the top achievement slots (Linney. 1978). Combined with the fact that black children who are transferred to white schools are often less well accepted by their new peers and teachers has led one investigator to argue that "desegregation may be more detrimental to their academic and psychological development than the segregated situation" (Linney, 1978, p. 163). Unraveling the complexities of desegregation is far from finished. Understanding desegregation will require investigation of a multitude of factors including busing, voluntary and mandatory integration, attitudes and values of teachers and families, and ethnic ratios. By considering these issues we may begin to ask not whether desegregation works, but under what conditions can it work.

Conclusion

The school is an extremely influential, although often neglected, socialising force. In this chapter several factors that affect the kind and extent of the school's influence were examined. First, the physical structure of the school environment came under scrutiny. School sise, for example, determines the extent of involvement in extracurricular activities; children at small high schools are not only more likely to participate but also more likely to occupy positions of prestige and importance. One result is that there are few potential dropouts in small schools. Next, the impact of the size, shape, and seating arrangements of the classroom was examined. Both class size and the pupil's location in the class determine the extent to which he or she participates in classroom activities. While participation is higher in smaller classrooms, the child located in the front and center of the class, the action zone, participates more than children seated in other parts of the room. In examining the effects of different classroom organisations it was found that students generally prefer a group-centered or open classroom in which they are allowed some opportunity to participate in the decision making. While conventional achievement does not appear to be affected, imaginative play and novelty of answers increase.

However, this is still an unresolved issue, and in the final analysis, any conclusion about the advantages of a traditional, authoritarian regime over more pupil-oriented arrangements must take into account the kind of pupils involved. Different personalities apparently function better under different types of classroom organisational arrangements. Teachers play a variety of roles, namely evaluators, disciplinarians, and models. Teachers' early impressions and expectations concerning a pupil's probable success can affect the child's academic progress.

A self-fulfilling prophecy is evident: children succeed when teachers believe they will do well, while pupils are likely to perform poorly when instructors expect them to fail. The types of evaluation conditions that teachers arrange can affect student performance, and anxious children may improve their performance under optimal test-taking conditions. Recent applications of behaviour modification techniques for controlling children's classroom behaviour were examined and found to be successful. This is particularly true when these programmes have used material or token reinforcers for shaping appropriate behaviour. Caution in the use of external rewards is necessary, since children's intrinsic interest in school activities, under some conditions, may be undermined by external reinforcers.

Finally, the teacher may influence students by serving as a social model. Evidence was presented indicating that a rewarding teacher tends to be imitated more than a negative instructor tends to be. Again, the sex and social class of the child observers must be considered. Middle-class girls, for example, tend to imitate a teacher-model to the greatest extent, while lower-class boys are influenced relatively little by a teacher-model. The impact of the teacher as model is not restricted to reinforcing style; the typical problem-solving style of the teacher is often imitated by students as well. One promising technique in classroom organisations is the peer-teacher approach, where older children are cast in the role of assistant teachers and given responsibility for teaching younger peers. Evaluations indicate that both the tutor and the child who is assisted benefit from this arrangement. After this discussion of teachers and their tactics, primary school textbooks were examined. Texts are important vehicles for learning and reinforcing attitudes and social values.

Unfortunately, most current primers are grossly inadequate,' rather than presenting a realistic picture of American culture, the typical text offers a Pollyannaish substitute. This is not merely an adult evaluation: children's library choices indicate that children themselves prefer very different kinds of books than those usually available as primary readers. Tentative evidence indicated that children provided with more reality-oriented interesting readers scored higher on a variety of reading and language measures. Although texts are changing, many of the white, middle-class, suburban biases still persist in more recent "new look" primers.

Special children, such as the retarded, often require special treatment. The controversy over mainstreaming, which involves placing children of varying abilities in regular classrooms rather than segregating low-ability children in special classes, was discussed. Next, another special group, gifted children, was considered, and recent evidence favouring academic acceleration was presented: The impact of the schools on the academic progress of the lower-class child was examined. A number of factors militate against the success of the lower-class child. In this chapter, some of the reasons underlying the school's inability to effectively educate lower-class children were presented. The incongruity between the attitudes and motivations of the lower-class child and the middle-class school was seen as an important factor. The school is a strange and often hostile environment for lower-class children. Even if they do succeed, they are unlikely to receive either parental support or peer acceptance for their accomplishments.

Some have blamed the teachers for their failure to appreciate the differences in background, experience, and values of the disadvantaged pupil. In fact, comparisons of middle-class white and lower-class black instructors suggests that this charge has validity, teachers from lower-class origins were more accepting and less pessimistic in their evaluations of their lower-class charges than were middle-class teachers. Clearly, any programme aimed at solving the problems of the lower-class child's chronic academic failure must include alterations in teacher preparation. Curriculum and content changes are not enough; teacher attitudes toward children must change as well.

REFERENCES

Allen, V.L., and Feldman, R. S. Learning through tutoring: Low achieving children as tutors. *Journal of Educational Psychology,* 1973, 42, 1-5.

Barker, R.G., and Gump, P.V. *Big school, small school,* Stanford, Calif.: Stanford University Press, 1964.

Bates, J.E. Effects of a child's imitation versus non-imitation on adults verbal and nonverbal positivity. *Journal of Personality and Social Psychology,* 1975, 31, 840-51.

Brenton, M. Mainstreaming the handicapped. *Today's Education,* 1974, 63, 20-25.

Cervantes, L.F. Family background, primary relationships and the high school dropout. *Journal of Marriage and the Family,* 1965, 5, 218-223.

Glick, J. Cognitive development in cross-cultural perspective. In F.D.

Horowitz (Ed.), *Review of child development research* (Vol. 4). Chicago: University of Chicago Press, 1975.

Hess, R., and Shipman, V. Cognitive elements in maternal behaviour. In J. Hill (Ed.).

Lewin, L., Lippitt, R., and White, R.K. Patterns of aggressive behaviour in experimentally created 'social climates.' *Journal of Social Psychology*. 1939, 10, 271-299.

McCandless, B.R., Roberts, A., and Starnes, T. Teachers' marks, achievement test scores and aptitude relations with respect to social class, race and sex. *Journal of Educational Psychology*. 1972,63, 153-159.

Sheehan, L., Feldman, R.S., and Allen, V.L. Research on children tutoring children: A critical review. *Review of Educational Research*, 1976,46, 355-385.

Sherif, M., and Sherif, C.W. *Groups in harmony and tension. An integration of studies on intergroup relations*. New York: Harper and Row, 29-53.

Walberg, H.J., and Rasher, S.P. The ways schooling makes a difference. *Phi Delta Kappa*, 1977, 58, 703-707.

Weinberg, M. The relationship between school desegregation and academic achievement: A review of the research. *Law and Contemporary Problems*, 1975, 39, 241-270.

Yando, R.M., and Kagan, J. The effect of teacher tempo on the child. *Child Development*, 1968, 39, 27-34.

Bibliography

Atwood, G. and Stolorow R. (1984). *Structures of Subjectivity*. Hillsdale, NJ: The Analytic Press.

Barker, R.G., and Gump, P.V. (1964). *Big school, small school,* Stanford, Calif.: Stanford University Press.

Bartlett, Harriett M. (1957). *Fifty Years of Social Work in a Medical Setting*. New York: National Association of Social Workers.

Basch, M.F. (1976). The concept of affect: A re-examination. *Journal of the American Psychoanalytic Association*, 24:759-777.

Basch, M.F. (1980). *Doing Psychotherapy*. New York: Basic Books, Inc.

Basch, M.F. (1989). *Understanding Psychotherapy*. New York: Basic Books.

Beebe, B. & Lachmann, F.M. (1988). Mother-infant mutual influence and precursors of psychic structure. In *Progress in Self Psychology*, vol. III, ed. A. Goldberg. New York: Guilford Press (pp. 3-25).

Bibring, E. (1941). The development and problems of the theory of instincts. *International Journal of Psychoanalysis*, 21:

Bowlby, J. (1969). *Attachment and loss, Vol. I: Attachment*. New York: Basic Books.

Bracht, Neil F. (1978). *Social Work in Health Care: A Guide to Professional Practice.* New York: The Haworth Press.

Brandschaft, B. (1983). The negativism of the negative

therapeutic reaction and the psychology of the self. In *The Future of Psychoanalysis* (Ed.) A. Goldberg. (pp. 327-359). New York: International Universities Press, Inc.

Breuer, J. and Freud, S. (1893-95). Studies on hysteria. *Standard Edition*, 2:3-305. London: Hogarth Press, 1955.

Coburn, W.J. (1998). Patient unconscious communication and analyst narcissistic vulnerability in the countertransference experience. In *Progress in Self Psychology* (Ed.) A. Goldberg, Vol. 14, 1998.

Coburn, W.J. (2000). The organising forces of contemporary psychoanalysis: Reflections on nonlinear dynamic systems theory. *Psychoanalytic Psychology*, Vol. 17, No. 3.

Coburn, W.J. (2001). Subjectivity, emotional resonance and the sense of the real. *Psychoanalytic Psychology*, Vol. 18, No. 2.

Fosshage, J. (1983). The psychological function of dreams: A revised psychoanalytic perspective. *Psychoanalysis and Contemporary Thought*, 6:641-669.

Fosshage, J. (1987). New vistas on dream interpretation. In M. Glucksman (Ed.), *Dreams in new perspective: The royal road revisited*. New York: Human Sciences Press.

Fosshage, J. (1992). Discussion on Morrison's Paper "On Shame". *Psychoanalytic Dialogues*. Vol. 4, l: 37-44, (1994).

Fosshage, J. (1992). Self psychology: The self and its vicissitudes within a relational matrix. In N. Skolnick and S. Warshaw (Eds.), *Relational perspectives* (pp. 21-42). Hillsdale, NJ: Analytic Press.

Fosshage, J. (1994). Toward reconceptualising transference: Theoretical and clinical considerations. *International Journal of Psycho-Analysis*, 75, 2: 265-280.

Fosshage, J. (1997). 'Compensatory' or 'primary': An alternative view: Discussion of Marian Tolpin's Compensatory structures: Paths to the restoration of the self. In A. Goldberg (Ed.), *Progress in self psychology* (pp. 21-27), Vol. 13. Hillsdale, NJ: The Analytic Press.

Fosshage, J. (1997). Listening/experiencing perspectives and the quest for a facilitative responsiveness. In A. Goldberg (Ed.), *Progress in self psychology* (pp. 33-55), Vol. 13. Hillsdale, NJ: The Analytic Press.

Fosshage, J. (1998). Discussion of Anna Ornstein's, "The fate of narcissistic rage in psychotherapy." *Psychoanalytic Inquiry*, Vol. 1, 1: 71-81.

Fosshage, J. (1998). On aggression: Its forms and functions. *Psychoanalytic Inquiry*. Vol. 18, 1: 45-54.

Fosshage, J. and Loew, C. (1987). *Dream interpretation: A comparative study: Revised edition*. Costa Mesa, CA: PMA Publications. (Also translated into Japanese and published in Japan).

Freud, S. (1900). The interpretation of dreams. *Standard Edition*, 4 & 5. London: Hogarth Press, 1953.

Freud, S. (1905). Three essays on the Theory of Sexuality. *Standard Edition*, 7. London: Hogarth Press, 1953.

Freud, S. (1926). Inhibitions, symptoms and anxiety. *Standard Edition*, 20:87-179. London, Hogarth Press, 1959

Freud, S. (1933). New introductory lectures on psychoanalysis. *Standard Edition*, 22:5-182. London: Hogarth Press, 1964.

Gunderson, J.G. (1984). *Borderline personality disorder*. Washington, DC: American Psychiatric Press.

Gunderson, J.G. (1989). Borderline personality disorder. In H. I. Kaplan and B. J. Sadock (Eds.), *Comprehensive textbook of psychiatry I V.* Baltimore, MD: Williams & Wilkins.

Kadushin, A. (1976). *Supervision in Social Work.* New York: Columbia University Press.

Kindler, J. (1995). Helping the Helpers: Mental Health Professional on Site of Disasters. *Disaster Response News.* Washington, DC: *APA Practice Directorate, 4,* 1, p. 3.

Kindler, J., Duncan, J., & Knapp, S. (1991). The process of helping. *The Pennsylvania Psychologist, 51,* 15-17.

Kirk, U. (1993). *Psychological First Aid and Other Human Support, A Guide for the Non-Professional Therapist.* Danish Red Cross.

Knudsen, L., Hogsted, R., & Berliner, P. (1997). *Psychological First Aid and Human Support.* Danish Red Cross.

Kohut, H. (1979). The Two Analyses of Mr. Z. *International Journal of Psychoanalysis.* 60:3-27.

Kohut, H. (1980). Summarising reflections. In *Advances in Self Psychology*, ed. A. Goldberg, New York: International Universities Press.

Krug, E. G., Kresnow, M., Peddicord, J. P., Dahlberg, L. L., Powell, K. E., Crosby, A. E., & Annest, J. L. (1998). Suicide After Natural Disasters. *The New England Journal of Medicine, 338,* 6, 373-378.

Lee, K., Furukawa, P., Malinoski, G., Kaplan, K., & Furuto, S. (1993). *Between Crisis and Chronicity: The Crucial Phase of Disaster Response.* Workshop presented at the National Association of Social Workers Annual Meeting, Orlando, FL.

Lee, R.& Martin, C. (1991). Psychotherapy after Kohut: A textbook of psychology. Hillsdale, NJ: The Analytic Press.

Leider, R.J. (1983). Analytic neutrality - a historical review. *Psychoanalytic Inquiry*, 3:665-674.

Lichtenberg, J.D. (1983). *Psychoanalysis and Infant Research*. Hillsdale, NJ: The Analytic Press.

Lichtenberg, J.D. (1984). The empathetic mode of perception and alternative vantage points for psychoanalytic work. In: *Empathy II* (ed.) Lichtenberg, Bornstein and Silver. Hillsdale, NJ: The Analytic Press.

Lindenberg, Steven Phillip (1983). *Group Psychotherapy with People Who are Dying*. Springfield, III.: Charles C. Thomas.

Lonsdale, Gill, Peter Elfer, and rod Ballard (1979). *Children, Grief and Social Work.* Oxford, England: Basil Blackwell.

Mechanic, David, ed. (1983). *Handbook of Health, Health Care, and the Health Professions.* New York: Free Press.

Ornstein, A. (1981). Self pathology in childhood: Developmental and clinical considerations. *Psychiatric Clinics of North America* 4:435-453.

Ornstein, A. and Ornstein, P. (1984). Empathy and the therapeutic dialogue. *The Lydia Rapoport Lectures* #11, available from Smith School of Social Work, Northampton, MA. (Ornstein and Lachmann 8/12).

Palombo, J. (2001). *Learning Disorders and Disorders of the Self in Children and Adolescents*. New York: W. W. Norton.

Panel (1981). The neutrality of the analyst in the analytic situation, R.J. Leider, reporter. *Journal of the American Psychoanalytic Association*, 32:573-585.

Papousek, H., & Papousek, M. (1979). Early ontogeny of human social interaction. In M. von Cranach, K. Koppa, W. Lepenies, & P. Ploog, eds. *Human*

Ethology: Claims and Limits of a New Discipline. Cambridge: Cambridge University Press.

Parens, H. (1979). *The Development of Aggression in Early Childhood*. New York: Aronson.

Perlman, Stuart (1999). *The Therapist's Emotional Survival: Dealing with the Pain of Exploring Trauma*. New York: Aronson.

Racker, H. (1968). *Transference and Countertransference*. New York: Int Univ. Press.

Reed, G. (1987). Rules of clinical understanding in classical psychoanalysis and in self psychology: A comparison. *Journal of the American Psychoanalytic Association*, 35:421-446.

Ringstrom, P.A. (1994) "An Intersubjective Approach to Conjoint Therapy," Progress in Self Psychology, Vol. 10, Hillsdale NJ: The Analytic Press.

Ringstrom, P.A. (1995) "Exploring the Model Scene: An Intersubjective Approach to Brief Psychotherapy." Psychoanalytic Inquiry.

Ringstrom, P.A. (1998) "An Interview with Bernard Brandchaft" Self Psychology Newsletter (June).

Ringstrom, P.A. (1998) "Competing Selfobject Functions: The Bane of the Conjoint Therapist," The Bulletin of the Menninger's Clinic.

Ringstrom, P.A. (1999) "News from the Western Division" Self Psychology Newsletter (June).

Ringstrom, P.A. (1999) "Self-Psychology Integrating and Evolving Therapeutic Action or, How Does Analysis Cure" Self Psychology Newsletter (June).

Rowe, C. & MacIsaac, D. (1989). Empathic Attunement: The "Technique" of Psychoanalytic Self Psychology. Northvale, NJ: Jason Aronson.

Rowe, C. (1992). Development from archaic to mature selfobject transferences. Clinical Social Work Journal, Vol 20, No. 1 (Spring).

Rowe, C. (1992). Development from archaic to mature selfobject transferences. Clinical Social Work Journal, Vol 20, No. 1.

Rubovits-Seitz, R. (1988). Kohut's method of interpretation: A critique. *Journal of the American Psychoanalytic Association*, 36:933-959.

Schafer, R. (1976). *A New Language for Psychoanalysis*. New Haven: Yale University Press.

Scheidlinger, Saul, *Psychoanalysis and Group Behaviour* (W.W. Norton & Company, Inc., New York, 1952).

Schore, A.N. (1994). Affect regulation and the origin of the self: The neurobiology of emotional development. Mahwah, NJ: Lawrence Erlbaum Associates. [Not primarily self psychology, but helpful with understanding affective development of the self. - P. Ornstein.].

Shane, M., & Shane, E. (1980). Psychoanalytic developmental theories of the self: An integration. In *Advances in Self Psychology*., ed. A. Goldberg, New York: International Universities Press, pp. 19-46.

Shane, M., & Shane, E. (1986). Self change and development in the analysis of an adolescent patient. In *Progress in Self Psychology, vol., 2*, ed. A. Goldberg, New York: Guilford Press, pp. 142-160.

Shane, M., & Shane, E. (1988). Pathways to integration: Adding to the self psychology model. In *Progress in Self Psychology, vol., 4*, ed. A. Goldberg, New York: Guilford Press, pp. 71-78.

Shapiro, S. (1995). *Talking with Patients: A Self Psychological View of Creative Intuition and Analytic Discipline*. Northvale, NJ: Jason Aronson Inc.

Socarides, D. and Stolorow, R. (1984/85). Affects and selfobjects. *Annual of Psychoanalysis*. 12/13:105-119. New York: International Universities Press.

Spence, D. (1982). *Narrative Truth and Historical Truth*. New York: Norton.

Steele, R. (1979). Psychoanalysis and hermeneutics. *International Review of Psychoanalysis*, 6:389-411.

Stepansky, P.E. & Goldberg, A., eds. (1984). *Kohut's Legacy: Contributions to Self Psychology*. Hillsdale, NJ: Analytic Press.

Stern, D. (1985). *The Interpersonal World of the Infant*. New York: Basic Books.

Stolorow, R. and Lachmann, F. (1980). *Psychoanalysis and Developmental Arrests: Theory and Treatment*. New York: International Universities Press.

Tolpin, M. (1971). On the beginnings of a cohesive self. In: *The Psychoanalytic Study of the Child*, 25:273-305. New Haven: Yale University Press.

Tolpin, P. (1983). Self psychology and the interpretation of dreams. In *The Future of Psychoanalysis* (ed.) A. Goldberg. (pp. 255-271).

Wolf, E.S. (1976). Ambience and Abstinence. In: *The Annual of Psychoanalysis*, 4:101-115. New York: International Universities Press.

Index

■■■